JAVA

PROGRAMMER'S REFERENCE

Herbert Schildt

with Joe O'Neil

Osborne **McGraw-Hill**

Berkeley   New York   St. Louis   San Francisco
Auckland   Bogotá   Hamburg   London   Madrid
Mexico City   Milan   Montreal   New Delhi   Panama City
Paris   São Paulo   Singapore   Sydney
Tokyo   Toronto

Osborne **McGraw-Hill**
2600 Tenth Street
Berkeley, California 94710
U.S.A.

For information on translations or book distributors outside of the U.S.A.,
or to arrange bulk purchase discounts for sales, promotions, premiums, or
fundraisers, please write to Osborne **McGraw-Hill** at the above address.

Java Programmer's Reference

Publisher   Brandon A. Nordin
Editor in Chief   Scott Rogers
Acquisitions Editor   Megg Bonar
Technical Editor   Greg Guntle
Design and Composition   Publication Services
Senior Project Coordinator   Rhonda Zachmeyer
Copy Editor   Karen Bojda
Indexer   Sheryl Schildt

1234567890   DOC   9987

ISBN 0-07-882368-4

CONTENTS

6 The Language Classes and Interfaces **85**

7   The Utility Classes and Interfaces ... 175

8 The Input/Output Classes
and Interfaces **227**

---

12 The Event Classes and Interfaces .. 437

INTRODUCTION

Java is the language of the Internet. It is also the next step in the evolution of programming languages. Java traces its roots to C and C++, building on the benefits of each. Invented by James Gosling, Patrick Naughton, Chris Warth, Ed Frank, and Mike Sheridan at Sun Microsystems, Inc., starting in 1991, Java was originally called Oak, but was renamed Java in 1995. Shortly after its release Java achieved mainstream status, and it is, without a doubt, one of today's most important programming languages.

This book describes the most commonly used features of Java. As you probably know, Java defines many classes and hundreds of methods. It is, of course, not possible to cover all of these in this quick reference. However, we have selected the classes and methods that the programmer needs on a day-to-day basis.

Chapter 1—Data Types and Variables

Java provides a rich assortment of built-in data types to the programmer. You may create individual variables or arrays of these types. You may also use them as return types for methods.

Java is a strongly typed language. Indeed, part of Java's safety and robustness comes from this fact. Every variable has a type, every expression has a type, and every type is strictly defined. All assignments, whether explicit or via parameter passing in method calls, are checked for type compatibility. There are no automatic coercions or conversions of conflicting types as in some languages. The Java compiler checks all expressions and parameters to ensure that the types are compatible. Any type mismatches are errors, which must be corrected before the compiler will finish compiling the class.

THE SIMPLE TYPES

Java defines eight simple (that is, atomic or elemental) types of data: **byte**, **short**, **int**, **long**, **char**, **float**, **double**, and **boolean**. The atomic types represent single values—not complex objects. They can be put in four groups:

- Integers: **byte**, **short**, **int**, and **long**, which are for whole-valued signed numbers

- Floating-point numbers: **float** and **double**, which represent numbers with fractional components

- Characters: **char**, which represent symbols in a character set such as letters and digits

- Boolean: **boolean**, which is a special type for representing true/false values

You can use these types as-is or to construct arrays or your own class types. Thus, they form the basis for all other types of data that you can create.

Each simple type is described next.

Integers

Java defines four integer types: **byte**, **short**, **int**, and **long**. All of these are signed quantities; Java does not support unsigned, positive-only integers.

The width in bits and ranges of the integer types are shown here:

Name	Width in Bits	Range
long	64	−9,223,372,036,854,775,808 to 9,223,372,036,854,775,807
int	32	−2,147,483,648 to 2,147,483,647
short	16	−32,768 to 32,767
byte	8	−128 to 127

Floating-point Types

Floating-point numbers, also known as *real* numbers, are used when evaluating expressions that require fractional precision. For example, calculations such as square root or transcendentals such as sine and cosine require a floating-point type. There are two kinds of floating-point types, **float** and **double**, which represent single and double precision numbers, respectively. Their width and ranges are shown here:

Name	Width in Bits	Range
double	64	1.7e−308 to 1.7e+308
float	32	3.4e−038 to 3.4e+038

Characters

In Java, the data type used to store characters is **char**. However, C/C++ programmers beware: **char** in Java is not the same as **char** in C or C++. In C/C++, **char** is an integer type that is 8 bits wide. This is *not* the case in Java. Instead, Java uses *Unicode* to represent characters. Unicode defines a full international character set that can represent all of the characters found in all human languages. For this purpose, it requires 16 bits. Thus, in Java **char** is a 16-bit type. The range of a **char** is 0 to 65,536. There are no negative **char**s. The standard ASCII character set still ranges from 0 to 127 as it always has, and the extended 8-bit character set, ISO-Latin-1, ranges from 0 to 255. Thus, you can still think in terms of ASCII if you want, even though Java uses Unicode.

Booleans

Java has a simple type for logical values, called **boolean**. It can have only one of two possible values, **true** or **false**, which are keywords. This is the type returned by all relational operators, such as **a** < **b**. **boolean** is also the type *required* by the conditional expressions that govern the control statements such as **if** and **for**.

LITERALS

In Java, a constant value used in a program is called a *literal*. There are literals for each of Java's elemental types.

Integer Literals

Integers are probably the most commonly used literal in the typical program. Any whole number value is an integer literal.

Examples are 1, 2, 3, and 42. These are all decimal values. Integer literals can also be represented in octal (base 8) and in hexadecimal (base 16). Octal values are denoted in Java by a leading zero and may use only the digits 0 through 7. For example, 011 is the octal equivalent of the decimal value 9. Hexadecimal constants begin with a leading zero and x (**0x** or **0X**) and may consist of the digits 0 to 9 and the letters A through F (or a through f), which stand for 10 through 15. Thus, 255 in decimal is 0xFF in hexadecimal.

Floating-point Literals

Floating-point numbers represent decimal values with a fractional component. They can be expressed in either standard or scientific notation. Standard notation consists of a whole number component followed by a decimal point followed by a fractional component. For example, 2.0, 3.14159, and 0.6667 represent valid standard-notation, floating-point numbers. Scientific notation uses a standard-notation, floating-point number plus a suffix that specifies a power of 10 by which the number is to be multiplied. The exponent is indicated by an **E** or **e** followed by a decimal number, which can be positive or negative. Examples are 6.022E23, 314159E−05, and 2e+100.

Floating-point literals in Java default to **double** precision. To specify a **float** literal, you must append an **F** or **f** to the constant. You may also explicitly specify a **double** literal by appending a **D** or **d**. Doing so is, of course, redundant. The default **double** type consumes 64 bits of storage, while the less accurate **float** type requires only 32 bits.

Boolean Literals

There are only two logical values that a **boolean** value can have, **true** and **false**. The values of **true** and **false** do not convert into any numerical representation. The **true** keyword in Java does not equal 1, nor does the **false** keyword equal 0. In Java, **true** and **false** can only be assigned to variables declared as **boolean** or used in expressions with Boolean operators.

Character Literals

A character literal is represented inside a pair of single quotes. All of the visible ASCII characters can be directly entered inside the quotes, such as 'a', 'z', and '@'. For characters that are impossible to enter directly, there are several escape sequences, which allow you to enter the character you need, such as '\ '' for the single-quote character itself, and '\ n' for the newline character. You can also specify a character in octal or hexadecimal. For octal notation, use the backslash followed by the three-digit number. For example, '\ 141' is the letter *a*. For hexadecimal, enter a backslash and u (\ **u**) then exactly four hexadecimal digits. The following table shows character escape sequences:

Escape Sequence	Description
\ *ddd*	Octal character (*ddd*)
\ u*xxxx*	Hexadecimal Unicode character (*xxxx*)
\ '	Single quote
\ "	Double quote
\ \	Backslash
\ r	Carriage return
\ n	Newline (also known as linefeed)
\ f	Form feed
\ t	Tab
\ b	Backspace

String Literals

String literals in Java are specified as they are in most other languages: by enclosing a sequence of characters between a pair of double quotes. The escape sequences that apply to character literals also work within string literals. Examples of string literals are

"I like Java"

"one\ntwo\nthree"

"this is tabbed:\tover"

One important thing to note about Java strings is that they must begin and end on the same line. There is no line-continuation escape sequence as there is in other languages.

VARIABLES

The variable is the basic unit of storage in a Java program. A variable is defined by the combination of an identifier, a type, and an optional initializer. In addition, all variables have a scope, which defines their visibility, and a lifetime. These issues are examined here.

Declaring a Variable

In Java, all variables must be declared before they can be used. The basic form of a variable declaration is shown here:

type identifier [= *value*][, *identifier* [= value] ...] ;

The *type* is one of Java's atomic types or the name of a class or interface. The *identifier* is the name of the variable. To declare more than one variable of the specified type, use a comma-separated list. Here are some examples:

```
int a;
double balance;
char c1, c2, c3;
```

You may initialize a variable by including an equal sign and a value. Keep in mind that the initialization expression must result in a value of the same (or compatible) type as that specified for the variable. For example, the following declaration assigns **count** the initial value of 10:

```
int count = 10;
```

Programming Tip

Java allows variables to be initialized dynamically, using any expression valid at the time the variable is declared. For example, here is a short program that computes the length of the hypotenuse of a right triangle given the lengths of its two opposing sides:

```
// Demonstrate dynamic initialization.
class DynInit {
    public static void main(String args[]) {
        double a = 3.0, b = 4.0;

        // c is dynamically initialized
        double c = Math.sqrt(a * a + b * b);

        System.out.println("Hypotenuse is " + c);
    }
}
```

Here, three local variables, **a**, **b**, and **c**, are declared. The first two, **a** and **b**, are initialized by constants. However, **c** is initialized dynamically to the length of the hypotenuse (using the Pythagorean theorem). The program uses one of Java's built-in methods—**sqrt( )**, which is a member of the **Math** class—to compute the square root of its argument. The key point here is that the initialization expression may use any element valid at the time of the initialization, including calls to methods, other variables, or literals.

The Scope and Lifetime of Variables

Java allows variables to be declared within any block. A block is begun with an opening curly brace and ended by a closing curly brace. A block defines a *scope*. Thus, each time you start a new block, you are creating a new scope. A scope determines what objects are visible to other parts of your program. It also determines the lifetime of those objects.

The scope defined by a method begins with its opening curly brace. However, if that method has parameters, they too are included within the method's scope.

As a general rule, variables declared inside a scope are not visible (i.e., accessible) by code that is defined outside that scope. Thus, when you declare a variable within a scope, you are localizing that variable and protecting it from unauthorized access and/or modification. Indeed, the scope rules provide the foundation for encapsulation.

Scopes can be nested. Each time you create a new, nested scope, the outer scope encloses the inner scope. This means that objects declared in the outer scope will be visible to code within the inner scope. However, the reverse is not true. Objects declared within the inner scope will not be visible outside it.

A variable's scope affects its lifetime. Variables are created when their scope is entered and destroyed when their scope is exited. This means that a variable will not hold its value once it has gone out of scope. Therefore, variables declared within a method will not hold their values between calls to that method. Also, a variable declared within a block will lose its value when the block is exited. Thus, the lifetime of a variable is confined to its scope.

TYPE CONVERSION AND CASTING

It is common to assign a value of one type to a variable of another type. If the two types are compatible, then Java will perform the conversion automatically. For example, it is always possible to assign an **int** value to a **long** variable. However, not all types are compatible, and thus not all type conversions are implicitly allowed. For instance, there is no conversion defined from **double** to **byte**. Fortunately, it is still possible to obtain a conversion between incompatible types. To do so, you must use a *cast,* which performs an explicit conversion between incompatible types. Each situation is described in the following sections.

Java's Automatic Conversions

When assigning one type of data to another type of variable, an *automatic type conversion* will take place if the following two conditions are met:

- The two types are compatible.

- The destination type is larger than the source type.

In this case, a *widening conversion* takes place. For example, the **int** type is always large enough to hold all valid **byte** values, so no explicit cast statement is required.

For widening conversions, the numeric types, including integer and floating-point types, are compatible with each other. However, the numeric types are not compatible with **char** or **boolean**. Also, **char** and **boolean** are not compatible with each other.

Java also performs an automatic type conversion when storing a literal integer constant into variables of type **byte**, **short**, or **long**.

Casting Incompatible Types

In cases where Java's automatic conversions do not apply, you will need to use an explicit cast. For example, you will need to use a cast when assigning an **int** value to a **byte** variable, because a **byte** is smaller than an **int**. This kind of conversion is sometimes called a *narrowing conversion,* because the target type is smaller than the source.

A cast is simply an explicit type conversion. It has this general form:

   (target-type) value

Here, *target-type* specifies the desired type to convert the specified value to. For example, the following fragment casts an **int** to a **byte**:

```
int i;
byte b;
// ...
b = (byte) i;
```

If the integer's value is larger than the range of a **byte**, the high order bits will be lost.

A different type of conversion will occur when a floating-point value is assigned to an integer type: *truncation.* As you know, integers do not have fractional components. Thus, when a floating-point value is assigned to an integer type, the fractional component is lost. For example, if the value 1.23 is assigned to an integer, the resulting value will simply be 1. The 0.23 will have been truncated. Of course, if the size of the whole number component is too large to fit into the target integer type, then that value will be reduced modulo the target type's range.

AUTOMATIC TYPE PROMOTION IN EXPRESSIONS

Java defines several *type promotion rules* that apply to expressions. They are as follows. First, all **byte** and **short** values are promoted to **int**. Then, if one operand is a **long**, the whole expression is promoted to **long**. If one operand is a **float**, the entire expression is promoted to **float**. If any of the operands is **double**, the result is **double**.

ARRAYS

An array is a group of like-typed variables that are referred to by a common name. Arrays of any type can be created and may have one or more dimensions. A specific element in an array is accessed by its index. Arrays offer a convenient means of grouping together related information.

Obtaining an array is a two-step process. First, you must declare a variable of the desired array type. Second, you must allocate the memory that will hold the array, using **new**, and assign it to the array variable. Thus, in Java all arrays are dynamically allocated.

One-Dimensional Arrays

A one-dimensional array is, essentially, a list of like-typed variables. To create an array, you first must create an array variable of the desired type. The general form of a one-dimensional array declaration is as follows:

type var-name[ ];

Here, *type* declares the base type of the array. The base type determines the data type of each element in the array. Thus, the base type for the array determines what type of data the array will hold.

Once you have created the array variable, you need to allocate storage for the array using **new**. Here is an example:

```
int iarray[];
iarray = new int[32];
```

This example declares an array named **iarray** and allocates storage for 32 elements. You can combine these two steps, as shown here:

```
int iarray[] = new int[32];
```

Once you have allocated an array, you can access a specific element in the array by specifying its index within square brackets. All array indexes start at zero.

Arrays can be initialized when they are declared. The process is much the same as that used to initialize the simple types. An array initializer is a list of comma-separated expressions surrounded by curly braces. The commas separate the values of the array elements. The array will automatically be created large enough to hold the number of elements you specify in the array initializer. There is no need to use **new**. For example, the following line does the declaration, allocation, and initialization for the array **intx**:

```
int intx[] = { 1, 2, 3, 4, 5 };
```

Multidimensional Arrays

In Java, multidimensional arrays are actually arrays of arrays. To declare a multidimensional array variable, specify each additional index using another set of square brackets. This example declares a two-dimensional array variable called **twoD**:

```
int twoD[][] = new int[4][5];
```

This declaration allocates a 4 × 5 array and assigns it to **twoD**. Internally this matrix is implemented as an *array of arrays* of **int**.

When you allocate memory for a multidimensional array, you need to specify the memory only for the first (leftmost) dimension. You can allocate the remaining dimensions separately. For example, the following fragment allocates memory for the first dimension of **twoD** when it is declared. It allocates the second dimension manually.

```
int twoD[][] = new int[4][];
twoD[0] = new int[5];
twoD[1] = new int[5];
twoD[2] = new int[5];
twoD[3] = new int[5];
```

While there is no advantage to individually allocating the second-dimension arrays in this situation, there may be in others. For example, when you allocate dimensions manually, you do not need to allocate the same number of elements for each dimension. As stated earlier, since multidimensional arrays are actually arrays of arrays, the length of each array is under your control. The following fragment creates a two-dimensional array in which the sizes of the second dimension are unequal:

```
int twoD[][] = new int[4][];
twoD[0] = new int[1];
twoD[1] = new int[2];
twoD[2] = new int[3];
twoD[3] = new int[4];
```

Programming Tip

There is a second form that can be used to declare an array, shown here:

type [ ] *var-name;*

Here, the square brackets follow the type specifier and not the name of the array variable. For example, the following two declarations are equivalent:

```
int a1[] = new int[3];
int[] a2 = new int[3];
```

The following declarations are also equivalent:

```
char twod1[][] = new char[3][4];
char[][] twod2 = new char[3][4];
```

This form of array declaration is often a convenient alternative.

STRINGS

Java's string type, called **String**, is not a simple type. Nor is it simply an array of characters (as are strings in C/C++). Rather, **String** defines an object and is discussed under **java.lang**.

Chapter 2—Classes and Methods

The class is at the core of Java. It is the logical construct upon which the entire Java language is built because it defines the shape and nature of an object. As such, the class forms the basis for object-oriented programming in Java. Any concept you wish to implement in a Java program must be encapsulated within a class. Within a class, all program actions occur within methods. The method is Java's way of creating a named subroutine. Topics relating to both classes and methods are examined here.

CLASS FUNDAMENTALS

A class is a *template* for an object and an object is an *instance* of a class. When you define a class, you declare its exact form and nature. You do this by specifying the data that it contains and the code that operates on that data. While very simple classes may contain only code or only data, most real-world classes contain both.

A class is declared using the **class** keyword. The general form of a **class** definition is shown here:

```
class classname {
    type instance-variable1;
    type instance-variable2;
    // ...
    type instance-variableN;

    type methodname1(parameter-list) {
        // body of method
    }
    type methodname2(parameter-list) {
        // body of method
    }
```

```
// ...
type methodnameN(parameter-list) {
  // body of method
}
}
```

The data, or variables, defined within a **class** are called *instance variables.* The code is contained within *methods.* Collectively, the methods and variables defined within a class are called *members* of the class. In most classes, the instance variables are acted upon and accessed by the methods defined for that class. Thus, it is the methods that determine how a class's data may be used.

All methods are declared within classes, and all have this general form:

```
type name(parameter-list ) {
  // body of method
}
```

Here, *type* specifies the type of data returned by the method. This can be any valid type, including class types that you create. If the method does not return a value, its return type must be **void**. The name of the method is specified by *name.* This can be any legal identifier other than those already used by other items within the current scope. The *parameter-list* is a sequence of type and identifier pairs separated by commas. Parameters are essentially variables that receive the values of the *arguments* passed to the method when it is called. If the method has no parameters, then the parameter list will be empty.

Methods that have a return type other than **void** return a value to the calling routine using the following form of the **return** statement:

```
return value;
```

Here, *value* is the value returned.

Following is an example of a simple class.

```
class Sample {
   int a, b;

   int sum() {
      return a+b;
   }
}
```

This class is called **Sample**. It contains two instance variables called **a** and **b** and one method called **sum( )**.

DECLARING CLASS OBJECTS

When you create a class, you are creating a new data type. You can use this type to declare objects of that type. However, obtaining objects of a class is a two-step process. First, you must declare a variable of the class type. This variable does not define an object itself. Instead, it is simply a variable that can *refer to an object*. Second, you must acquire an actual, physical copy of the object and assign it to that variable. This is accomplished using the **new** operator. The **new** operator dynamically allocates (i.e., allocates at run time) memory for an object and returns a reference to it. This reference is, more or less, the address in memory of the object allocated by **new**. This reference is then stored in the variable. Thus, in Java, all class objects must be dynamically allocated.

Here is an example that creates an object of the **Sample** class (shown earlier):

```
Sample ob = new Sample();
```

This statement combines the two steps just described. It can be rewritten like this to show each step more clearly:

```
Sample ob; // declare reference to object
ob = new Sample(); // allocates an object
```

The first line declares **ob** as a reference to an object of type **Sample**. After this line executes, **ob** contains the value **null**, which indicates that it does not yet point to an actual object. Any attempt to use **ob** at this point will result in a compile-time error. The next line allocates an actual object and assigns a reference to it to **ob**. After the second line executes, you can use **ob** as if it were a **Sample** object itself. But in reality, **ob** simply holds the memory address of the actual **Sample** object.

Once you have obtained a class object, you access its members using the dot (.) operator. This is its general form:

object-name.member-name

For example, to assign the **a** member of **ob** the value 10, use the following statement:

```
ob.a = 10;
```

CONSTRUCTORS

A constructor initializes an object immediately upon creation. It has the same name as the class in which it resides and is syntactically similar to a method. However, constructors have no return type, not even **void**. This is because the implicit return type of a class's constructor is the class type itself. It is the constructor's job to initialize the internal state of an object so that the code creating an instance will have a fully initialized, usable object.

Constructors can have parameters. These parameters receive the arguments passed to the constructor when an object is created. Typically, the values contained in a constructor's parameters are used to initialize an object. The arguments that are passed to the constructor are specified when each object is created. For example, here a parameterized constructor has been added to the **Sample** class:

```
class Sample {
  int a, b;

  // constructor
  Sample(int x, int y) {
    a = x;
    b = y;
  }

  int sum() {
    return a+b;
  }
}
```

The following class creates an object of type **Sample**, passing it the values −99 and 88. This means that **a** will receive the value −99 and **b** will receive the value 88.

```
class Example {
  public static void main(String args[]) {
    Sample ob = new Sample(-99, 88);

    System.out.println(ob.sum());
  }
}
```

This program displays the value −11.

When no constructor is explicitly defined for a class, Java creates a default constructor. The default constructor automatically initializes all instance variables to zero. The default constructor is often sufficient for simple classes, but it usually won't do for more sophisticated ones. Once you define your own constructor, the default constructor is no longer used.

GARBAGE COLLECTION

In some languages, such as C++, dynamically allocated objects must be manually released by using a **delete** operator. Java takes a different approach; it handles deallocation for you automatically. The technique that accomplishes this is called *garbage collection*. It works like this: When no references to an object exist, that object is assumed to be no longer needed and the memory occupied by the object can be reclaimed. There is no explicit need to destroy objects as in C++. Garbage collection only occurs sporadically (if at all) during the execution of your program. It will not occur simply because one or more objects exist that are no longer used. Furthermore, different Java run-time implementations take various approaches to garbage collection, but for the most part, you should not have to think about it while writing your programs.

THE finalize( ) METHOD

Sometimes you will need to ensure that an object has performed some action before it is destroyed. For example, if an object had acquired some system resource, such as a file handle, then you might want to make sure this resource has been freed before the object is destroyed. To handle these types of situations, Java provides a mechanism called *finalization*. Using finalization, you can define specific actions that will occur when an object is just about to be reclaimed by the garbage collector.

To add a finalizer to a class, you simply define the **finalize( )** method. The Java run-time calls that method whenever it is about to recycle an object of that class. Inside the **finalize( )** method you specify those actions that must be performed before

2

an object is destroyed. The **finalize( )** method has this general form.

```
protected void finalize( )
{
  // finalization code here
}
```

It is important to understand that **finalize( )** is only called just prior to garbage collection. It is not called when an object goes out of scope, for example. This means that you cannot know when—or even if—**finalize( )** will be executed. Therefore, your program should provide other means of releasing system resources and so on used by the object. It must not rely on **finalize( )** for normal program operation.

Programming Tip

If you are familiar with C++, then you know that C++ allows you to define a destructor for a class, which is called when an object goes out of scope. Java does not support this idea or provide for destructors. Although the **finalize( )** method somewhat approximates the function of a destructor in a few cases, it is not equivalent. Therefore, if you are porting code from C++, you cannot use **finalize( )** as a substitute for a destructor.

OVERLOADING METHODS

In Java it is possible to define two or more methods within the same class that share the same name, as long as their parameter declarations are different. When this is the case, the methods are said to be *overloaded* and the process is referred to as *method overloading*. When an overloaded method is invoked,

Java uses the type and/or number of arguments as its guide to determine which version of the overloaded method to actually call. Thus, overloaded methods must differ in the type and/or number of their parameters. While overloaded methods may have different return types, the return type alone is insufficient to distinguish two versions of a method. When Java encounters a call to an overloaded method, it simply executes the version of the method whose parameters match the arguments used in the call.

In addition to overloading normal methods, you may also overload constructors.

Here is a simple example that illustrates method overloading.

```
// Demonstrate method overloading.
class OverloadDemo {
  void test( ) {
    System.out.println("No parameters");
  }

  // Overload test for one integer parameter.
  void test(int a) {
    System.out.println("a: " + a);
  }

  // Overload test for two integer parameters.
  void test(int a, int b) {
    System.out.println("a and b: " + a + " " + b);
  }

  // overload test for a double parameter
  double test(double a) {
    System.out.println("double a: " + a);
    return a*a;
  }
}
```

As you can see, **test( )** is overloaded four times. The first version takes no parameters, the second takes one integer parameter, the third takes two integer parameters, and the fourth takes one **double** parameter. The fact that the fourth version of **test( )** also returns a value is of no consequence relative to overloading, since return types do not play a role in overload resolution.

The following class demonstrates the overloaded **test( )** method.

```
class Overload {
  public static void main(String args[]) {
    OverloadDemo ob = new OverloadDemo();
    double result;

    // call all versions of test()
    ob.test();  // calls test()
    ob.test(10); // calls test(int)
    ob.test(10, 20); // calls test(int, int)
    result = ob.test(123.2); // calls test(double)
    // ...
  }
}
```

ARGUMENT PASSING

In general, there are two ways that a computer language can pass an argument to a subroutine. The first is called *call-by-value*. This method copies the *value* of an argument into the formal parameter of the subroutine. Therefore, changes made to the parameter of the subroutine have no effect on the argument used to call it. The second way an argument can be passed is called *call-by-reference*. In this method, a reference to an argument (not the value of the argument) is passed to the parameter. Inside the subroutine, this reference is used to access the actual argument specified in the call. This means that changes made to the parameter will affect the argument used to call the subroutine. Java uses both methods, depending upon what is passed.

In Java, when you pass a simple type to a method, it is passed by value. Thus, what occurs to the parameter that receives the argument has no effect outside the method.

When you pass an object to a method, the situation changes dramatically because objects are passed by reference. Remember, when you create a variable of a class type, you are creating only a reference to an object. Thus, when you pass this reference to a method, the parameter that receives it will refer to the same object as that referred to by the argument. This effectively means that objects are passed to methods using call-by-reference. Changes to the object inside the method *do* affect the object used as an argument.

RECURSION

Java supports *recursion*. Recursion is the process of defining something in terms of itself. As it relates to Java programming, recursion is the attribute that allows a method to call itself. A method that calls itself is said to be *recursive*.

The classic example of recursion is the computation of the factorial of a number. The factorial of a number N is the product of all the whole numbers between 1 and N. For example, 3 factorial is $1 \times 2 \times 3$, or 6. Here is how a factorial can be computed using a recursive method:

```
// A simple example of recursion.
class Factorial {
  // this is a recursive method
  int fact(int n) {
    int result;

    if(n==1) return 1;
    result = fact(n-1) * n;
    return result;
  }
}
```

```
class Recursion {
  public static void main(String args[]) {
    Factorial f = new Factorial();

    System.out.println("Factorial of 3 is " + f.fact(3));
    System.out.println("Factorial of 4 is " + f.fact(4));
    System.out.println("Factorial of 5 is " + f.fact(5));
  }
}
```

Following is the output from this program:

```
Factorial of 3 is 6
Factorial of 4 is 24
Factorial of 5 is 120
```

Here is how **fact( )** works. When called with an argument of 1,
fact( ) returns 1; otherwise it returns the product of **fact(n−1)*n**.
To evaluate this expression, **fact( )** is called with **n−1**. This
process repeats until **n** equals 1 and the calls to the method
begin returning.

When a method calls itself, new local variables and parameters
are allocated storage on the stack and the method code is
executed with these new variables from the start. A recursive
call does not make a new copy of the method. Only the
arguments are new. As each recursive call returns, the old
local variables and parameters are removed from the stack and
execution resumes at the point of the call inside the method.
Recursive methods could be said to "telescope" out and back.

Programming Tip

Although recursive methods are powerful, they should
be used with care. Recursive versions of many routines may
execute a bit more slowly than the iterative equivalent because
of the added overhead of the additional method calls. Many
recursive calls to a method could cause a stack overrun. Because

storage for parameters and local variables is on the stack and each new call creates a new copy of these variables, it is possible that the stack could be exhausted. If this occurs, the Java run-time system will cause an exception. However, you probably will not have to worry about this unless a recursive method runs wild.

When writing recursive methods, you must include a conditional statement somewhere that causes the method to return without executing the recursive call. If you don't, once you call the method, it will call itself until the stack is exhausted. This is a very common error when developing recursive routines. Use output statements liberally during development so that you can watch what is going on and abort execution if you see that you have made a mistake.

UNDERSTANDING static

When a class member is declared **static**, it may be accessed before any objects of its class are created and without reference to any object. Thus, a **static** member is for most intents and purposes global. You may declare both methods and variables to be **static**. The most common use of **static** is to declare the **main( )** method.

You may also use **static** to create a block in which you may initialize **static** variables. A **static** block is executed exactly once, when the class is first loaded.

Outside of the class in which they are defined, **static** methods and variables may be used independently of any object. To do so, you need only specify the name of their class followed by the dot operator. For example, if you wish to call a **static** method from outside its class, you may do so using this general form:

classname.method( )

Here, *classname* is the name of the class in which the **static** method is declared. As you can see, this format is similar to that used to call non-**static** methods through object reference variables. A **static** variable may be accessed in the same way: using the dot operator on the name of the class.

ACCESS CONTROL

How a class member can be accessed is determined by the access specifier that modifies its declaration. Java's access specifiers are **public**, **private**, and **protected**. A default access level is also defined.

These keywords are more fully described in Chapter 4, "Inheritance, Packages, and Interfaces."

THE main( ) METHOD

In a Java program, execution begins at **main( )**. It is typically declared as shown here:

```
public static void main(String args[]) {
```

The **main( )** method is declared as **public static** so that it can be called by code outside of the class in which it is declared and before any objects of its class are created.

Sometimes you will want to pass information into a program when you run it. This is accomplished by passing *command line arguments* to **main( )**. A command line argument is the information that directly follows the program's name on the command line when it is executed. To access the command line arguments inside a Java program is quite easy: They are stored as strings in the **String** array passed to **main( )**. For example, this program displays all of the command line arguments that it is called with:

```
// Display all command line arguments.
class CommandLine {
  public static void main(String args[]) {
    for(int i=0; i<args.length; i++)
      System.out.println("args[" + i + "]: " + args[i]);
  }
}
```

Try executing this program as shown here:

```
java CommandLine this is a test 100 -1
```

When you do, you will see the following output:

```
args[0]: this
args[1]: is
args[2]: a
args[3]: test
args[4]: 100
args[5]: -1
```

Remember, all arguments are passed as strings. You must convert numeric values to their internal forms manually.

Chapter 3—Operators

Java provides a rich operator environment. Most of its operators can be divided into the following four groups: *arithmetic, bitwise, relational,* and *logical.* Java also defines some additional operators that handle certain special situations.

ARITHMETIC OPERATORS

Arithmetic operators are used in mathematical expressions in the same way that they are used in algebra. The following table lists the arithmetic operators:

Operator	Result
+	Addition
−	Subtraction (also unary minus)
*	Multiplication
/	Division
%	Modulus
++	Increment
−−	Decrement

The operands of the arithmetic operators must be of a numeric type. You cannot use them on **boolean** types, but you can use them on **char** types, since the **char** type in Java is, essentially, a subset of **int.**

The Basic Arithmetic Operators

The basic arithmetic operations—addition, subtraction, multiplication, and division—all behave as you would expect for all numeric types. The minus operator also has a unary form, which negates its single operand. Remember that when the division operator is applied to an integer type, there will be no fractional component attached to the result.

The Modulus Operator

The modulus operator, %, returns the remainder of a division. It can be applied to floating-point types as well as integer types.

Increment and Decrement

The ++ and −− are Java's increment and decrement operators. The increment operator increases its operand by 1. The decrement operator decreases its operand by 1. These operators are unique in that they can appear both in *postfix* form, where they follow the operand, and *prefix* form, where they precede the operand. In the prefix form, the operand is incremented or decremented before the value is obtained for use in the expression. In postfix form, the previous value is obtained for use in the expression and then the operand is modified.

BITWISE OPERATORS

Java defines several *bitwise operators* that can be applied to the integer types: **long**, **int**, **short**, **char**, and **byte**. These operators act upon the individual bits of their operands. The bitwise operators fall into two general categories: logical and shift.

The Bitwise Logical Operators

The bitwise logical operators are shown next:

3

Operator	Result
~	Bitwise unary NOT
&	Bitwise AND
|	Bitwise OR
^	Bitwise exclusive OR

The following table shows the outcome of each operation. Keep in mind that the bitwise operators are applied to each individual bit within each operand.

A	B	A | B	A & B	A ^ B	~A
0	0	0	0	0	1
1	0	1	0	1	0
0	1	1	0	1	1
1	1	1	1	0	0

The Bitwise Shift Operators

The shift operators are shown here:

Operator	Result
>>	Shift right
>>>	Shift right, zero fill
<<	Shift left

The left-shift operator, <<, shifts all of the bits in a value to the left a specified number of times. This is its general form:

$$value << num$$

Here, *num* specifies the number of positions to left-shift *value*. That is, the << moves all of the bits in the specified value to the left by the number of bit positions specified by *num*. For each shift left, the high-order bit is shifted out (and lost) and a zero is brought in on the right.

The right-shift operator, >>, shifts all of the bits in a value to the right a specified number of times. This is its general form:

value >> *num*

Here, *num* specifies the number of positions to right-shift *value*. For each right shift, the low-order bit is shifted out (and lost), but the value of the sign bit (high-order bit) is preserved. That is, the >> operator automatically fills the high-order bit with its previous contents each time a shift occurs.

In some cases you will not want the sign bit preserved when performing a right shift. For example, if you are shifting something that does not represent a numeric value, you may not want sign extension to take place. In these cases you will generally want to shift a zero into the high-order bit no matter what its initial value was. This is known as an *unsigned shift*. To accomplish this you use Java's unsigned, shift-right operator, >>>, which always shifts zeros into the high-order bit.

RELATIONAL OPERATORS

The relational operators ascertain the relationship that one operand has to the other. The relational operators are shown here:

Operator	Result
==	Equal to
!=	Not equal to
>	Greater than
<	Less than
>=	Greater than or equal to
<=	Less than or equal to

The outcome of these operations is a **boolean** value. The relational operators are most frequently used in the expressions that control the **if** statement and the various loop statements.

Any type in Java, including integers, floating-point numbers, characters, and Booleans, can be compared using the equality test, $==$, and the inequality test, $!=$. Notice that in Java equality is denoted with two equal signs, not one. (Remember: A single equal sign is the assignment operator.) Only numeric types can be compared using the ordering operators. That is, only integer, floating-point, and character operands can be compared to see which is greater or less than the other.

Programming Tip

If you have a C/C++ background, please note the following. In C/C++, these types of statements are very common.

```
int done;
// ...
if(!done) ... // Valid in C/C++
if(num) ...   // but not in Java.
```

In Java, these statements must be written like this:

```
if(done == 0)) ... // This is Java style.
if(num != 0) ...
```

The reason for this difference is that Java does not define true and false in the same way as C/C++. In C/C++, true is any nonzero value and false is zero. In Java, **true** and **false** are nonnumeric values that do not relate to zero or nonzero. Therefore, to test for zero or nonzero values, you must explicitly employ one or more of the relational operators.

BOOLEAN LOGICAL OPERATORS

The Boolean logical operators summarized below operate only on **boolean** operands. All of the binary logical operators combine two **boolean** values to form a resultant **boolean** value.

Operator	Result
&	Logical AND
|	Logical OR
^	Logical XOR (exclusive OR)
||	Short-circuit OR
&&	Short-circuit AND
!	Logical unary NOT
==	Equal to
!=	Not equal to
?:	Ternary if-then-else

The logical Boolean operators **&**, **|**, and **^** operate on **boolean** values in the same way that they operate on the bits of an integer. The logical **!** operator inverts the Boolean state: **!true** == **false**, and **!false** == **true**. The following table shows the effect of each logical operation:

A	B	A | B	A & B	A ^ B	!A
false	false	false	false	false	true
true	false	true	false	true	false
false	true	true	false	true	true
true	true	true	true	false	false

Short-Circuit Logical Operators

The logical AND (**&**) and OR (**|**) operators always evaluate the expressions on both the right and left sides of the operator.

However, the short-circuit AND (**&&**) and OR (**||**) operators do not always evaluate the expression on the right side of the operator. As you can see from the preceding table, the OR operator results in **true** when **A** is **true**, no matter what **B** is. Similarly, the AND operator results in **false** when **A** is **false**, no matter what **B** is. If you use **||** and **&&** rather than the **|** and **&** forms of these operators, Java will not evaluate the right-hand operand when the outcome of the expression can be determined by the left operand alone. Here is an example:

```
if((income >= 40000) && (age >= 65)) {
  // ...
}
```

In this case, if **income** is less than 40,000, the test will be **false** regardless of the age. Therefore, it is not necessary to execute the right-side expression. Here is another example:

```
if((income >= 40000) || (age >= 65)) {
  // ...
}
```

In this case, if **income** is greater than 40,000, the test will be **true** regardless of the age. Again, it is not necessary to execute the right-side expression.

Employing the short-circuit operators helps you write more efficient code. In cases where the left operand can determine the outcome, time is not wasted also evaluating the operand on the right. However, be careful. If your code relies upon some side effect of the evaluation of the right operand, then you will not be able to use the short-circuit operators.

THE ASSIGNMENT OPERATOR

The assignment operator is the single equal sign, =. The assignment operator works in Java much as it does in any other computer language. Its general form is shown here:

   var = *expression*;

Here, the type of *var* must be compatible with the type of *expression*.

Java allows a convenient "shorthand" for assignments of this general form:

   var = *var op expression*;

Assignments of this type can be shortened to

   var op= *expression*;

For example, you can replace a sequence such as

```
a = a + b;
```

with

```
a += b;
```

Here are the shorthand assignment operators supported by Java:

Operator	Result
+=	Addition assignment
−=	Subtraction assignment
*=	Multiplication assignment
/=	Division assignment
%=	Modulus assignment
&=	Bitwise AND assignment
|=	Bitwise OR assignment
^=	Bitwise exclusive OR assignment
>>=	Shift right assignment
>>>=	Shift right, zero fill assignment

Operator	Result
<<=	Shift left assignment
&=	AND assignment
|=	OR assignment
^=	XOR assignment

Programming Tip

You can assign two or more variables a common value in a single statement by using a series of assignment operators. For example, the following is perfectly valid:

```
int a, b, c;
a = b = c = 100; // assign a, b, and c the value 100
```

After this statement executes, **a**, **b**, and **c** will each have the value 100.

THE ? OPERATOR

Java includes a special ternary (three-way) operator that can replace certain types of if-then-else statements. The **?** operator has this general form:

expression1 ? *expression2* : *expression3*

expression1 can be any expression that evaluates to a **boolean** value. If *expression1* is **true**, then *expression2* is evaluated; otherwise, *expression3* is evaluated. The result of the **?** operation is that of the expression evaluated. Both *expression2* and *expression3* are required to return the same type, which can't be **void**.

Here is an example in which the **?** operator is used to avoid a division by zero:

```
c = a!=0 ? b/a : 0;
```

If **a** is nonzero, then **c** is assigned the value of **b/a**. Otherwise, the division is avoided and **c** is assigned zero.

THE DOT OPERATOR

The dot operator (.) is used to refer to a member of a class. See Chapter 2, "Classes and Methods."

OPERATOR PRECEDENCE

Table 3-1 shows the order of precedence for the Java operators, from highest to lowest.

3

Table 3-1.   The Precedence of the Java Operators

		highest	
( )	[ ]	.	
++	——	~	!
*	/	%	
+	—		
>>	>>>	<<	
>	>=	<	<=
==	!=		
&			
^			
|			
&&			
||			
?:			
=	*op*=		
		lowest	

Chapter 4—Inheritance, Packages, and Interfaces

This section discusses three key Java features: inheritance, packages, and interfaces. Inheritance is the mechanism that allows one class to acquire the attributes of another. A package partitions the class name space. An interface defines a set of methods that other classes must implement.

INHERITANCE

In Java, it is possible for one class to inherit the characteristics of another class. In the terminology of Java, a class that is inherited is called a *superclass.* The class that does the inheriting is called a *subclass.* Therefore, a subclass is a specialized version of a superclass. It inherits all of the instance variables and methods defined by the superclass and adds its own, unique elements.

To inherit a class, you simply incorporate the definition of one class into another using the **extends** keyword using this general form:

```
class subclass-name extends superclass-name {
  // body of class
}
```

You can specify only one superclass for any subclass that you create. Java does not support the inheritance of multiple superclasses into a single subclass. You can, however, create a hierarchy of inheritance in which a subclass becomes a superclass of another subclass. But no class can be a superclass of itself.

Here is a simple example of inheritance. The following program creates a superclass called **A** and a subclass called **B**. Notice how the keyword **extends** is used to create a subclass of **A**.

```
// Create a superclass.
class A {
  int i, j;

  void showij() {
    System.out.println("i and j: " + i + " " + j);
  }
}

// Create a subclass by extending class A.
class B extends A {
  int k;

  void showk() {
    System.out.println("k: " + k);
  }
  void sum() {
    System.out.println("i+j+k: " + (i+j+k));
  }
}

class SimpleInheritance {
  public static void main(String args[]) {
    A superOb = new A();
    B subOb = new B();

    // The superclass can be used by itself.
    superOb.i = 38;
    superOb.j = 48;
    System.out.println("Contents of superOb: ");
    superOb.showij();
    System.out.println();

    /* The subclass has access to all public members of
       its superclass. */
    subOb.i = 46;
    subOb.j = 45;
    subOb.k = 19;
```

```
System.out.println("Contents of subOb: ");
subOb.showij();
subOb.showk();
System.out.println();

System.out.println("Sum of i, j and k in subOb:");
subOb.sum();
  }
}
```

As the example shows, the subclass **B** includes all of the members of its superclass, **A**. This is why **subOb** can access **i** and **j** and call **showij( )**. Also, inside **sum( )**, **i** and **j** can be referred to directly, as if they were part of **B**. Even though **A** is a superclass for **B**, it is also a completely independent, stand-alone class. Being a superclass for some subclass does not necessarily mean that the superclass cannot be used by itself.

USING super

Whenever a subclass needs to refer to its immediate superclass, it can do so using the keyword **super**. **super** has two general forms. The first calls the superclass' constructor. The second is used to access a member of the superclass that has been hidden by a member of a subclass. Each use is examined here.

Using super to Call Superclass Constructors

A subclass can call a constructor method defined by its superclass using the following form of **super**:

super(*parameter-list*);

Here, *parameter-list* specifies any parameters needed by the constructor in the superclass. **super( )** must always be the first statement executed inside a subclass' constructor.

Using super to Refer to a Superclass Member

The second form of **super** acts somewhat like **this**, except that it always refers to the superclass of the subclass in which it is used. This usage has the following general form:

super.*member*

Here, *member* can be either a method or an instance variable.

This second form of **super** is most applicable to situations in which member names of a subclass hide members by the same name in the superclass.

WHEN CONSTRUCTORS ARE CALLED

In a class hierarchy, constructors are called in order of derivation, from superclass to subclass. Further, since **super( )** must be the first statement executed in a subclass's constructor, this order is the same whether **super( )** is used or not. If **super( )** is not used, then the default or parameterless constructor of each superclass will be executed.

METHOD OVERRIDING

In a class hierarchy, when a method in a subclass has the same name and type signature as a method in its superclass, then the method in the subclass is said to *override* the method in the superclass. When an overridden method is called from within a subclass, it will always refer to the version of that method defined by the subclass. The version of the method defined by the superclass will be hidden.

Dynamic Method Dispatch

4

Method overriding forms the basis for one of Java's most powerful concepts: *dynamic method dispatch.* Dynamic method dispatch is the mechanism by which a call to an overridden function is resolved at run time, rather than compile time. Dynamic method dispatch is important because this is how Java implements run-time polymorphism.

Dynamic method dispatch is founded on an important principle: A superclass reference variable can refer to a subclass object. Java uses this fact to resolve calls to overridden methods at run time. Here is how: When an overridden method is called through a superclass reference, Java determines which version of that method to execute based upon the type of the object being referred to at the time the call occurs. Thus, this determination is made at run time. When different types of objects are referred to, different versions of an overridden method will be called. In other words, *it is the type of the object being referred to* that determines which version of an overridden method will be executed—not the type of the reference variable. Therefore, if a superclass contains a method that is overridden by a subclass, when different types of objects are referred to through a superclass reference variable, different versions of the method are executed.

Programming Tip

Overridden methods allow Java to support run-time polymorphism. Polymorphism is essential to object-oriented programming for one reason: It allows a general class to specify methods that will be common to all of its derivatives, while allowing those subclasses to define the specific implementation of some or all of those methods. Overridden methods are one way that Java implements the "one interface, multiple methods" aspect of polymorphism.

Part of the key to successfully applying polymorphism is understanding that the super- and subclasses form a hierarchy that moves from lesser to greater specialization. When used correctly, the superclass provides all elements that a subclass can use directly. It also defines those methods that the derived class must implement on its own. This allows the subclass the flexibility to define its own methods, yet still enforces a consistent interface. Thus, by combining inheritance with overridden methods, a superclass can define the generic methods that will be used by all of its subclasses.

ABSTRACT CLASSES

It is possible to define a superclass that declares its form and structure without providing a complete implementation of its methods. Such a class is referred to as *abstract*. An abstract class is a class in which at least one method has no implementation. A method that does not include an implementation (i.e., a body) is also called abstract.

An abstract method is declared using the **abstract** specifier and has no defined implementation. Thus, when a superclass contains an abstract method, any subclass must override the abstract method—it cannot simply use the version defined by the superclass, since it doesn't exist. To declare an abstract method, use this general form:

abstract *type name*(*parameter-list*);

As you can see, no method body is present.

4

Any class that contains one or more abstract methods must also be declared abstract. To do so, simply put the **abstract** keyword in front of the **class** keyword at the beginning of the class declaration.

Here is a very simple example that uses an abstract method and class:

```
// Demonstrate abstract method and class.
abstract class Square {
  abstract int square(int i); // abstract method
}

/* SqrIt must implement square. If it doesn't, a
     compile-time error will occur. */
class SqrIt extends Square {
  int square(int i) { return i*i; }
}

class AbstractDemo {
  public static void main(String args[]) {
    SqrIt ob = new SqrIt();
    System.out.println("10 squared is " + ob.square(10));
  }
}
```

As the comments indicate, since **square( )** is abstract, its class **Square** must also be abstract. This means that **SqrIt**, which extends **Square**, must implement **square( )**. Failure to do so would prevent the program from compiling.

There can be no objects of an abstract class. That is, an abstract class cannot be directly instantiated with the **new** operator. The reason for this is easy to understand. Such objects would be useless, because an abstract class is not fully defined. Also, you cannot declare abstract constructors or abstract static methods. Any subclass of an abstract class must either implement all of the abstract methods in the superclass or be declared **abstract** itself.

THE final KEYWORD

Java defines the keyword **final**, which has three uses. Two relate directly to inheritance. The third allows you to create named constants. All three uses are examined here.

Using final to Prevent Overriding

While method overriding is one of Java's most powerful features, there will be times when you will want to prevent it from occurring. To disallow a method from being overridden, specify **final** as a modifier at the start of its declaration. Here is an example:

```
class A {
  final void meth() {
    System.out.println("This is a final method.");
  }
}

class B extends A {
  void meth() { // ERROR! Can't override.
    System.out.println("Illegal!");
  }
}
```

Because **meth( )** is declared as **final**, it cannot be overridden in **B**. If you attempt to do so, a compile-time error will result. Also, methods declared as **final** can have their code generated in-line, thus avoiding the overhead of the normal call and return mechanism.

Using final to Prevent Inheritance

Sometimes you will want to prevent a class from being inherited. To do this, precede the class declaration with **final**. Declaring a class as **final** implicitly declares all of its methods as **final**, too. As you might expect, it is illegal to declare a class as both **abstract** and **final** since an abstract class is incomplete by itself and relies upon its subclasses to provide complete implementations.

4

Here is an example of a **final** class:

```
final class A {
  // ...
}

// The following class is illegal.
class B extends A { // ERROR! Can't subclass A
  // ...
}
```

As the comments imply, it is illegal for **B** to inherit **A** since **A** is declared as **final**.

Using final to Create Named Constants

The third use of **final** creates the equivalent of a named constant. If you precede a variable declaration with **final**, the variable cannot be modified. This means that you must initialize a **final** variable when it is declared. For example,

```
final int COUNT = 100;
```

Here, **COUNT** is a constant that has the value 100.

PACKAGES

Packages are containers for classes. They are used to keep the class name space compartmentalized. For this reason, the Java standard library is stored in a collection of packages.

The package is both a naming and a visibility control mechanism. You can define classes inside a package that are not accessible by code outside that package. You can also define class members that are exposed only to other members of the same package.

Defining a Package

To create a package, simply include a **package** command as the first statement in a Java source file. The **package** statement defines a name space in which classes are stored. If you omit the **package** statement, the class names are put into the default package, which has no name.

The general form of the **package** statement is shown here:

    package *pkg*;

Here, *pkg* is the name of the package.

Java uses file system directories to store packages. For example, a package called **MyPack** must be stored in a directory called **MyPack**. The directory name must match the package name exactly.

You can create a hierarchy of packages. To do so, simply separate each package name from the one above it using a period. The general form of a multilevel package statement is shown here.

    package *pkg1[.pkg2[.pkg3]]*;

The package hierarchy must be supported by equivalent subdirectories on disk.

Understanding CLASSPATH

The specific location that the Java compiler will consider as the root of any package hierarchy is controlled by **CLASSPATH**. The default current working directory (".") is usually in the **CLASSPATH** environmental variable defined for the Java run-time system. Remember, **CLASSPATH** sets the top of the class hierarchy.

IMPORTING PACKAGES

There are two ways to refer to a class that is contained within a package. First, you can specify its full name, which includes its package name or names. Of course, it could become tedious to type in long, dot-separated package path names for every class that you use within a program. This is the reason for the second way to access code in another package: the **import** statement.

The **import** statement brings certain classes, or entire packages, into the current name space. Once imported, a class can be referred to directly, using only its name. The **import** statement is a convenience to the programmer and is not technically needed to write a complete Java program.

In a Java source file, **import** statements occur immediately following the **package** statement (if it exists) and before any class definitions. The general form of the **import** statement is shown here:

import *pkg1*[.*pkg2*].(*classname*|*);

Here, *pkg1* is the name of a top-level package, *pkg2* is the name of a subordinate package inside the outer package separated by a dot (.). There is no practical limit on the depth of a package hierarchy, except the limit imposed by the file system. Finally, an explicit *classname* or a star (*) is specified; a star indicates that the Java compiler should search this entire package when it encounters a class name that does not have an explicit package associated with it.

ACCESS CONTROL

In general, Java implements access control using the keywords **public**, **private**, and **protected**. In addition, Java defines a default access level that is distinct from **public**. Both classes and packages provide access control, and interact with each other. Thus, Java provides these four categories of visibility for class members relative to packages:

- Subclasses in the same package
- Non-subclasses in the same package
- Subclasses in different packages
- Classes that are neither in the same package nor subclasses

The three access specifiers—**private**, **public**, and **protected**—provide a variety of ways to produce the many levels of access required by these categories. Table 4-1 sums up the interactions. The columns indicate the different access specifiers that can be applied to a member of a class. The rows specify the places from which each type of member can or cannot be accessed. The entry at the intersection of that row and column indicates if access is permitted.

In general, **public** grants access to anyone. **private** denies access to everyone except code within that same class. **protected** provides access to all code in the same package and to subclasses in different packages. The default access restricts access to within the same package.

Table 4-1 applies only to members of classes. A class itself has only two possible access levels: default and public. When a class is declared as **public**, it is accessible by any other code. If a class has default access, it can be accessed only by other code within its same package.

Table 4-1. Class Member Access

	private member	default member	protected member	public member
Visible within same class	yes	yes	yes	yes
Visible within same package by subclass	no	yes	yes	yes
Visible within same package by non-subclass	no	yes	yes	yes
Visible within different package by subclass	no	no	yes	yes
Visible within different package by non-subclass	no	no	no	yes

INTERFACES

An **interface** allows you to fully abstract a class from its implementation. Interfaces are syntactically similar to classes, but their methods are declared without any body. Using an **interface**, you can specify what a class must do, but not how it does it. Once defined, any number of classes can implement an interface. Also, one class can implement any number of interfaces. Since interfaces are in a different hierarchy from classes, it is possible for classes that are unrelated in terms of the class hierarchy to implement the same interface.

Defining an Interface

An interface is defined much like a class. The general form of an interface is shown here:

```
access interface name {
  return-type method-name1(parameter-list);
  return-type method-name2(parameter-list);
  type final-varname1 = value;
  type final-varname2 = value;
  // ...
  return-type method-nameN(parameter-list);
  type final-varnameN = value;
}
```

Here, *access* is either **public** or not used. When no access specifier is included, then default access results and the interface is available only to other members of the package in which it is declared. When it is declared as **public**, the interface can be used by any other code. *name* is the name of the interface and can be any valid identifier. Notice that the methods that are declared have no bodies. They end with a semicolon after the parameter list. They are, essentially, abstract methods; there can be no default implementation of any method specified within an interface. Each class that implements an interface must implement all of the methods. Variables can be declared inside of interface declarations. They are implicitly **final** and **static**, meaning they cannot be changed by the implementing class. They must also be initialized with a constant value. All methods and variables are implicitly public if the interface itself is declared as **public**.

Here is an example of an interface definition:

```
interface Series {
  int nextNumber(); // get next number in series
  void setStart(int i); // set starting point
}
```

Here, **Series** is the name of the interface. It defines two methods, called **nextNumber( )** and **setStart( )**, which must be created by any class that implements **Series**.

Implementing Interfaces

Once an **interface** has been defined, one or more classes can implement that interface. To implement an interface, include the **implements** clause in a class definition and then create the methods defined by the interface. The general form of a class that includes the **implements** clause looks like this:

```
access class classname implements interface {
  // class-body
}
```

Here, *access* is either **public** or not used. If a class implements more than one interface, the interfaces are separated with a comma. The methods that implement an interface must be declared **public**. Also, the type signature of the implementing method must match exactly the type signature specified in the **interface** definition.

For example, the following class implements the **Series** interface:

```
class MySeries implements Series {
  int num;

  // count by 2s
  public int nextNumber() {
    num += 2;
    return num;
  }

  public void setStart(int i) { num = i; }
}
```

Interfaces Can Be Extended

One interface can inherit another using the keyword **extends**. The syntax is the same as for inheriting classes. When a class implements an interface that inherits another interface, it must provide implementations for all methods defined within the interface inheritance chain.

Programming Tip

You can declare variables as object references that use an interface rather than a class type. Any instance of any class that implements the declared interface can be stored in such a variable. When you call a method through one of these references, the correct version will be called based on the actual instance of the interface being referred to. For example, here is another implementation of **Series**:

```
class AnotherSeries implements Series {
  int num;

  // count by 3s
  public int nextNumber() {
    num += 3;
    return num;
  }

  public void setStart(int i) { num = i; }
}
```

Now the following code is perfectly valid:

```
class TestSeries {
  public static void main(String args[]) {
    Series ob = new MySeries();
      // ob references MySeries object
    ob.setStart(10);
    System.out.println(ob.nextNumber() + " "
                     + ob.nextNumber());
```

```
   ob = new AnotherSeries();
     // ob references AnotherSeries object
   ob.setStart(22);
   System.out.println(ob.nextNumber() + " " +
                      ob.nextNumber());
 }
}
```

Here, **ob** is an interface reference. Therefore, the version of
setStart( ) and **nextNumber( )** that will be executed is determined
by what type of object **ob** refers to. This is one of the key features
of interfaces. The method to be executed is looked up
dynamically at run time. This is another way that Java supports
run-time polymorphism, and it is similar to using a superclass
reference to access a subclass object, as described earlier.

Chapter 5—Keyword Summary

The Java language reserves the following keywords:

abstract	default	if	package	synchronized
boolean	do	implements	private	this
break	double	import	protected	throw
byte	else	instanceof	public	throws
case	extends	int	return	transient
catch	final	interface	short	try
char	finally	long	static	void
class	float	native	super	volatile
const	for	new	switch	while
continue	goto			

The keywords **const** and **goto** are reserved but not used. In addition to the keywords, Java reserves the following: **true**, **false**, and **null**. These values are predefined by Java. You cannot use these words for the names of variables, classes, or other items.

A synopsis of each keyword follows.

abstract

The **abstract** keyword can be applied to a method or a class. An **abstract** method does not define an implementation. (That is, an **abstract** method has no body.) An implementation must be provided by a subclass. This is the general form of an **abstract** method:

    abstract *ret-type name*(*parameter-list*);

As you can see, no method body is present.

An **abstract** class is one that contains one or more abstract methods. Abstract classes cannot be instantiated. To declare a class as abstract, precede its declaration with the **abstract** keyword.

See Chapter 4 for additional details about **abstract** classes and methods.

boolean

boolean is one of the eight elemental data types in Java. It is used to declare Boolean variables and return values.

break

break exits from a **do**, **for**, or **while** loop, bypassing the normal loop condition. It is also used to exit from a **switch** statement.

This is an example of **break** in a loop:

```
int x = 5;

while(true) {
   if(x < 0) break;
   System.out.println("x = " + x);
   x--;
}
```

Here, if **x** is negative, the loop is terminated.

A **break** terminates only the **for, do, while**, or **switch** statement that contains it. It will not break out of nested loops or **switch** statements. In a **switch** statement, **break** effectively keeps program execution from "falling through" to the next **case**. (See "**switch**" for details.)

byte

byte is one of the eight elemental data types in Java. It is used to declare byte (i.e., 8-bit) variables and return types.

case

See "**switch**."

catch

See "**try**."

char

char is one of the eight elemental data types in Java. It is used to declare character variables and return types.

class

The **class** keyword starts the definition of a class, as in the following example:

```
class Sphere {
  double radius;
  Sphere(double radius) {
    this.radius = radius;
  }
  double area() {
    return 4 * Math.PI * radius * radius;
  }
}
```

The **class** keyword can be preceded by the **abstract** or **final** keywords. A superclass is designated via the **extends** keyword. Interfaces implemented by a class are designated with the **implements** keyword.

For more information on classes, see Chapter 2.

continue

The keyword **continue** bypasses the remaining portion of code in a loop and forces the conditional test to be performed. For example, the following **for** loop prints out the numbers less than 100 that are multiples of both 3 and 5:

```
for(int i=0; i<100; i++) {
  if((i%3 != 0) || (i%5 != 0)) continue;
  System.out.println("A multiple of both 3 and 5 is " + i)
}
```

Here, if **i** is not evenly divisible by 3 or 5, the loop continues. Otherwise, the **println( )** statement executes.

default

See **"switch."**

do

The **do** loop is one of three loop constructs available in Java. This is the general form of the **do** loop:

```
do {
    statement block
} while(condition);
```

If only one statement is repeated, the braces are not necessary, but they do add clarity. The *condition* must be a Boolean expression. The **do** loop repeats as long as the condition is true.

The **do** loop is the only loop in Java that will always have at least one iteration, because the condition is tested at the bottom of the loop.

Here is an example of the **do** loop:

```
int x = 10;
do {
  System.out.println("x = " + x);
  x -= 2;
} while(x > 0);
```

This loop exits when **x** becomes negative.

double

double is one of the eight elemental data types in Java. It is used to declare double-precision floating-point variables and return values.

else

See "**if.**"

extends

The **extends** keyword is used to specify the superclass of a class. Its general form is as follows:

class *class-name* extends *inherited-class-name* {

Here is an example:

```
// Create a superclass.
class A {
   int a;
}

// Create a subclass by extending class A.
class B extends A {
   int b;
}
```

Here, class **B** inherits class **A**. This means that an object of type **B** will also include the instance variable **a**.

It is also possible for one interface to inherit another using the keyword **extends**. The syntax is the same as for inheriting classes. When a class implements an interface that inherits another interface, it must provide implementations for all methods defined within the interface inheritance chain, as in this example:

```
// One interface can extend another.
interface A {
  void a1();
  void a2();
}

// B now includes a1() and a2()--it adds b1().
interface B extends A {
  void b1();
}

// This class must implement all of A and B.
class MyClass implements B {
  public void a1() {
    System.out.println("Implement a1().");
  }

  public void a2() {
    System.out.println("Implement a2().");
  }

  public void b1() {
    System.out.println("Implement b1().");
  }
}
```

Here, interface **B** inherits interface **A**. Thus, when **MyClass** implements **B**, it must implement the methods specified by both **A** and **B**.

false

false is one of the two possible **boolean** values. The other is **true**.

final

The **final** keyword can be applied to classes, methods, or variables. A class designated as **final** cannot be subclassed. A method designated as **final** cannot be overridden. A variable designated as **final** cannot be changed and is effectively a constant.

finally

See "**try**."

float

float is one of the eight elemental data types in Java. It is used to declare single-precision floating-point variables and return values.

for

The **for** loop allows automatic initialization and incrementation of a loop-control variable. This is its most common general form:

```
for(initialization; condition; increment) {
  statement block
}
```

If only one statement is being repeated, the braces are not necessary.

Although the **for** loop allows a number of variations, generally the *initialization* is used to set a loop-control variable to its starting value. The *condition* is generally a relational statement that checks the control variable against a termination value, and *increment* increments (or decrements) the control variable. The loop will run until the condition is **false**. If the condition is **false** to begin with, the body of the **for** will not execute even once.

The following code prints the message "hello" ten times:

```
for(int t = 0; t < 10; t++) System.out.println("hello");
```

if

The **if** is Java's conditional statement. It has this general form:

```
if(condition) {
  statement block 1
}
else {
  statement block 2
}
```

If single statements are used, the braces are not needed. The **else** is optional.

The *condition* must be a Boolean expression. If that expression evaluates to **true**, then statement block 1 will be executed; otherwise, if statement block 2 exists, it will be executed.

The following fragment checks the value of a variable that references a color object:

```
Color c = Color.blue;
if(c == Color.red) {
  System.out.println("color is red");
}
else {
  System.out.println("color is not red");
}
```

implements

The **implements** keyword specifies one or more interfaces that will be implemented by a class. This is its general form:

> class *class-name* implements *interface-name* {

To implement more than one interface, use a comma-separated list of interfaces.

See Chapter 4 for additional information about implementing interfaces.

import

import statements can be placed at the beginning of a Java source file (after the optional package statement). An **import**

statement has this general form:

import *pkg1*[.*pkg2*].(*classname*|*);

Here, *pkg1* is the name of a top-level package, *pkg2* is the name of a subordinate package inside the outer package separated by a dot (.). There is no practical limit on the depth of a package hierarchy, except the limit imposed by the file system. Finally, an explicit *classname* is specified, or a star (*), which indicates that the Java compiler should search this entire package when it encounters a class name that does not have an explicit package associated with it.

An **import** statement allows you to use the names of the classes and interfaces in the package directly, avoiding the use of the package name and the dot operator, as in this example:

```
import java.awt.*;
```

This **import** statement allows you to refer to **java.awt.Button** as **Button** in your program.

The **import** keyword can also import individual classes, as in this example:

```
import java.awt.TextField;
```

This statement allows you to refer to **java.awt.TextField** as **TextField**.

The package **java.lang** is imported automatically into your source files. **import** statements do not cause your **.class** files to become any larger. However, importing packages with large numbers of classes and interfaces may cause compilation time to increase.

instanceof

The **instanceof** operator tests whether an object is an instance of a particular class or whether an object implements a particular interface. The operator returns **true** or **false**. Here is an example:

```
Component c = new Button("Start");

if(c instanceof Button) {
    . . .
}
```

Here, the **if** statement succeeds because **c** is, indeed, an instance of **Button**.

int

int is one of the eight elemental data types in Java. It is used to declare integer variables and return values.

interface

The **interface** keyword starts the definition of an interface. Interfaces are syntactically similar to classes, but they lack instance variables and their methods are declared without any body.

See Chapter 4 for additional information.

long

long is one of the eight elemental data types in Java. It is used to declare long integer variables and return values.

native

The keyword **native** specifies that a method is implemented in native code rather than Java bytecode. (Native code is the instructions that a CPU actually executes.) Here is an example:

```
class Alarm {
  public native void activate();
}
```

Here, **activate( )** is a public method of the **Alarm** class that is implemented in native code.

Most native code methods are implemented in C.

new

The **new** operator creates an instance of an object. The **new** operator has this general form:

> *class-var* = new *class-name*( );

Here, *class-var* is the name of a reference variable, and *class-name* is the name of the class being instantiated. Here is an example:

```
Button b = new Button("Start");
```

The variable **b** holds a reference to a new **Button** object.

null

The **null** keyword specifies a null reference. An instance variable that has the value **null** does not refer to an object, as in this example:

```
Button b = null;
```

The variable **b** is declared to hold a reference to a **Button** object and is given the initial value of **null**, which means that it does not yet refer to a **Button** object.

A method also can return a **null**.

package

A **package** statement can be placed at the beginning of a Java source file to specify that all of the classes and interfaces in that source file are to be placed in the designated **package**. This is the general form of **package**:

package *pkg*;

Here, *pkg* is the name of the package. Here is an example:

```
package MyPack;
```

This statement indicates that the classes and interfaces in this source file are to be placed in the package **MyPack**.

See Chapter 4 for additional details.

private

The **private** modifier can be applied to a method or variable. A **private** method or variable is not visible outside the class in which it is defined.

5

protected

The **protected** modifier can be applied to a method or variable. A **protected** method or variable is visible only to code within the same package and to any subclasses in different packages.

public

The **public** modifier can be applied to a class, interface, method, or variable. A **public** class or interface can be accessed from any code in your program. A **public** method or variable is visible to any code that may access its class or interface.

return

The **return** statement forces a return from a method and can be used to transfer a value back to the calling method. For example, the following function returns the product of its two integer arguments:

```
public int multiply(int a, int b) {
  return a * b;
}
```

Keep in mind that as soon as a **return** is encountered, the method will return, skipping any other code that may remain in the method. Remember also that a method can contain more than one **return** statement.

short

short is one of the eight elemental data types in Java. It is used to declare short integer variables and return values.

static

The **static** modifier can be applied to either a variable or method. A variable designated as **static** exists only once in memory and is shared by all instances of the class of which it is a member. A **static** variable can be accessed directly through its class name, without the use of an object. Here is an example:

```
double pi = Math.PI;
```

Here, **Math.PI** is a **static** variable defined within the **Math** class.

A method designated as **static** can be accessed directly using its class name. No object of its class is required, as in this example:

```
double y = Math.sin(degrees * Math.PI/180);
```

Here, **sin( )** is a **static** method defined by **Math**.

Methods declared as **static** have several restrictions. First, a **static** method can call only other **static** methods. Second, it must access only **static** data. Third, a **static** method cannot refer to **this** or **super** in any way.

You can also declare a **static** block. A **static** block gets executed only once, when its class is first loaded.

> ## super

The **super** keyword allows a subclass to refer to its immediate superclass. **super** has two general forms. The first calls the superclass constructor, as in this example:

```
class MyButton extends Button {
  MyButton(String label) {
    super(label);
    // ...
  }
}
```

Here, the statement **super(label)** invokes **Button's** constructor.

The second use of **super** is to access a member of the superclass that has been hidden by a member of a subclass, as in this example:

```
class X {
  int a;
  // ...
}

class Y extends X {
  int a;  // This variable hides the a in X.
  void f() {
    // ...
    int b = super.a;  // b gets the a from X.
    int c = a;  // c gets the a from Y.
    // ...
  }
}
```

See Chapter 4 for additional information about **super**.

switch

The **switch** statement is Java's multiway branch statement. It is used to route execution one of several different ways. This is its general form:

```
switch(expression) {
  case constant1:
    statement-sequence1
    break;
  case constant2:
    statement-sequence2
    break
    . . .
  case constantN:
    statement-sequenceN
    break;
  default:
    default statements
}
```

Each statement sequence can be from one to several statements long. The default portion is optional.

switch works by checking the *expression* against the constants in the **case** statements. If a match is found, the sequence of statements associated with that **case** is executed. If the statement sequence does not contain a **break**, execution will continue on to the next case. Put differently, from the point of the match, execution will continue until either a **break** statement is found or the **switch** ends. If no match is found and a **default** case exists, its statement sequence is executed. Otherwise, no action takes place. The following example processes a menu selection:

```
switch(c) {
  case 'e':
    enter();
    break;
  case 'l':
    list();
    break;
  case 's':
    sort();
    break;
  default:
    System.out.println("Unknown command");
}
```

5

synchronized

The **synchronized** keyword provides two ways to coordinate the access of multiple threads to a shared resource. First, a method can be designated as **synchronized**. When a thread *T* is executing a **synchronized** method, all other threads that try to call it (or any other **synchronized** method) on the same instance have to wait until thread *T* returns from the **synchronized** method. This is the syntax for designating a **synchronized** method:

> synchronized *ret-type method1*(*parameter-list*) {

The second way that **synchronized** can be used is to designate a synchronized block. This is the syntax for designating a **synchronized** statement block:

> synchronized(*object*) {
>   *statements to be synchronized*
> }

Here, *object* is a reference to the object being synchronized. When a thread *T* is executing in a **synchronized** block, all other threads have to wait until thread *T* exits the **synchronized** block before another thread can call a method on *object*.

this

The keyword **this** can be used inside any method to refer to the current object. In other words, **this** is a reference to the object on which the method was invoked.

throw

See "**try**."

throws

An *exception* is an object that describes an exceptional (that is, error) condition that has occurred in a piece of code. If a method is capable of causing an exception that it does not handle, it must specify this behavior so that callers of the method can guard themselves against that exception. You do this by including a **throws** clause in the method's declaration. A **throws** clause lists the types of exceptions that a method might throw. It has the following general form:

```
ret-type method-name(parameter-list) throws exception-list {
   // ...
}
```

Here, *exception-list* is a comma-separated list of the exceptions that can be thrown by the method.

Here is an example:

```
void method1() throws MalformedURLException,
                      SocketException {
  // ...
}
```

This example indicates that **method1( )** is capable of throwing a **MalformedURLException** and **SocketException**.

You are required to catch or declare all non-run-time exceptions.

Also see **"try."**

transient

When an instance variable is declared as **transient**, its value need not persist when an object is stored. Here is an example:

```
class T {
  transient int a; // will not persist
  int b; // will persist
}
```

Here, if an object of type **T** is written to a persistent storage area, the contents of **b** would be saved, but the contents of **a** would not.

true

true is one of the two possible **boolean** values. The other is **false**.

try

The **try** keyword is part of Java's exception-handling mechanism. An *exception* is an object that describes an exceptional (that is, error) condition that has occurred in a piece of code. Java's exception handling is managed by five keywords: **try, catch, throw, throws,** and **finally**. Program statements that you want to monitor for exceptions are contained within a **try** block. If an exception occurs within the **try** block, it is thrown. Your code can catch this exception (using **catch**) and handle it in some rational manner. You must have a **catch** statement for each type of exception that you wish to catch. System-generated exceptions are automatically thrown by the Java run-time system. To manually throw an exception, use the keyword **throw**. Any exception that is thrown out of a method must be specified as such by a **throws** clause. Any code that absolutely must be executed before a method returns is put in a **finally** block.

The following general form illustrates how **try, catch, throw,** and **finally** are used:

```
try {
  // block of code to monitor for errors
  throw ExceptionType; // throw an exception
}
catch (ExceptionType1 exOb) {
  // exception handler for ExceptionType1
}
catch (ExceptionType2 exOb) {
  // exception handler for ExceptionType2
}
// ...
finally {
  // block of code to be executed before try block ends
}
```

Here, *ExceptionType* is the type of exception that has occurred. When an exception is thrown, the type of the exception determines which **catch** statement will be executed.

Also see **"throws."**

5

Programming Tip

Although Java's built-in exceptions handle most common errors, you will probably want to create your own exception types to handle situations specific to your applications. This is quite easy to do: Just define a subclass of **Exception,** which is a subclass of **Throwable**. Your subclasses don't need to actually implement anything themselves—their existence in the type system allows you to use them as exceptions. Of course, you might want to add features that relate to the type of exception that you are handling.

The **Exception** class does not define any methods of its own, but it does inherit those methods provided by **Throwable**. Thus, the methods defined by **Throwable** are available to all exceptions, including those that you create. (See **Throwable** in Chapter 6.)

Here is an example that declares a new subclass of **Exception** and then uses that subclass to throw an exception:

```
// Creating your own exceptions.
class MyException extends Exception {
  int pass;

  MyException(int x) { pass = x; }
}
```

```
class Except {
  public static void main(String args[]) {
    try {
      for(int i=0; i<10; i++) {
        if(i==4) throw new MyException(i);
        System.out.println("pass #" + i + "\n");
      }
    }
    catch(MyException e) {
      System.out.println("Exception on pass #"
                         + e.pass);
    }
  }
}
```

The output produced by this program is shown here.

```
pass #0
pass #1
pass #2
pass #3
Exception on pass #4
```

This example defines a subclass of **Exception** called **MyException**. This subclass is quite simple: It has only a constructor plus an integer variable called **pass**. The **Except** class creates a **for** loop that runs from 1 to 10. But when 4 is reached, a **MyException** object is created and thrown. The constructor is passed the value of **i**, which is stored in **pass**. When this exception is caught, the number of the pass in which the exception occurred is displayed.

void

The keyword **void** indicates that a method does not return a value. Here is an example:

```
void x1() {
  // ...
}
```

Here, **x1( )** does not return anything.

volatile

The **volatile** modifier tells the compiler that a variable's contents may be altered in ways not explicitly defined by the program. For example, variables that are changed by hardware such as real-time clocks, interrupts, or other inputs, should be declared as **volatile**.

while

The **while** loop has the following general form:

```
while(condition) {
  statement block
}
```

If a single statement is the object of the **while**, then the braces can be omitted. The *condition* must be a Boolean expression. The **while** loop repeats until the condition is false.

The **while** loop tests its condition at the top of the loop. Therefore, if the condition is false at the beginning, the loop will not execute even once.

5

An example of a **while** loop is shown here:

```
int x = 10;
while (x > 0) {
   System.out.println("x = " + x);
   x -= 2;
}
```

Chapter 6—The Language Classes and Interfaces

This section discusses those classes and interfaces defined by **java.lang**. It contains classes and interfaces that are fundamental to virtually all of Java programming. **java.lang** is automatically imported into all programs. It includes the following classes:

Boolean	Double	Object	StringBuffer
Byte	Float	Process	System
Character	Integer	Runtime	Thread
Class	Long	SecurityManager	ThreadGroup
ClassLoader	Math	Short	Throwable
Compiler	Number	String	Void

java.lang also defines the following interfaces:

Cloneable   Runnable

The following classes are new to Java specification 1.1: **Byte**, **Short**, and **Void**.

The following classes are infrequently used and are not discussed in this book: **ClassLoader**, **Compiler**, and **SecurityManager**.

THE BOOLEAN CLASS

The **Boolean** class encapsulates a **boolean** value. **Boolean** defines two **Boolean** constants: **FALSE** and **TRUE**.

In Java specification 1.1, **Boolean** also defines one constant named **TYPE**. This constant holds a reference to the **Class** object that represents the type **boolean**.

Boolean

public Boolean(boolean *b*)

This constructor creates an object whose value is equivalent to the **boolean** *b*.

public Boolean(String *str*)

This constructor creates an object whose value is equivalent to the **String** *str* (i.e., if *str* equals "true", the **Boolean** object holds the value **true**).

booleanValue

public boolean booleanValue( )

This method returns the value of the invoking object as a **boolean**.

equals

public boolean equals(Object *obj*)

This method tests whether the invoking object and *obj* have the same value.

getBoolean

public static boolean getBoolean(String *propName*)

This method returns **true** if the system property named *propName* exists and is equal to "true". Otherwise, it returns **false**. The comparison is performed in a case-insensitive manner.

hashCode

public int hashCode( )

This method returns the hash code of the invoking object.

toString

public String toString( )

This method returns the **String** equivalent of the invoking object.

valueOf

public static Boolean valueOf(String *str*)

This method returns a **Boolean** object whose value corresponds to the input argument.

THE BYTE CLASS

The **Byte** class encapsulates a **byte** value. **Byte** defines two **byte** constants: **MIN_VALUE** and **MAX_VALUE**. **MIN_VALUE** equals the minimum possible value of a **byte**. **MAX_VALUE** equals the maximum possible value of a **byte**.

Byte also defines one constant named **TYPE**. This constant holds a reference to the **Class** object that represents the type **byte**.

This class was introduced in Java specification 1.1.

Byte

public Byte(byte *b*)

This constructor creates an object whose value is equivalent to the **byte** *b*.

public Byte(String *str*)

This constructor creates an object whose value is equivalent to the **String** *str*. It can throw a **NumberFormatException**.

byteValue

public byte byteValue( )

This method returns the value of the invoking object as a **byte**.

decode

public static Byte decode(String *number*)

This method returns a **Byte** object that is equivalent to the **String** *number*. *number* can be in octal, hexadecimal, or decimal format. This method can throw a **NumberFormatException**.

doubleValue

public double doubleValue( )

This method returns the value of the invoking object as a **double**.

equals

public boolean equals(Object *obj*)

This method tests whether the invoking object and *obj* have the same value.

floatValue

public float floatValue( )

This method returns the value of the invoking object as a **float**.

hashCode

public int hashCode( )

This method returns the hash code of the invoking object.

intValue

public int intValue( )

This method returns the value of the invoking object as an **int**.

longValue

public long longValue( )

This method returns the value of the invoking object as a **long**.

parseByte

public static byte parseByte(String *str*)

This method returns a **byte** that is equivalent to the value represented by the **String** *str*. Radix 10 is used. It can throw a **NumberFormatException**.

public static byte parseByte(String *str*, int *radix*)

This method returns a **byte** that is equivalent to the value represented by the **String** *str*. *radix* is the radix to use when converting *str*. This method can throw a **NumberFormatException**.

shortValue

public short shortValue( )

This method returns the value of the invoking object as a **short**.

toString

public String toString( )

This method returns the **String** equivalent of the invoking object.

public static String toString(byte *b*)

This method returns a **String** object representing the value of the **byte** *b*. Radix 10 is used.

valueOf

public static Byte valueOf(String *str*)

This method returns a **Byte** object whose value is equivalent to the **String** object *str*. Radix 10 is used. This method can throw a **NumberFormatException.**

public static Byte valueOf(String *str*, int *radix*)

This method returns a **Byte** object whose value is equivalent to the **String** object *str*. *radix* is the radix to be used. This method can throw a **NumberFormatException.**

6

THE CHARACTER CLASS

The **Character** class encapsulates a character value. **Character** defines two **int** constants: **MAX_RADIX** and **MIN_RADIX**.

In Java specification 1.1, several additional fields have been added. **TYPE** is a constant that holds a reference to the **Class** object that represents the type **char**. **MIN_VALUE** and **MAX_VALUE** are **char** constants that specify the minimum and maximum values of a **char**. The following **byte** constants also exist: **COMBINING_SPACING_MARK**, **CONNECTOR_PUNCTUATION**, **CONTROL**, **CURRENCY_SYMBOL**, **DASH_PUNCTUATION**, **DECIMAL_DIGIT_NUMBER**, **ENCLOSING_MARK**, **END_PUNCTUATION**, **FORMAT**, **LETTER_NUMBER**, **LINE_SEPARATOR**, **LOWERCASE_LETTER**, **MATH_SYMBOL**, **MODIFIER_LETTER**, **MODIFIER_SYMBOL**, **NON_SPACING_MARK**, **OTHER_LETTER**, **OTHER_NUMBER**, **OTHER_PUNCTUATION**, **OTHER_SYMBOL**, **PARAGRAPH_SEPARATOR**, **PRIVATE_USE**, **SPACE_SEPARATOR**, **START_PUNCTUATION**, **SURROGATE**, **TITLECASE_LETTER**, **UNASSIGNED**, and **UPPERCASE_LETTER**. These constants are used to indicate a character category.

The most commonly used methods in this class are described here.

Character

public Character(char *ch*)

This constructor creates an object whose value is equivalent to the **char** *ch*.

charValue

public char charValue( )

This method returns the value of the invoking object as a **char**.

digit

public static int digit(char *ch*, int *radix*)

The **digit( )** method returns an **int** equivalent to a character in a specified radix.

equals

public boolean equals(Object *obj*)

This method tests whether the invoking object and *obj* have the same value.

hashCode

public int hashCode( )

This method returns the hash code of the invoking object.

isDigit

public static boolean isDigit(char *ch*)

This method tests whether a character is a digit.

isLetter

public static boolean isLetter(char *ch*)

This method tests whether a character is a letter.

This method was introduced in Java specification 1.1.

isLowerCase

public static boolean isLowerCase(char *ch*)

This method tests whether a character is lowercase.

isSpace

public static boolean isSpace(char *ch*)

This method tests whether a character is a space.

This method is deprecated in Java specification 1.1. You should use **isWhitespace( )**.

isUpperCase

public static boolean isUpperCase(char *ch*)

This method tests whether a character is uppercase.

isWhitespace

public static boolean isWhitespace(char *ch*)

This method tests whether a character is white space.

This method was introduced in Java specification 1.1.

toLowerCase

public static char toLowerCase(char *ch*)

This method converts a character to lowercase.

toString

public String toString( )

This method returns the **String** equivalent of the invoking object.

toUpperCase

public static char toUpperCase(char *ch*)

This method converts a character to uppercase.

THE CLASS CLASS

Class encapsulates the run-time state of an object or interface. Objects of type **Class** are created automatically, when classes are loaded. You cannot explicitly declare a **Class** object. Generally, you obtain a **Class** object by calling the **getClass( )** method defined by **Object**.

The most commonly used methods in this class are described here.

forName

public static native Class forName(String *name*)

This method returns a **Class** object given its complete name. It can throw a **ClassNotFoundException**.

getInterfaces

public native Class[ ] getInterfaces( )

When invoked on a class, this method returns an array of interfaces implemented by that class. When invoked on an interface, this method returns an array of interfaces extended by that interface.

getName

public native String getName( )

This method returns the complete name of the type of the invoking object.

getSuperclass

public native Class getSuperclass( )

This method returns the superclass of the invoking object. The return value is **null** if the invoking object is of type **Object**.

isInterface

public native boolean isInterface( )

This method tests whether the invoking object is an interface.

newInstance

public native Object newInstance( )

This method creates a new instance (that is, a new object) that
is of the same type as the invoking object. This is equivalent to
using **new** with the class' default constructor. The new object
is returned. This method can throw an **IllegalAccessException**
or **InstantiationException**.

toString

public String toString( )

This method returns the **String** equivalent of the invoking
object.

THE CLONEABLE INTERFACE

When a class implements the **Cloneable** interface, this indicates
that the **clone( )** method that is inherited from class **Object** can
make bitwise copies of objects of that class. The **Cloneable**
interface has no methods.

The **CloneNotSupportedException** is thrown if the **clone( )**
method is invoked on an instance that does not support the
Cloneable interface.

THE DOUBLE CLASS

The **Double** class encapsulates a **double** value. **Double**
defines five **double** constants: **MIN_VALUE**, **MAX_VALUE**,

NEGATIVE_INFINITY, **NaN**, and **POSITIVE_INFINITY**. These represent the minimum positive value, the maximum positive value, negative infinity, not a number, and positive infinity.

In Java specification 1.1, **Double** also defines one constant named **TYPE**. This constant holds a reference to the **Class** object that represents the type **double**.

Double

public Double(double *d*)

This constructor creates an object whose value is equivalent to the **double** d.

public Double(String *str*)

This constructor creates an object whose value is equivalent to the **String** str. It can throw a **NumberFormatException**.

byteValue

public byte byteValue( )

This method returns the value of the invoking object as a **byte**.

This method was introduced in Java specification 1.1.

doubleToLongBits

public native static long doubleToLongBits(double *value*)

This method returns the IEEE-compatible, double-precision bit pattern that corresponds to the input argument.

doubleValue

public double doubleValue( )

This method returns the value of the invoking object as a **double**.

equals

public boolean equals(Object *obj*)

This method tests whether the invoking object and *obj* have the same value.

floatValue

public float floatValue( )

This method returns the value of the invoking object as a **float**.

hashCode

public int hashCode( )

This method returns the hash code of the invoking object.

intValue

public int intValue( )

This method returns the value of the invoking object as an **int**.

isInfinite

public boolean isInfinite( )

This method tests whether the invoking object represents **Double.POSITIVE_INFINITY** or **Double.NEGATIVE_INFINITY**.

public static boolean isInfinite(double *d*)

This method tests whether *d* is **Double.POSITIVE_INFINITY** or **Double.NEGATIVE_INFINITY**.

isNaN

public boolean isNaN( )

This method tests whether the invoking object represents **Double.NaN**.

6

public static boolean isNaN(double *d*)

This method tests whether *d* is **Double.NaN**.

longBitsToDouble

public static native double longBitsToDouble(long *bits*)

This method returns the **double** equivalent of the IEEE-compatible, double-precision bit pattern specified by the argument.

longValue

public long longValue( )

This method returns the value of the invoking object as a **long**.

shortValue

public short shortValue( )

This method returns the value of the invoking object as a **short**.

This method was introduced in Java specification 1.1.

toString

public String toString( )

This method returns the **String** equivalent of the invoking object.

public static String toString(double *d*)

This method returns the **String** equivalent of *d*.

valueOf

public static Double valueOf(String *str*)

This method returns a **Double** object that contains the value specified by the input argument. It can throw a **NumberFormatException**.

THE FLOAT CLASS

The **Float** class encapsulates a **float** value. **Float** defines five **float** constants: **MIN_VALUE**, **MAX_VALUE**, **NEGATIVE_INFINITY**, **NaN**, and **POSITIVE_INFINITY**. These represent the minimum positive value, the maximum positive value, negative infinity, not a number, and positive infinity.

In Java specification 1.1, **TYPE** is a constant that holds a reference to the **Class** object that represents the type **float**.

Float

public Float(double *d*)

This constructor creates an object whose value is equivalent to the **double** *d*.

public Float(float *f*)

This constructor creates an object whose value is equivalent to the **float** *f*.

public Float(String *str*)

This constructor creates an object whose value is equivalent to the **String** *str*. It can throw a **NumberFormatException**.

byteValue

public byte byteValue( )

This method returns the value of the invoking object as a **byte**.

This method was introduced in Java specification 1.1.

doubleValue

public double doubleValue( )

This method returns the value of the invoking object as a **double**.

equals

public boolean equals(Object *obj*)

This method tests whether the invoking object and *obj* have the same value.

floatToIntBits

public static native int floatToIntBits(float *f*)

This method returns the IEEE-compatible, single-precision bit pattern that corresponds to the input argument.

floatValue

public float floatValue( )

This method returns the value of the invoking object as a **float**.

hashCode

public int hashCode( )

This method returns the hash code of the invoking object.

intBitsToFloat

public static native float intBitsToFloat(int *bits*)

This method returns the **float** equivalent of the IEEE-compatible, single-precision bit pattern specified by the argument.

intValue

public int intValue( )

This method returns the value of the invoking object as an **int**.

isInfinite

public boolean isInfinite( )

This method tests whether the invoking object represents **Float.POSITIVE_INFINITY** or **Float.NEGATIVE_INFINITY**.

public static boolean isInfinite(float *f*)

This method tests whether *f* is **Float.POSITIVE_INFINITY** or **Float.NEGATIVE_INFINITY**.

isNaN

public boolean isNaN( )

This method tests whether the invoking object represents **Float.NaN**.

public static boolean isNaN(float *f*)

This method tests whether *f* is **Float.NaN**.

longValue

public long longValue( )

This method returns the value of the invoking object as a **long**.

shortValue

public short shortValue( )

This method returns the value of the invoking object as a **short**.

toString

public String toString( )

This method returns the **String** equivalent of the invoking object.

public static String toString(float *f*)

This method returns the **String** equivalent of *f.*

valueOf

public static Float valueOf(String *str*)

This method returns a **Float** object that contains the value specified by the input argument. It can throw a **NumberFormatException**.

THE INTEGER CLASS

The **Integer** class encapsulates an **int** value. **Integer** defines two **int** constants: **MIN_VALUE** and **MAX_VALUE**. **MIN_VALUE** equals the minimum possible value of an **int**. **MAX_VALUE** equals the maximum possible value of an **int**.

In Java specification 1.1, **Integer** also defines one constant named **TYPE**. This constant holds a reference to the **Class** object that represents the type **int**.

The most commonly used methods in this class are described here.

Integer

public Integer(int *i*)

This constructor creates an object whose value is equivalent to the **int** *i*.

public Integer(String *str*)

This constructor creates an object whose value is equivalent to the **String** *str*. It can throw a **NumberFormatException**.

byteValue

public byte byteValue( )

This method returns the value of the invoking object as a **byte**.

This method was introduced in Java specification 1.1.

decode

public static Integer decode(String *number*)

This method returns an **Integer** object that is equivalent to the **String** *number*. *number* can be in octal, hexadecimal, or decimal format. This method can throw a **NumberFormatException**.

This method was introduced in Java specification 1.1.

doubleValue

public double doubleValue( )

This method returns the value of the invoking object as a **double**.

equals

public boolean equals(Object *obj*)

This method tests whether the invoking object and *obj* have the same value.

floatValue

public float floatValue( )

This method returns the value of the invoking object as a **float**.

hashCode

public int hashCode( )

This method returns the hash code of the invoking object.

intValue

public int intValue( )

This method returns the value of the invoking object as an **int**.

longValue

public long longValue( )

This method returns the value of the invoking object as a **long**.

parseInt

public static int parseInt(String *str*)

This method returns an **int** that is equivalent to the value represented by the **String** *str*. Radix 10 is used. This method can throw a **NumberFormatException**.

public static int parseInt(String *str*, int *radix*)

This method returns an **int** that is equivalent to the value represented by the **String** *str*. *radix* is the radix to use when converting *str*. This method can throw a **NumberFormatException**.

shortValue

public short shortValue( )

This method returns the value of the invoking object as a **short**.

This method was introduced in Java specification 1.1.

toString

public String toString( )

This method returns the **String** equivalent of the invoking object.

public static String toString(int *i*)

This method returns the **String** equivalent of the **int** *i*.

public static String toString(int *i*, int *radix*)

This method returns the **String** equivalent of the **int** *i* using the specified *radix*.

valueOf

public static Integer valueOf(String *str*)

This method returns an object whose value is equivalent to the **String** object *str*. Radix 10 is used. This method can throw a **NumberFormatException**.

public static Integer valueOf(String *str*, int *radix*)

This method returns an object whose value is equivalent to the **String** object *str*. *radix* is the radix to be used. This method can throw a **NumberFormatException**.

THE LONG CLASS

The **Long** class encapsulates a **long** value. **Long** defines two **long** constants: **MIN_VALUE** and **MAX_VALUE**. **MIN_VALUE** represents the minimum possible value of a **long**. **MAX_VALUE** represents the maximum possible value of a **long**.

In Java specification 1.1, **Long** also defines one constant named **TYPE**. This constant holds a reference to the **Class** object that represents the type **long**.

The most commonly used methods in this class are described here.

Long

public Long(long *l*)

This constructor creates an object whose value is equivalent to the **long** *l*.

public Long(String *str*)

This constructor creates an object whose value is equivalent to the **String** *str*. It can throw a **NumberFormatException**.

byteValue

public byte byteValue( )

This method returns the value of the invoking object as a **byte**.

This method was introduced in Java specification 1.1.

doubleValue

public double doubleValue( )

This method returns the value of the invoking object as a **double**.

equals

public boolean equals(Object *obj*)

This method tests whether the invoking object and *obj* have the same value.

floatValue

public float floatValue( )

This method returns the value of the invoking object as a **float**.

getLong

public static Long getLong(String *propertyName*)

The **getLong( )** method returns the value associated with the environmental property specified by *propertyName*. A **null** is returned on failure.

public static Long getLong(String *propertyName*, long *default*)

The **getLong( )** method returns the value associated with the environmental property specified by *propertyName*. A **Long** object with the value of *default* is returned on failure.

public static Long getLong(String *propertyName*, Long *default*)

The **getLong( )** method returns the value associated with the environmental property specified by *propertyName*. The value of *default* is returned on failure.

hashCode

public int hashCode( )

This method returns the hash code of the invoking object.

intValue

public int intValue( )

This method returns the value of the invoking object as an **int**.

longValue

public long longValue( )

This method returns the value of the invoking object as a **long**.

parseLong

public static long parseLong(String *str*)

This method returns the **long** equivalent of the number contained in the string specified by *str*. Radix 10 is used. This method can throw a **NumberFormatException**.

public static long parseLong(String *str*, int *radix*)

This method returns the **long** equivalent of the number contained in the string specified by *str* using the specified radix. This method can throw a **NumberFormatException**.

shortValue

public short shortValue( )

This method returns the value of the invoking object as a **short**.

This method was introduced in Java specification 1.1.

toString

public String toString( )

This method returns the **String** equivalent of the invoking object.

public static String toString(long *num*)

This method returns a **String** that contains the decimal equivalent of *num* using radix 10.

public static String toString(long *num*, int *radix*)

This method returns a **String** that contains the decimal equivalent of *num* using the specified radix.

valueOf

public static Long valueOf(String *str*)

This method returns a **Long** object whose value corresponds to the input argument. It can throw a **NumberFormatException**.

public static Long valueOf(String *str*, int *radix*)

This method returns a **Long** object whose value corresponds to the input argument using the specified radix. It can throw a **NumberFormatException**.

THE MATH CLASS

The **Math** class encapsulates mathematical operations. **Math** defines two **double** constants: **E** and **PI**.

abs

public static double abs(double *arg*)

This method returns the absolute value of *arg*.

public static float abs(float *arg*)

This method returns the absolute value of *arg*.

public static int abs(int *arg*)

This method returns the absolute value of *arg*.

public static long abs(long *arg*)

This method returns the absolute value of *arg*.

acos

public static native double acos(double *arg*)

This method returns the angle whose cosine is specified by *arg*.

asin

public static native double asin (double *arg*)

This method returns the angle whose sine is specified by *arg*.

atan

public static native double atan(double *arg*)

This method returns the angle whose tangent is specified by *arg*.

atan2

public static native double atan2(double *x*, double *y*)

This method returns the angle whose tangent is specified by x/y.

ceil

public static native double ceil(double *arg*)

This method returns the smallest whole number greater than or equal to *arg*.

cos

public static native double cos(double *radians*)

This method returns the cosine of its argument, which is specified in radians.

exp

public static native double exp(double *arg*)

This method returns **E** raised to the power *arg*.

floor

public static native double floor(double *arg*)

This method returns the largest whole number less than or equal to *arg*.

IEEEremainder

public static native double IEEEremainder(double *f1*, double *f2*)

This method returns the remainder of *f1* divided by *f2*.

log

public static native double log(double *arg*)

This method returns the natural logarithm of *arg*.

max

public static double max(double *x*, double *y*)

This method returns the maximum of *x* and *y*.

public static float max(float *x*, float *y*)

This method returns the maximum of *x* and *y*.

public static int max(int *x*, int *y*)

This method returns the maximum of *x* and *y*.

public static long max(long *x*, long *y*)

This method returns the maximum of *x* and *y*.

min

public static double min(double *x*, double *y*)

This method returns the minimum of *x* and *y*.

public static float min(float *x*, float *y*)

This method returns the minimum of *x* and *y*.

public static int min(int *x*, int *y*)

This method returns the minimum of *x* and *y*.

public static long min(long *x*, long *y*)

This method returns the minimum of *x* and *y*.

pow

public static native double pow(double *x*, double *y*)

This method returns *x* raised to the power *y*. It can throw an **ArithmeticException**.

random

public static synchronized double random( )

This method returns a random number between 0.0 and 1.0.

rint

public static native double rint(double *arg*)

This method returns the integer nearest in value to *arg*.

round

public static int round(float *arg*)

This method returns *arg* rounded up to the nearest **int**.

public static long round(double *arg*)

This method returns *arg* rounded up to the nearest **long**.

sin

public static native double sin(double *radians*)

This method returns the sine of its argument, which is expressed in radians.

6

sqrt

public static native double sqrt(double *arg*)

This method returns the square root of *arg*.

tan

public static native double tan(double *radians*)

This method returns the tangent of its argument, which is specified in radians.

THE NUMBER CLASS

The **Number** class is the superclass of the **Byte**, **Double**, **Float**, **Integer**, **Long**, and **Short** classes. It is an abstract class, which is never directly instantiated.

Number

public Number( )

This is the default constructor.

byteValue

public abstract byte byteValue( )

An implementation of the **byteValue( )** method must be provided by a subclass.

This method was introduced in Java specification 1.1.

doubleValue

public abstract double doubleValue( )

An implementation of the **doubleValue( )** method must be provided by a subclass.

floatValue

public abstract float floatValue( )

An implementation of the **floatValue( )** method must be provided by a subclass.

intValue

public abstract int intValue( )

An implementation of the **intValue( )** method must be provided by a subclass.

longValue

public abstract long longValue( )

An implementation of the **longValue( )** method must be provided by a subclass.

shortValue

public abstract short shortValue( )

An implementation of the **shortValue( )** method must be provided by a subclass.

This method was introduced in Java specification 1.1.

THE OBJECT CLASS

The **Object** class is the root of the class hierarchy. It is the only class that has no superclass.

Object

public Object( )

This is the default constructor.

clone

protected native Object clone( )

This method returns a new object that is the same as the invoking object. This method can throw a **CloneNotSupportedException** or **OutOfMemoryError**.

equals

public boolean equals(Object *obj*)

This method tests whether the invoking object and *obj* refer to the same object.

finalize

protected void finalize( )

This method is usually overridden by subclasses. It provides any special cleanup code and is executed just prior to the invoking object being garbage-collected. It can throw a **Throwable** object.

getClass

public final native Class getClass( )

This method returns the **Class** object that is associated with the invoking object.

hashCode

public native int hashCode( )

This method returns the hash code of the invoking object.

notify

public final native void notify( )

This method resumes execution of a thread waiting on the invoking object. It can throw an **IllegalMonitorStateException**.

notifyAll

public final native void notifyAll( )

This method resumes execution of all threads waiting on the invoking object. It can throw an **IllegalMonitorStateException**.

toString

public String toString( )

This method returns the **String** equivalent of the invoking object.

wait

public final void wait( )

This method waits indefinitely on another thread of execution. It can throw an **IllegalMonitorStateException** or **InterruptedException**.

public final native void wait(long *ms*)

This method waits up to *ms* milliseconds on another thread of execution. It can throw an **IllegalArgumentException**, **IllegalMonitorStateException**, or **InterruptedException**.

public final void wait(long *ms*, int *ns*)

This method waits up to *ms* milliseconds plus *ns* nanoseconds on another thread of execution. It can throw an **IllegalArgumentException**, **IllegalMonitorStateException**, or **InterruptedException**.

6

Programming Tip

When an object is used in a context in which a string is required, Java obtains the string representation of the object by calling its **toString( )** method. Every class implements **toString( )** because it is defined by **Object**. However, the default implementation of **toString( )** is seldom sufficient. For most classes

that you create, you will want to override **toString( )** and provide
your own string representations. Fortunately, this is easy to do. To
implement **toString( )**, simply return a **String** object that contains
the human-readable string that appropriately describes an object
of your class.

By overriding **toString( )** for classes that you create, you allow the
resulting strings to be fully integrated into Java's programming
environment. For example, they can be used in **print( )** and
println( ) statements and in concatenation expressions. The
following program demonstrates this by overriding **toString( )**
for the **Force** class.

```java
// Override toString() for Force class.
class Force {
  double mass;
  double accel;

  Force(double m, double a) {
    mass = m;
    accel = a;
  }

  public String toString() {
    // Force = mass * acceleration
    return "Force is " + (mass * accel);
  }
}

class Demo {
  public static void main(String args[]) {
    Force ob1 = new Force(2000, 60);
    Force ob2 = new Force(1, 88);

    System.out.println(ob1);
    System.out.println(ob2);

    String str = ob1 + " newtons";
    System.out.println(str);
```

```
      str = ob2 + " pounds";
      System.out.println(str);
   }
}
```

The output of this program is shown here.

```
Force is 120000.0
Force is 88.0
Force is 120000.0 newtons
Force is 88.0 pounds
```

As you can see, **Force**'s **toString( )** method is automatically invoked when a **Force** object is used in a concatenation expression or in a call to **println( )**.

THE PROCESS CLASS

The **Process** class encapsulates a running program. It is used primarily as a superclass for the type of objects created by **exec( )** in the **Runtime** class. **Process** is an abstract class.

Process

public Process( )

This is the default constructor.

destroy

public abstract void destroy( )

This method terminates the process.

exitValue

public abstract int exitValue( )

This method returns an exit code obtained from a subprocess. It can throw an **IllegalThreadStateException**.

getErrorStream

public abstract InputStream getErrorStream( )

This method returns an input stream that reads input from the process' **err** output stream.

getInputStream

public abstract InputStream getInputStream( )

This method returns an input stream that reads input from the process' **out** output stream.

getOutputStream

public abstract OutputStream getOutputStream( )

This method returns an output stream that writes output to the process' **in** input stream.

waitFor

public abstract int waitFor( )

This method returns the exit code returned by the process. This method does not return until the process on which it is called terminates. It can throw an **InterruptedException**.

THE RUNNABLE INTERFACE

The **Runnable** interface defines the **run( )** method that provides the body of a thread. To create a new thread, your program will either extend **Thread** or implement the **Runnable** interface.

Related classes: **Thread, ThreadGroup**

6

run

public abstract void run( )

The implementation of the **run( )** method must be provided by classes that implement the **Runnable** interface.

THE RUNTIME CLASS

The **Runtime** class encapsulates the run-time environment. You cannot instantiate a **Runtime** object. However, you can get a reference to the current **Runtime** object by calling the static method **getRuntime( )**. Once you obtain a reference to the current **Runtime** object, you can call several methods that control the state and behavior of the Java Virtual Machine. Applets and other untrusted code typically cannot call any of the **Runtime** methods without raising a **SecurityException**.

exec

public Process exec(String *progName*)

This method executes the program specified by *progName* as a separate process. An object of type **Process** is returned that describes the new process. This method can throw an **IOException** or a **SecurityException**.

public Process exec(String *progName*, String *environment*[ ])

This method executes the program specified by *progName* as a separate process. An object of type **Process** is returned that describes the new process with the environment specified by *environment*. This method can throw an **IOException** or a **SecurityException**.

public Process exec(String *comLineArray*[ ])

This method executes the command line specified by the strings in *comLineArray* as a separate process. An object of type **Process** is returned that describes the new process. This method can throw an **IOException** or a **SecurityException**.

public Process exec(String *comLineArray*[ ], String *environment*[ ])

This method executes the command line specified by the strings in *comLineArray* as a separate process with the environment specified by *environment*. An object of type **Process** is returned that describes the new process. This method can throw an **IOException** or a **SecurityException**.

exit

public void exit(int *exitCode*)

This method halts execution and returns the value of *exitCode* to the parent process. By convention, zero indicates normal termination. All other values indicate some form of error.

freeMemory

public native long freeMemory( )

This method returns the approximate number of bytes of free memory available to the Java run-time system.

gc

public native void gc( )

This method initiates garbage collection.

getLocalizedInputStream

public InputStream getLocalizedInputStream(InputStream *in*)

This method creates and returns a localized input stream that has the same characteristics as *in* except that it performs automatic conversions from the user's character set to Unicode.

This method is deprecated in Java specification 1.1.

getLocalizedOutputStream

public OutputStream getLocalizedOutputStream(OutputStream *out*)

This method creates and returns a localized output stream that has the same characteristics as *out* except that it performs automatic conversions from Unicode to the user's character set.

This method is deprecated in Java specification 1.1.

getRuntime

public static Runtime getRuntime( )

This method returns the current **Runtime** object.

load

public synchronized void load(String *libraryFileName*)

This method loads the dynamic library whose file is specified by *libraryFileName*, which must specify its complete path. It can throw a **SecurityException** or an **UnsatisfiedLinkError**.

loadLibrary

public synchronized void loadLibrary(String *libraryName*)

This method loads the dynamic library whose name is associated with *libraryName*. *libraryName* is mapped to an actual file in a platform-dependent manner. This method can throw a **SecurityException** or an **UnsatisfiedLinkError**.

runFinalization

public native void runFinalization( )

This method initiates calls to the **finalize( )** methods of unused, but not yet recycled objects.

runFinalizersOnExit

public static void runFinalizersOnExit(boolean *runFinalizers*)

This method is used to affect the behavior of the Java run-time system on exit. If *runFinalizers* is **true**, the **finalizer( )** methods for all objects are executed before the Java run-time system exits.

This method was introduced in Java specification 1.1.

totalMemory

public native long totalMemory( )

This method returns the total number of bytes of memory available to the program.

traceInstructions

public native void traceInstructions(boolean *traceOn*)

This method turns instruction tracing on or off, depending upon the value of *traceOn*. If *traceOn* is **true**, the trace is displayed. If it is **false**, tracing is turned off.

traceMethodCalls

public native void traceMethodCalls(boolean *traceOn*)

This method turns method call tracing on or off, depending upon the value of *traceOn*. If *traceOn* is **true**, the trace is displayed. If it is **false**, tracing is turned off.

THE SHORT CLASS

The **Short** class encapsulates a **short** value. **Short** defines two **short** constants: **MIN_VALUE** and **MAX_VALUE**. **MIN_VALUE** equals the minimum possible value of a **short**. **MAX_VALUE** equals the maximum possible value of a **short**.

Short also defines one constant named **TYPE**. This constant holds a reference to the **Class** object that represents the type **short**.

This class was introduced in Java specification 1.1.

Short

public Short(short *s*)

This constructor creates an object whose value is equivalent to the **short** *s*.

public Short(String *str*)

This constructor creates an object whose value is equivalent to the **String** *str*. It can throw a **NumberFormatException**.

byteValue

public byte byteValue( )

This method returns the value of the invoking object as a **byte**.

decode

public static Short decode(String *number*)

This method returns a **Short** object that is equivalent to the **String** *number. number* can be in octal, hexadecimal, or decimal format. This method can throw a **NumberFormatException**.

doubleValue

6

public double doubleValue( )

This method returns the value of the invoking object as a **double**.

equals

public boolean equals(Object *obj*)

This method tests whether the invoking object and *obj* have the same value.

floatValue

public float floatValue( )

This method returns the value of the invoking object as a **float**.

hashCode

public int hashCode( )

This method returns the hash code of the invoking object.

intValue

public int intValue( )

This method returns the value of the invoking object as an **int**.

longValue

public long longValue( )

This method returns the value of the invoking object as a **long**.

parseShort

public static short parseShort(String *str*)

This method returns a **short** that is equivalent to the value represented by the **String** *str*. It can throw a **NumberFormatException**.

public static short parseShort(String *str*, int *radix*)

This method returns a **short** that is equivalent to the value represented by the **String** *str*. *radix* is the radix to use when converting *str*. This method can throw a **NumberFormatException**.

shortValue

public short shortValue( )

This method returns the value of the invoking object as a **short**.

toString

public String toString( )

This method returns the **String** equivalent of the invoking object.

public static String toString(short *s*)

This method returns a **String** object representing the value of the **short** *s*.

valueOf

public static Short valueOf(String *str*)

This method returns a **Short** object whose value is equivalent to the **String** object *str*. It can throw a **NumberFormatException**.

public static Short valueOf(String *str*, int *radix*)

This method returns a **Short** object whose value is equivalent to the **String** object *str*. *radix* is the radix that is used. This method can throw a **NumberFormatException**.

THE STRING CLASS

The **String** class provides a set of methods to manipulate a string. Note that strings are immutable. There are no methods to modify the contents of a **String** object after it has been created.

Related classes: **StringBuffer**

The most commonly used methods in this class are described here.

String

public String( )

This constructor creates an empty **String** object.

public String(byte *asciiChars*[ ])

This constructor creates an object from the **byte** array *asciiChars*. The **byte**-to-**char** conversion is done by using the default character encoding on the platform.

This constructor was introduced in Java specification 1.1.

public String(byte *asciiChars*[ ], int *highOrderByte*)

This constructor creates an object from the **byte** array *asciiChars*. *highOrderByte* specifies the high-order byte of each character in the **String** object that is created.

This constructor is deprecated in Java specification 1.1.

public String(byte *asciiChars*[ ], int *start*, int *size*)

This constructor creates an object from the **byte** array *asciiChars*. *start* specifies the position of the first byte in *asciiChars* that is to be used. *size* specifies the number of bytes to use. The **byte**-to-**char** conversion is done using the default character encoding on the platform.

This constructor was introduced in Java specification 1.1.

public String(byte *asciiChars*[ ], int *highOrderByte*, int *start*, int *size*)

This constructor creates an object from the **byte** array *asciiChars*. *highOrderByte* specifies the high-order byte of each character in the **String** object that is created. *start* specifies the position of the first byte in *asciiChars* that is to be used. *size* specifies the number of bytes to use. This constructor can throw a **StringIndexOutOfBoundsException**.

This constructor is deprecated in Java specification 1.1

6

public String(byte *asciiChars*[ ], int *start*, int *size*, String *encode*)

This constructor creates an object from the **byte** array *asciiChars*. *start* specifies the position of the first byte in *asciiChars* that is to be used. *size* specifies the number of bytes to use. *encode* specifies the name of the character encoding to use. This constructor can throw an **UnsupportedEncodingException**.

This constructor was introduced in Java specification 1.1.

public String(byte *asciiChars*[ ], String *encode*)

This constructor creates an object from the **byte** array *asciiChars*. *encode* specifies the name of the character encoding to use. This constructor can throw an **UnsupportedEncodingException**.

This constructor was introduced in Java specification 1.1.

public String(char *asciiChars*[ ])

This constructor creates an object from the **char** array *asciiChars*.

public String(char *asciiChars*[ ], int *start*, int *size*)

This constructor creates an object from the **char** array *asciiChars*. *start* specifies the position of the first byte in *asciiChars* that is to be used. *size* specifies the number of bytes to use. The **byte**-to-**char** conversion is done using the default character encoding on the platform. This constructor can throw a **StringIndexOutOfBoundsException**.

public String(String *str*)

This constructor creates an object whose contents are equivalent to **String** *str*.

public String(StringBuffer *sb*)

This constructor creates an object whose contents are equivalent to **StringBuffer** *sb*.

charAt

public char charAt(int *position*)

This method returns the character at index *position*. It can throw a **StringIndexOutOfBoundsException**.

compareTo

public int compareTo(String *str*)

This method does a lexicographical comparison of the invoking object and **String** *str*. If the strings are equal, it returns zero. If the invoking object is lexicographically greater than *str*, the method returns a positive value. Otherwise, it returns a negative value.

concat

public String concat(String *str*)

This method returns a new **String** object that is the equivalent of **String** *str* appended to the end of the invoking object.

copyValueOf

public static String copyValueOf(char *asciiChars*[ ])

This method returns a new **String** object that is equivalent to the **char** array *asciiChars*.

public static String copyValueOf(char *asciiChars*[ ], int *start*, int *size*)

This method returns a new **String** object that is equivalent to a subset of the **char** array *asciiChars*. *start* specifies the position of the first byte in *asciiChars* that is to be used. *size* specifies the number of bytes to use.

endsWith

public boolean endsWith(String *str*)

This method tests whether the invoking object ends with the characters represented by *str*.

equals

public boolean equals(Object *obj*)

This method tests whether the invoking object and *obj* have the same value.

equalsIgnoreCase

public boolean equalsIgnoreCase(String *str*)

This method tests whether the invoking object and *str* each have the same value. This comparison is done independent of case.

getBytes

public byte[ ] getBytes( )

This method returns a byte array that contains the information from the invoking object. The **char**-to-**byte** conversion is done using the default character encoding on the platform.

This method was introduced in Java specification 1.1.

public byte[ ] getBytes(String *encodeName*)

This method returns a byte array that contains the information from the invoking object. The **char**-to-**byte** conversion is done using the character encoding *encodeName*. This method can throw an **UnsupportedEncodingException**.

This method was introduced in Java specification 1.1.

public void getBytes(int *srcStart*, int *srcEnd*, byte *destination*[ ], int *desStart*)

This method copies characters from the invoking object to a **byte** array. *srcStart* is the position at which to start copying characters from the invoking object. *srcEnd* is the position at which to stop copying characters from the invoking object. Therefore, a total of *srcEnd* − *srcBegin* characters are copied. *destination* is the **byte** array into which the characters should be copied. *desStart* is the position in *destination* at which to begin the copy. This method can throw a **StringIndexOutOfBoundsException**.

This method is deprecated in Java specification 1.1.

getChars

public void getChars(int *srcStart*, int *srcEnd*, char *destination*[ ], int *desStart*)

This method copies characters from the invoking object to a **char** array. *srcStart* is the position at which to start copying characters from the invoking object. *srcEnd* is the position at which to stop copying characters from the invoking object. Therefore, a total of *srcEnd − srcBegin* characters are copied. *destination* is the **char** array into which the characters should be copied. *desStart* is the position in *destination* at which to begin the copy. This method can throw a **StringIndexOutOfBoundsException**.

hashCode

public int hashCode( )

This method returns the hash code of the invoking object.

indexOf

public int indexOf(int *c*)

This method returns the index within the invoking object at which the first instance of *c* is located. If *c* is not found, −1 is returned.

public int indexOf(int *c*, int*start*)

This method returns the index within the invoking object at which the first instance of *c* is located. *start* specifies the position at which to start the search. If c is not found, -1 is returned.

public int indexOf(String *str*)

This method returns the index within the invoking object at which the first instance of *str* is located. If *str* is not found, -1 is returned.

public int indexOf(String *str*, int *start*)

This method returns the index within the invoking object at which the first instance of *str* is located. *start* specifies the position at which to start the search. If *str* is not found, -1 is returned.

lastIndexOf

public int lastIndexOf(int *c*)

This method returns the index within the invoking object at which the last instance of c is located. If c is not found, -1 is returned.

public int lastIndexOf(int *c*, int *start*)

This method returns the index within the invoking object at which the last instance of c is located. *start* specifies the position at which to start the search. The search proceeds backward from *start*. If c is not found, -1 is returned.

public int lastIndexOf(String *str*)

This method returns the index within the invoking object at which the last instance of *str* is located. If *str* is not found, -1 is returned.

public int lastIndexOf(String *str*, int *start*)

This method returns the index within the invoking object at which the last instance of *str* is located. *start* specifies the position at which to start the search. The search proceeds backward from *start*. If *str* is not found, −1 is returned.

length

public int length( )

This method returns the number of characters in the invoking object.

regionMatches

public boolean regionMatches(int *start*, String *str*, int *sStart*, int *number*)

This method tests whether two regions in two **String** objects match. *start* is the position in the invoking object at which to begin the comparison. *str* is the **String** object that will be compared with the invoking object. *sStart* is the position in *str* at which to begin the comparison. *number* is the number of characters to compare.

public boolean regionMatches(boolean *ignoreCaseFlag*, int *start*, String *str*, int *sStart*, int *number*)

This method tests whether two regions in two **String** objects match. If *ignoreCaseFlag* is **true**, case is ignored when performing the comparison. Otherwise, case is significant. *start* is the position in the invoking object at which to begin the comparison. *str* is the **String** object that will be compared with the invoking object. *sStart* is the position in *str* at which to begin the comparison. *number* is the number of characters to compare.

replace

public String replace(char *oldc*, char *newc*)

If the invoking object does not have any instances of *oldc*, this method returns a reference to that object. Otherwise, this method returns a new **String** object in which each occurrence of *oldc* is replaced with *newc*.

startsWith

public boolean startsWith(String *str*)

This method tests whether the invoking object starts with the character sequence in *str.*

public boolean startsWith(String *str*, int *start*)

This method tests whether the invoking object starts with the character sequence in *str. start* specifies the position in the invoking object at which to begin the search.

substring

public String substring(int *start*)

This method returns a substring of the invoking object. *start* specifies the position that begins the substring. The substring continues until the end of the invoking object. This method can throw a **StringIndexOutOfBoundsException**.

public String substring(int *start*, int *end*)

This method returns a substring of the invoking object. *start* is the position at which to start copying characters from the invoking object. *end* is the position at which to stop copying characters from the invoking object. Therefore, a total of *end* − *start* characters are copied. It can throw a **StringIndexOutOfBoundsException**.

toCharArray

public char[ ] toCharArray( )

This method returns a **char** array that contains the characters in the invoking object.

6

toLowerCase

public String toLowerCase( )

If all characters in the invoking object are already lowercase, this method returns a reference to that object. Otherwise, this method returns a new **String** object in which all characters have been converted to lowercase.

public String toLowerCase(Locale *localeObj*)

If all characters in the invoking object are already lowercase, this method returns a reference to that object. Otherwise, this method returns a new **String** object in which all characters have been converted to lowercase. *localeObj* contains rules that are to be used for doing this conversion.

This method was introduced in Java specification 1.1.

toString

public String toString( )

This method returns the **String** equivalent of the invoking object.

toUpperCase

public String toUpperCase( )

If all characters in the invoking object are already uppercase, this method returns a reference to that object. Otherwise, this method returns a new **String** object in which all characters have been converted to uppercase.

public String toUpperCase(Locale *localeObj*)

If all characters in the invoking object are already uppercase, this method returns a reference to that object. Otherwise, this method returns a new **String** object in which all characters have been converted to uppercase. *localeObj* contains rules that are to be used for doing this conversion.

This method was introduced in Java specification 1.1.

trim

public String trim( )

This method returns a new **String** object that has the same characters as the invoking object without any white space at the beginning or end of the invoking object.

valueOf

public static String valueOf(boolean *b*)

This method returns a **String** object equivalent to the **boolean** *b*.

public static String valueOf(char *c*)

This method returns a **String** object equivalent to the **char** *c*.

public static String valueOf(char *carray*[ ])

This method returns a **String** object equivalent to the **char** array *carray*.

public static String valueOf(char *carray*[ ], int *start*, int *size*)

This method returns a **String** object that is equivalent to the **char** array *carray*. *start* specifies the position of the first byte in *carray* that is to be used. *size* specifies the number of bytes to use.

6

public static String valueOf(double *d*)

This method returns a **String** object equivalent to the **double** *d*.

public static String valueOf(float *f*)

This method returns a **String** object equivalent to the **float** *f*.

public static String valueOf(int *i*)

This method returns a **String** object equivalent to the **int** *i*.

public static String valueOf(long *l*)

This method returns a **String** object equivalent to the **long** *l*.

public static String valueOf(Object *o*)

This method returns a **String** object equivalent to the **Object** *o*.

THE STRINGBUFFER CLASS

The **StringBuffer** class represents growable and writable character sequences. **StringBuffer** can have characters and substrings inserted in the middle, or appended to the end. **StringBuffer** will automatically grow to make room for such additions and often has more characters preallocated than are actually needed, to allow room for growth.

Related class: **String**

StringBuffer

public StringBuffer( )

This constructor creates an object with room for 16 characters without reallocation.

public StringBuffer(int *size*)

This constructor accepts an integer argument that explicitly sets the size of the buffer. It can throw a **NegativeArraySizeException**.

public StringBuffer(String *str*)

This constructor accepts a **String** argument that sets the initial contents of the **StringBuffer** object and reserves room for 16 additional characters without reallocation.

append

Each of these methods returns a reference to the invoking object.

public StringBuffer append(boolean *b*)

This method concatenates the string representation of *b* to the end of the invoking object.

public synchronized StringBuffer append(char *c*)

This method concatenates the string representation of *c* to the end of the invoking object.

public synchronized StringBuffer append(char *carray*[ ])

This method concatenates the string representation of *carray* to the end of the invoking object.

public synchronized StringBuffer append(char *carray*[ ], int *start*, int *size*)

This method concatenates the string representation of some of the characters in *carray* to the end of the invoking object. *start* specifies the position in *carray* at which to begin reading characters. *size* specifies the number of characters to read from *carray*.

public StringBuffer append(double *d*)

This method concatenates the string representation of *d* to the end of the invoking object.

public StringBuffer append(float *f*)

This method concatenates the string representation of *f* to the end of the invoking object.

public StringBuffer append(int *num*)

This method concatenates the string representation of *num* to the end of the invoking object.

public StringBuffer append(long *l*)

This method concatenates the string representation of *l* to the end of the invoking object.

public synchronized StringBuffer append(Object *obj*)

This method concatenates the string representation of *obj* to the end of the invoking object.

public synchronized StringBuffer append(String *str*)

This method concatenates the string representation of *str* to the end of the invoking object.

capacity

public int capacity( )

This method returns the total allocated capacity of the invoking object.

charAt

public synchronized char charAt(int *where*)

This method returns the value of a single character from the **StringBuffer**. *where* specifies the index of the character being obtained. It can throw a **StringIndexOutOfBoundsException**.

ensureCapacity

public synchronized void ensureCapacity(int *capacity*)

This method sets the size of the buffer. This is useful if you know in advance that you will be appending a large number of small strings to a **StringBuffer**.

getChars

public synchronized void getChars(int *sourceStart*, int *sourceEnd*, char *target*[ ], int *targetStart*)

This method copies a substring of a **StringBuffer** into an array. *sourceStart* specifies the index of the beginning of the substring and *sourceEnd* specifies an index that is one past the end of the desired substring. This means that the substring contains the characters from *sourceStart* through *sourceEnd*−1. The array that will receive the characters is specified by *target*. The index within *target* at which the substring will be copied is passed in *targetStart*. Care must be taken to ensure that the *target* array is large enough to hold the number of characters specified. This method can throw a **StringIndexOutOfBoundsException**.

insert

Each of these methods returns a reference to the invoking object.

public StringBuffer insert(int *index*, boolean *b*)

This method inserts the information from the **boolean** *b* into the invoking object starting at position *index*. It can throw a **StringIndexOutOfBoundsException**.

public synchronized StringBuffer insert(int *index*, char *c*)

This method inserts the information from the **char** *c* into the invoking object starting at position *index*. It can throw a **StringIndexOutOfBoundsException.**

public synchronized StringBuffer insert(int *index*, char *carray*[ ])

This method inserts the information from *carray* into the invoking object starting at position *index*. It can throw a **StringIndexOutOfBoundsException.**

public StringBuffer insert(int *index*, double *d*)

This method inserts the information from the **double** *d* into the invoking object starting at position *index*. It can throw a **StringIndexOutOfBoundsException.**

public StringBuffer insert(int *index*, float *f*)

This method inserts the information from the **float** *f* into the invoking object starting at position *index*. It can throw a **StringIndexOutOfBoundsException.**

public StringBuffer insert(int *index*, int *i*)

This method inserts the information from the **int** *i* into the invoking object starting at position *index*. It can throw a **StringIndexOutOfBoundsException.**

public StringBuffer insert(int *index*, long *l*)

This method inserts the information from the **long** *l* into the invoking object starting at position *index*. It can throw a **StringIndexOutOfBoundsException.**

public synchronized StringBuffer insert(int *index*, Object *obj*)

This method inserts the information from the **Object** *obj* into the invoking object starting at position *index*. It can throw a **StringIndexOutOfBoundsException**.

public synchronized StringBuffer insert(int *index*, String *str*)

This method inserts the information from the **String** object *str* into the invoking object starting at position *index*. It can throw a **StringIndexOutOfBoundsException**.

length

public int length( )

This method returns the current length of the invoking object.

reverse

public synchronized StringBuffer reverse( )

This method reverses the sequence of characters in the invoking object.

This method was introduced in Java specification 1.1.

setCharAt

public synchronized void setCharAt(int *where*, char *ch*)

This method sets the value of a character within the invoking object. *where* specifies the index of the character being set. *ch* specifies the new value of that character. This method can throw a **StringIndexOutOfBoundsException**.

setLength

public synchronized void setLength(int *len*)

This method sets the length of the buffer within the invoking object. *len* specifies the length of the buffer. This value must be positive. When you increase the size of the buffer, null characters will be added to the end of the existing buffer. If you call **setLength( )** with a value less than the current value returned by **length( )**, then the characters stored beyond the new length will be lost. This method can throw a **StringIndexOutOfBoundsException**.

toString

public String toString( )

This method returns the **String** equivalent of the invoking object.

THE SYSTEM CLASS

The **System** class provides an interface to system functionality. The standard input, output, and error streams of the Java run-time system are stored in the **in**, **out**, and **err** variables.

The most commonly used methods in this class are described here.

arraycopy

public static void arraycopy(Object *source,* int *sourceStart*, Object *target*, int *targetStart*, int *size*)

This method copies an array. The array to be copied is passed in *source* and the index at which the copy will begin within *source* is passed in *sourceStart.* The array that will receive the copy is passed in *target* and the index at which the copy will begin within *target* is passed in *targetStart. size* elements are copied. This method can throw **ArrayIndexOutOfBoundsException** or **ArrayStoreException**.

currentTimeMillis

public static native long currentTimeMillis( )

This method returns the current time in terms of milliseconds since midnight, January 1, 1970.

exit

public static void exit(int *exitCode*)

This method halts execution and returns the value of *exitCode* to the parent process (usually the operating system). By convention, zero indicates normal termination. All other values indicate some form of error. This method can throw a **SecurityException**.

gc

public static void gc( )

This method initiates garbage collection.

getenv

public static String getenv(String *envVariable*)

This method returns the environment variable specified by *envVariable.*

This method is deprecated in Java specification 1.1.

getProperties

public static Properties getProperties( )

This method returns the properties associated with the Java run-time system. It can throw a **SecurityException**.

getProperty

public static String getProperty(String *which*)

This method returns the property associated with *which*. A **null** is returned if the desired property is not found. This method can throw a **SecurityException**.

public static String getProperty(String *which*, String *default*)

This method returns the property associated with *which*. *default* is returned if there is no property associated with *which*. This method can throw a **SecurityException**.

getSecurityManager

public static SecurityManager getSecurityManager( )

This method returns the current security manager or a **null** if no security manager is installed.

load

public static void load(String *libraryFileName*)

This method loads the dynamic library whose file is specified by *libraryFileName*, which must specify its complete path. This method can throw a **SecurityException** or an **UnsatisfiedLinkError**

loadLibrary

public static void loadLibrary(String *libraryName*)

This method loads the dynamic library whose name is associated with *libraryName*. *libraryName* is mapped to an actual file in a platform-dependent manner. This method can throw a **SecurityException** or an **UnsatisfiedLinkError**.

runFinalization

public static void runFinalization( )

This method initiates calls to the **finalize( )** methods of unused, but not yet recycled objects.

runFinalizersOnExit

public static void runFinalizersOnExit(boolean *runFinalizers*)

This method is used to affect the behavior of the Java run-time system on exit. If *runFinalizers* is **true**, the **finalizer( )** methods for all objects are executed before the Java run-time system exits. Finalization on exit is disabled by default.

This method was introduced in Java specification 1.1.

setErr

public static void setErr(PrintStream *pstream*)

This method assigns *pstream* as the standard error stream.

This method was introduced in Java specification 1.1.

6

setIn

public static void setIn(InputStream *istream*)

This method assigns *istream* as the standard input stream.

This method was introduced in Java specification 1.1.

setOut

public static void setOut(PrintStream *ostream*)

This method assigns *ostream* as the standard output stream.

This method was introduced in Java specification 1.1.

setProperties

public static void setProperties(Properties *sysProperties*)

This method sets the current system properties as specified by *sysProperties*. It can throw a **SecurityException**.

setSecurityManager

public static void setSecurityManager(SecurityManager *secMan*)

This method sets the security manager to that specified by *secMan*. It can throw a **SecurityException**.

THE THREAD CLASS

The **Thread** class encapsulates a thread of execution and provides several methods that help manage threads. **Thread** defines three **int** constants: **MAX_PRIORITY**, **MIN_PRIORITY**, and **NORM_PRIORITY**. These represent the maximum, minimum, and normal priority of a thread.

Related classes: **ThreadGroup**

Related interfaces: **Runnable**

Thread

public Thread( )

This constructor creates a **Thread** object.

public Thread(Runnable *threadOb*)

This constructor creates a **Thread** object. *threadOb* is an object that implements the **Runnable** interface.

public Thread(Runnable *threadOb*, String *threadName*)

This constructor creates a **Thread** object. *threadOb* is an object that implements the **Runnable** interface. *threadName* is the name of the thread.

public Thread(String *threadName*)

This constructor creates a **Thread** object. *threadName* is the name of the thread.

public Thread(ThreadGroup *group*, Runnable *threadOb*)

This constructor creates a **Thread** object. *group* is the **ThreadGroup** to which this thread is to be added. *threadOb* is an object that implements the **Runnable** interface. This constructor can throw a **SecurityException**.

public Thread(ThreadGroup *group*, Runnable *threadOb*, String *threadName*)

This constructor creates a **Thread** object. *group* is the **ThreadGroup** to which this **Thread** is to be added. *threadOb* is an object that implements the **Runnable** interface. *threadName* is the name of the thread. This constructor can throw a **SecurityException**.

public Thread(ThreadGroup *group*, String *threadName*)

This constructor creates a **Thread** object. *group* is the **ThreadGroup** to which this **Thread** is to be added. *threadName* is the name of the thread. This constructor can throw a **SecurityException**.

activeCount

public static int activeCount( )

This method returns the number of threads in the group to which the invoking object belongs.

checkAccess

public void checkAccess( )

This method causes the security manager to verify that the current thread may access and/or change the invoking object. It can throw a **SecurityException**.

countStackFrames

public native int countStackFrames( )

This method returns the number of stack frames used by the invoking object. It can throw an **IllegalThreadStateException** if the invoking object is not suspended.

currentThread

public static native Thread currentThread( )

This method returns a reference to the thread that is now executing.

destroy

public void destroy( )

This method destroys the invoking object without any cleanup.

This method was introduced in Java specification 1.1.

dumpStack

public static void dumpStack( )

This method displays the call stack for the thread that is now executing.

enumerate

public static int enumerate(Thread *threads*[ ])

This method puts copies of all **Thread** objects that are in the current thread's group into *threads.* The number of threads is returned.

getName

public final String getName( )

This method returns the name of the invoking object.

getPriority

public final int getPriority( )

This method returns the priority of the invoking object.

getThreadGroup

public final ThreadGroup getThreadGroup( )

This method returns the **ThreadGroup** object of which the invoking object is a member.

interrupt

public void interrupt( )

This method interrupts the invoking object.

interrupted

public static boolean interrupted( )

This method tests whether the thread that is now executing has been interrupted.

isAlive

public final native boolean isAlive( )

This method tests whether the invoking object is still active.

isDaemon

public final boolean isDaemon( )

This method tests whether the invoking object is a daemon thread.

isInterrupted

public boolean isInterrupted( )

This method tests whether the invoking object has been interrupted.

join

public final void join( )

This method waits indefinitely for the thread on which it is called to terminate. It can throw an **InterruptedException**.

public final synchronized void join(long *ms*)

This method waits up to *ms* milliseconds for the thread on which it is called to terminate. It can throw an **InterruptedException**.

public final synchronized void join(long *ms*, int *ns*)

This method waits up to *ms* milliseconds plus *ns* nanoseconds for the thread on which it is called to terminate. It can throw an **IllegalArgumentException** or **InterruptedException**.

resume

public final void resume( )

This method resumes the invoking object. It can throw a **SecurityException**.

run

public void run( )

This method runs the invoking object.

setDaemon

public final void setDaemon(boolean *state*)

This method flags the thread as a daemon thread. When only daemon threads are executing, the Java Virtual Machine exits. This method can throw an **IllegalThreadStateException**.

setName

public final void setName(String *threadName*)

This method sets the name of the thread to that specified by *threadName*. It can throw a **SecurityException**.

setPriority

public final void setPriority(int *priority*)

This method sets the priority of the thread to that specified by *priority*. It can throw an **IllegalArgumentException** or a **SecurityException**.

sleep

public static native void sleep(long *ms*)

This method suspends execution of the executing thread for the specified number of milliseconds. It can throw an **InterruptedException**.

public static void sleep(long *ms*, int *ns*)

This method suspends execution of the executing thread for the specified number of milliseconds plus nanoseconds. It can throw an **IllegalArgumentException** or **InterruptedException**.

start

public native synchronized void start( )

This method starts execution of the invoking object. It can throw an **IllegalThreadStateException** if the thread was already started.

stop

6

public final void stop( )

This method terminates the invoking object. It can throw a **SecurityException**.

public final synchronized void stop(Throwable *e*)

This method terminates the invoking object and throws e. It can throw a **SecurityException**.

suspend

public final void suspend( )

This method suspends the invoking object. It can throw a **SecurityException**.

toString

public String toString( )

This method returns the **String** equivalent of the invoking object.

yield

public static native void yield( )

This method causes the executing thread to pause. Other threads can then run.

> ### Programming Tip
>
> The easiest way to create a thread is to create a class that implements the **Runnable** interface because you can construct a thread on any object that implements **Runnable.** To implement **Runnable** you need to implement only a single method called **run( ),** which is declared like this:
>
> public abstract void run( )
>
> Inside **run( ),** you will define the code that constitutes the new thread. It is important to understand that **run( )** can call other methods, use other classes, and declare variables just like the main thread. The only difference is that **run( )** establishes the entry point for another, concurrent thread of execution within your program. This thread will end when **run( )** returns.
>
> After you have created a class that implements **Runnable,** you instantiate an object of type **Thread** from within that class. Once created, the new thread will not start running until you call its **start( )** method, which is declared within **Thread.** In essence, **start( )** executes a call to **run( ).**
>
> Here is an example that creates a new thread and starts it running:
>
> ```
> // Create a thread.
> class NewThread implements Runnable {
>   Thread t;
> ```

```
  NewThread() {
    // Create a new, second thread
    t = new Thread(this, "Second Thread");
    System.out.println("Child thread: " + t);
    t.start(); // Start the thread
  }

  // This is the entry point for the second thread.
  public void run() {
    try {
      for(int i = 5; i > 0; i--) {
        System.out.println("Child Thread: " + i);
        Thread.sleep(500);
      }
    } catch (InterruptedException e) {
      System.out.println("Child interrupted.");
    }
    System.out.println("Exiting child thread.");
  }
}

class ThreadDemo {
  public static void main(String args[]) {
    new NewThread(); // create a new thread

    try {
      for(int i = 5; i > 0; i--) {
        System.out.println("Main Thread: " + i);
        Thread.sleep(1000);
      }
    } catch (InterruptedException e) {
      System.out.println("Main thread interrupted.");
    }
    System.out.println("Main thread exiting.");
  }
}
```

Inside **NewThread**'s constructor, a new **Thread** object is created using the following statement:

```
t = new Thread(this, "Second Thread");
```

Passing **this** as the first argument causes the new thread to call the **run( )** method on **this** object. Next, **start( )** is called, which starts the thread of execution beginning at the **run( )** method. This causes the child thread's **for** loop to begin. After calling **start( ), NewThread**'s constructor returns to **main( ).** When the main thread resumes, it enters its **for** loop. Both threads continue running, sharing the CPU, until their loops finish. Here is the output produced by this program:

```
Child thread: Thread[Second Thread,5,main]
Main Thread: 5
Child Thread: 5
Child Thread: 4
Main Thread: 4
Child Thread: 3
Child Thread: 2
Main Thread: 3
Child Thread: 1
Exiting child thread.
Main Thread: 2
Main Thread: 1
Main thread exiting.
```

One last point: In a multithreaded program, the main thread must be the last thread to finish running. If the main thread finishes before a child thread has completed, then the Java run-time system may "hang." The preceding program ensures that the main thread will finish last because the main thread sleeps for 1,000 milliseconds between iterations, but the child thread sleeps for only 500 milliseconds. This causes the child thread to terminate earlier than the main thread. Of course, Java provides more sophisticated methods of thread synchronization.

THE THREADGROUP CLASS

Thread groups offer a convenient way to manage groups of threads as a unit.

The most commonly used methods in this class are described here.

Related class: **Thread**

ThreadGroup

public ThreadGroup(String *gname*)

This constructor creates a **ThreadGroup** object whose name is equivalent to *gname*.

public ThreadGroup(ThreadGroup *parent*, String *gname*)

This constructor creates a **ThreadGroup** object that is a child of the *parent* thread group. The **ThreadGroup** object has a name equivalent to *gname*. The constructor can throw a **NullPointerException** or **SecurityException**.

activeCount

public int activeCount( )

This method returns the number of threads in the group, plus any groups for which this thread is a parent.

activeGroupCount

public int activeGroupCount( )

This method returns the number of groups for which the invoking thread is a parent.

checkAccess

public final void checkAccess( )

This method causes the security manager to verify that the currently running thread may access and/or change the invoking object. It can throw a **SecurityException**.

destroy

public final void destroy( )

This method destroys the thread group (and any child groups) on which it is called. It can throw an **IllegalThreadStateException** or **SecurityException**.

enumerate

public int enumerate(Thread *group*[ ])

The threads that constitute the invoking thread group are put into the *group* array. This method returns the number of threads that were entered into *group.* Use the **activeCount( )** method to determine how large *group* should be before invoking this method.

public int enumerate(Thread *group*[ ], boolean *all*)

The threads that constitute the invoking thread group are put into the *group* array. If *all* is **true**, then threads in all subgroups are also put into *group.* The method returns the number of threads that were entered into *group.* Use the **activeCount( )** method to determine how large *group* should be before invoking this method.

public int enumerate(ThreadGroup *group*[ ])

The subgroups of the invoking thread group are put into the *group* array. The method returns the number of thread groups that were entered into *group*. Use the **activeGroupCount( )** method to determine how large *group* should be before invoking this method.

public int enumerate(ThreadGroup *group*[ ], boolean *all*)

The subgroups of the invoking thread group are put into the *group* array. If *all* is **true**, then all subgroups of the subgroups (and so on) are also put into *group*. The method returns the number of thread groups that were entered into *group*. Use the **activeGroupCount( )** method to determine how large *group* should be before invoking this method.

getMaxPriority

public final int getMaxPriority( )

This method returns the maximum priority setting for the group.

getName

public final String getName( )

This method returns the name of the group.

getParent

public final ThreadGroup getParent( )

This method returns **null** if the invoking object has no parent. Otherwise, it returns the parent of the invoking object.

isDaemon

public final boolean isDaemon( )

This method tests whether the invoking object is a daemon thread group.

isDestroyed

public synchronized boolean isDestroyed( )

This method tests whether the thread group has been destroyed.

This method was introduced in Java specification 1.1.

list

public void list( )

This method displays information about the group to the standard output.

parentOf

public final boolean parentOf(ThreadGroup *group*)

This method tests whether the invoking object is equal to *group* or is an ancestor of *group*.

resume

public final void resume( )

This method resumes all the threads in the invoking group. It can throw a **SecurityException**.

setDaemon

public final void setDaemon(boolean *isDaemon*)

This method sets all of the threads in the invoking object to be daemon threads. (A daemon thread group is automatically destroyed when it has no running threads.) It can throw a **SecurityException**.

setMaxPriority

6

public final void setMaxPriority(int *priority*)

This method sets the maximum priority of the invoking group to *priority*. It can throw a **SecurityException**.

stop

public final void stop( )

This method terminates all threads in the invoking group. It can throw a **SecurityException**.

suspend

public final void suspend( )

This method suspends all threads in the invoking group. It can throw a **SecurityException**.

toString

public String toString( )

This method returns the **String** equivalent of the invoking object

uncaughtException

public void uncaughtException(Thread *thread*, Throwable *e*)

This method is called by the Java Virtual Machine when a thread in the invoking object does not catch an exception.

THE THROWABLE CLASS

The **Throwable** class provides functionality applicable to all other classes that provide exception and error handling. Those classes indirectly inherit from **Throwable**.

Throwable

public Throwable( )

This is the default constructor.

public Throwable(String *information*)

This constructor returns a **Throwable** object initialized with *information*.

fillInStrackTrace

public native Throwable fillInStackTrace( )

This method returns a **Throwable** object that contains a completed stack trace. This object can be rethrown.

getMessage

public String getMessage( )

This method returns a description of the exception.

printStackTrace

public void printStackTrace( )

This method displays the stack trace.

public void printStackTrace(PrintStream *stream*)

This method sends the stack trace to the specified stream.

public void printStackTrace(PrintWriter *pw*)

This method sends the stack trace to the specified stream.

toString

public String toString( )

This method returns a **String** object containing a description of the exception. This method is called by **println( )** when outputting a **Throwable** object.

THE VOID CLASS

The **Void** class defines one variable named **TYPE**. This variable holds a reference to the **Class** object that represents the type **void.** You do not instantiate the **Void** class.

This class was introduced in Java specification 1.1.

Chapter 7—The Utility Classes and Interfaces

The Java library includes an assortment of utility classes. These classes are used throughout the core Java packages and are also available for programs that you write. Their uses include storing collections of objects, generating pseudorandom numbers, manipulating date and time, and tokenizing strings.

The classes found in **java.util** are shown here:

BitSet	**Properties**
Calendar	**PropertyResourceBundle**
Date	**Random**
Dictionary	**ResourceBundle**
EventObject	**SimpleTimeZone**
GregorianCalendar	**Stack**
Hashtable	**StringTokenizer**
ListResourceBundle	**TimeZone**
Locale	**Vector**
Observable	

java.util also defines these interfaces:

Enumeration   **EventListener**   **Observer**

The following classes and interfaces are new to Java specification 1.1: **Calendar**, **EventListener**, **EventObject**, **GregorianCalendar**, **ListResourceBundle**, **Locale**, **PropertyResourceBundle**, **ResourceBundle**, **SimpleTimeZone**, and **TimeZone**.

The following classes are less frequently used and are not discussed in this book: **ListResourceBundle**, **PropertyResourceBundle**, and **ResourceBundle**.

THE BITSET CLASS

The **BitSet** class creates a special type of array that holds bit values. Each element equals a **boolean** value (i.e., **true** or **false**). When a bit is cleared, it has the value **false**. When a bit is set, it has the value **true**. A **BitSet** can increase in size as needed. This makes it similar to a vector of bits.

Bit Set

public BitSet( )

This constructor creates an object with a default size and clears all bits.

public BitSet(int *size*)

This constructor creates an object of *size* bits and clears all bits.

and

public void and(BitSet *bitSet*)

This method ANDs the contents of the invoking object with that specified by *bitSet*. The result is placed into the invoking object.

clear

public void clear(int *index*)

This method clears the bit at *index*. It can throw an
IndexOutOfBoundsException.

clone

public Object clone( )

This method duplicates the invoking object.

equals

public boolean equals(Object *bitSet*)

This method tests whether the invoking object and *bitSet* have
the same value.

get

public boolean get(int *index*)

This method returns the current state of the bit at *index*.

hashCode

public int hashCode( )

This method returns the hash code of the invoking object.

or

public void or(BitSet *bitSet*)

This method ORs the contents of the invoking object with that specified by *bitSet*. The result is placed into the invoking object.

set

public void set(int *index*)

This method sets the bit at *index*.

size

public int size( )

This method returns the number of bits in the invoking object.

toString

public String toString( )

This method returns the **String** equivalent of the invoking object.

xor

public void xor(BitSet *bitSet*)

This method XORs the contents of the invoking object with that specified by *bitSet*. The result is placed into the invoking object.

THE CALENDAR CLASS

The abstract **Calendar** class provides a set of methods that allow you to convert a time in milliseconds to a number of useful components. Some examples of the type of information that can be provided are year, month, day, hour, minute, and second.

It is intended that subclasses of **Calendar** will provide the specific functionality to interpret time information according to their own rules. This is one aspect of the Java class library that allows you to write programs that can operate in several international environments. One example of such a subclass is **GregorianCalendar**.

7

Calendar defines several **int** constants that are used when you get or set components of the calendar. These are **AM, AM_PM, APRIL, AUGUST, DATE, DAY_OF_MONTH, DAY_OF_WEEK, DAY_OF_WEEK_IN_MONTH, DAY_OF_YEAR, DECEMBER, DST_OFFSET, ERA, FEBRUARY, FIELD_COUNT, FRIDAY, HOUR, HOUR_OF_DAY, JANUARY, JULY, JUNE, MARCH, MAY, MILLISECOND, MINUTE, MONDAY, MONTH, NOVEMBER, OCTOBER, PM, SATURDAY, SECOND, SEPTEMBER, SUNDAY, THURSDAY, TUESDAY, UNDECIMBER, WEDNESDAY, WEEK_OF_MONTH, WEEK_OF_YEAR, YEAR,** and **ZONE_OFFSET.**

Calendar defines several protected instance variables. **areFieldsSet** is a **boolean** that indicates whether the time components have been set. **fields** is an array of **int**s that hold the components of the time. **isSet** is a **boolean** array that indicates whether a specific time component has been set. **time** is a **long** that holds the current time for this object. **isTimeSet** is a **boolean** that indicates whether the current time has been set.

Related classes: **Date, GregorianCalendar, Locale, TimeZone, SimpleTimeZone**

This class was introduced in Java specification 1.1.

The most commonly used methods in this class are described here.

Calendar

protected Calendar( )

This constructor creates an object initialized with the default time zone and locale.

protected Calendar(TimeZone *zoneObj*, Locale *localeObj*)

This constructor creates an object initialized with the time zone *zoneObj* and the locale *localeObj*.

after

public abstract boolean after(Object *calendarObj*)

This method tests whether the time of the invoking object is after the time of *calendarObj*.

before

public abstract boolean before(Object *calendarObj*)

This method tests whether the time of the invoking object is before the time of *calendarObj*.

equals

public abstract boolean equals(Object *calendarObj*)

This method tests whether the time of the invoking object is equal to the time of *calendarObj*.

get

public final int get(int *calendarField*)

This method returns the value of one component of the invoking object. *calendarField* specifies the component. Some examples of the components that can be requested are: **Calendar.YEAR**, **Calendar.MONTH**, **Calendar.MINUTE**, and so forth.

getTime

public final Date getTime( )

This method returns a **Date** object equivalent to the time of the invoking object.

set

public final void set(int *year*, int *month*, int *date*, int *hour*, int *minute*, int *second*)

This method sets various date and time components of the invoking object.

setTime

public final void setTime(Date *d*)

This method sets various date and time components of the invoking object. This information is obtained from the **Date** object *d*.

THE DATE CLASS

The **Date** class represents a date and time. It provides methods that allow you to set and get different components of the date or time.

Related classes: **Calendar**, **GregorianCalendar**, **TimeZone**, **SimpleTimeZone**

Date

public Date( )

This constructor creates an object initialized with the current date and time.

public Date(long *milliseconds*)

This constructor creates an object initialized according to the number of milliseconds that have elapsed since midnight, January 1, 1970, GMT.

public Date(int *year*, int *month*, int *dayOfMonth*)

This constructor creates an object initialized with the information supplied in its arguments. The time components represent 12 A.M. local time.

This constructor is deprecated in Java specification 1.1.

public Date(int *year*, int *month*, int *dayOfMonth*, int *hours*, int *minutes*)

This constructor creates an object initialized with the information supplied in its arguments.

This constructor is deprecated in Java specification 1.1.

public Date(int *year*, int *month*, int *dayOfMonth*, int *hours*, int *minutes*, int *seconds*)

This constructor creates an object initialized with the information supplied in its arguments.

This constructor is deprecated in Java specification 1.1.

public Date(String *str*)

This constructor creates an object initialized with the information supplied in its **String** argument. For example, **new Date("Thu Feb 15 1996 22:24:34")** will construct an object with the specified date and time. **Date** parses many formats of string dates, but you should adhere to the standard date syntax just shown.

This constructor is deprecated in Java specification 1.1.

after

public boolean after(Date *date*)

This method returns **true** if the invoking object contains a date that is later than the one specified by *date*. Otherwise, it returns **false**.

before

public boolean before(Date *date*)

This method returns **true** if the invoking object contains a date that is earlier than the one specified by *date*. Otherwise, it returns **false**.

equals

public boolean equals(Object *date*)

This method returns **true** if the invoking object contains the same time and date as the one specified by *date*. Otherwise, it returns **false**.

getDate

public int getDate( )

This method returns the day of the month, which will be in the range 1 through 31.

This method is deprecated in Java specification 1.1.

getDay

public int getDay( )

This method returns the day (Monday, Tuesday, etc.) encoded as an integer. Sunday is 0, Monday is 1, and so on.

This method is deprecated in Java specification 1.1.

getHours

public int getHours( )

This method returns the hour. Hours are represented using a 24-hour clock.

This method is deprecated in Java specification 1.1.

getMinutes

public int getMinutes( )

This method returns the minutes.

This method is deprecated in Java specification 1.1.

getMonth

public int getMonth( )

This method returns the month encoded as an integer. January is 0.

This method is deprecated in Java specification 1.1.

getSeconds

public int getSeconds( )

This method returns the seconds.

This method is deprecated in Java specification 1.1.

getTime( )

public long getTime( )

This method returns the number of milliseconds that have elapsed since January 1, 1970, GMT.

getTimezoneOffset

public int getTimezoneOffset( )

This method returns the number of minutes that must be added to Greenwich Mean Time to obtain the local time. The effect of daylight saving time is taken into account.

This method is deprecated in Java specification 1.1.

getYear

public int getYear( )

This method returns the number of years since 1900. Thus, the current year is this value plus 1900.

This method is deprecated in Java specification 1.1.

hashCode

public int hashCode( )

This method returns the hash code of the invoking object.

parse

public static long parse(String *str*)

Translates a time and date string into the number of milliseconds that have elapsed since midnight, January 1, 1970, GMT. This value is returned.

This method is deprecated in Java specification 1.1.

setDate

public void setDate(int *dayOfMonth*)

This method sets the day of the month to that specified by *dayOfMonth* (1-31).

This method is deprecated in Java specification 1.1.

setHours

public void setHours(int *hours*)

This method sets the hours to that specified by *hours*. A 24-hour clock is used (0 through 23).

This method is deprecated in Java specification 1.1.

setMinutes

public void setMinutes(int *minutes*)

This method sets the minutes to that specified by *minutes*.

This method is deprecated in Java specification 1.1.

setMonth

public void setMonth(int *month*)

This method sets the month to that specified by *month.*

This method is deprecated in Java specification 1.1.

setSeconds

public void setSeconds(int *seconds*)

This method sets the seconds to that specified by *seconds.*

This method is deprecated in Java specification 1.1.

setTime

public void setTime(long *ms*)

This method sets the time and date as specified by *ms*, which represents an elapsed time in milliseconds from midnight, January 1, 1970, GMT.

setYear

public void setYear(int *year*)

This method sets the year as specified by *year.* This value specifies the number of years that have elapsed since 1900.

This method is deprecated in Java specification 1.1.

toGMTString

public String toGMTString( )

This method returns the **String** equivalent of the invoking object. The time and date are represented in Greenwich Mean Time.

This method is deprecated in Java specification 1.1.

toLocaleString

public String toLocaleString( )

This method returns the **String** equivalent of the invoking object. The time and date are represented in a form compatible with the current locale.

This method is deprecated in Java specification 1.1.

toString

public String toString( )

This method returns the **String** equivalent of the invoking object.

UTC

public static long UTC(int *year*, int *month*, int *dayOfMonth*, int *hours*, int *minutes*, int *seconds*)

This method returns the number of milliseconds between midnight, January 1, 1970, GMT and the specified time and date.

This method is deprecated in Java specification 1.1.

THE DICTIONARY CLASS

Dictionary is an abstract class that represents a key/value storage repository. A *key* is a name you use to retrieve a *value* at a later date. Given a key and value, you can store the value in a **Dictionary** object. Once stored, you can retrieve the value, using its key. Thus, a dictionary can be thought of as a list of key/value pairs.

Related class: **Hashtable**

Dictionary

public Dictionary( )

This is the default constructor.

elements

public abstract Enumeration elements( )

This method returns an enumeration of the values contained in the dictionary.

get

public abstract Object get(Object *key*)

This method returns the object that contains the value associated with *key*. If *key* is not in the dictionary, a null object is returned.

isEmpty

public abstract boolean isEmpty( )

This method returns **true** if the dictionary is empty and **false** if it contains at least one key.

keys

public abstract Enumeration keys( )

This method returns an enumeration of the keys contained in the dictionary.

put

public abstract Object put(Object *key*, Object *value*)

This method inserts a key and its value into the dictionary. It returns null if *key* is not already in the dictionary, or the previous value associated with *key* if it is already in the dictionary. It can throw a **NullPointerException**.

remove

public abstract Object remove(Object *key*)

This method removes *key* and its value. It returns the value associated with *key*. If *key* is not in the dictionary, a null object is returned.

size

public abstract int size( )

This method returns the number of entries in the dictionary.

THE ENUMERATION INTERFACE

The **Enumeration** interface defines the methods by which you can enumerate (obtain one at a time) the elements in a collection of objects.

hasMoreElements

public abstract boolean hasMoreElements( )

This method returns **true** while there are still more elements to extract, and **false** when all of the elements have been enumerated.

nextElement

public abstract Object nextElement( )

This method returns the next object in the enumeration as a generic **Object** reference. That is, each call to **nextElement( )** obtains the next object in the enumeration. The calling routine must cast that object into the object type held in the enumeration. It can throw a **NoSuchElementException**.

THE EVENTLISTENER INTERFACE

The **EventListener** interface must be extended by all event listener interfaces. It contains no methods but is used to identify whether an object is listening to events.

This interface was introduced in Java specification 1.1.

THE EVENTOBJECT CLASS

The **EventObject** class is the superclass of all events. It has one instance variable. **source** holds a protected reference to an **Object** that is the source of this event.

Related classes: **AWTEvent**

This class was introduced in Java specification 1.1.

EventObject

public EventObject(Object *obj*)

This constructor creates an object that holds a reference to *obj*. *obj* is the source of the event.

getSource

public Object getSource( )

This method returns a reference to the object that is the source of the event.

toString

public String toString( )

This method returns a **String** equivalent of the invoking object.

THE GREGORIANCALENDAR CLASS

GregorianCalendar is a concrete implementation of a **Calendar**.

GregorianCalendar defines two **int** constants: **AD** and **BC**.

Related classes: **Calendar, Date, TimeZone, SimpleTimeZone**

This class was introduced in Java specification 1.1.

The most commonly used constructors and methods in this class are described here.

GregorianCalendar

public GregorianCalendar( )

This is the default constructor. It builds an object by using the current time in the default locale and default time zone.

public GregorianCalendar(int *year*, int *month*, int *date*, int *hour*, int *minute*, int *second*)

This constructor builds an object by using the date and time parameters supplied as arguments. The default locale and time zone are used.

public GregorianCalendar(TimeZone *zoneObj*, Locale *localeObj*)

This constructor builds an object by using the current time in the time zone specified by *zoneObj* and the locale specified by *localeObj*.

after

public boolean after(Object *calendarObj*)

This method tests whether the time of the invoking object is after the time of *calendarObj*.

before

public boolean before(Object *calendarObj*)

This method tests whether the time of the invoking object is before the time of *calendarObj*.

equals

public boolean equals(Object *calendarObj*)

This method tests whether the time of the invoking object is equal to the time of *calendarObj*.

isLeapYear

public boolean isLeapYear(int *year*)

This method tests whether *year* is a leap year.

7

THE HASHTABLE CLASS

Hashtable is a concrete implementation of a **Dictionary**. A **Hashtable** instance can be used to store arbitrary objects that are indexed by any other arbitrary object. A hash table stores information using a mechanism called *hashing*. In hashing, the informational content of a key is used to determine a unique value, called its *hash code*. The hash code is then used as the index at which the data associated with the key is stored.

When using a **Hashtable**, you specify an object that is used as a key and the value (i.e., data) that you want linked to that key. The key is then hashed and the resulting hash code is used as the index at which the value is stored within the table. The transformation of the key into its hash code is performed automatically—you never see the hash code itself. Also, it is not possible for your code to directly index the hash table. Through the use of hashing, you can efficiently store and access information using whatever type of key (object) is most convenient for your application.

A hash table can store only objects that override the **hashCode( )** and **equals( )** methods defined by **Object**. The **hashCode( )**

method must compute and return the hash code for the object. Of course, **equals( )** compares two objects. Fortunately, many of Java's built-in classes already implement the **hashCode( )** method. For example, the most common type of **Hashtable** uses a **String** object as the key. **String** implements both **hashCode( )** and **equals( )**.

Related class: **Dictionary**

Hashtable

public Hashtable( )

This is the default constructor.

public Hashtable(int *size*)

This constructor creates a hash table that has an initial size specified by *size*.

public Hashtable(int *size*, float *fillRatio*)

This constructor creates a hash table that has an initial size specified by *size* and a fill ratio specified by *fillRatio*. This ratio must be between 0.0 and 1.0, and it determines how full the hash table can be before it is made larger. Specifically, when the number of elements is greater than the capacity of the hash table multiplied by its fill ratio, the hash table is expanded. If you do not specify a fill ratio, then 0.75 is used. This constructor can throw an **IllegalArgumentException**.

clear

public synchronized void clear( )

This method resets and empties the hash table.

clone

public synchronized Object clone( )

This method returns a duplicate of the invoking object.

contains

public synchronized boolean contains(Object *value*)

This method returns **true** if some value equal to *value* exists within the hash table. It returns **false** if the value is not found. It can throw a **NullPointerException**.

containsKey

public synchronized boolean containsKey(Object *key*)

This method returns **true** if some key equal to *key* exists within the hash table. It returns **false** if the key is not found.

elements

public synchronized Enumeration elements( )

This method returns an enumeration of the values contained in the hash table.

get

public synchronized Object get(Object *key*)

This method returns the object that contains the value associated with *key*. If *key* is not in the hash table, a null object is returned.

isEmpty

public boolean isEmpty( )

This method returns **true** if the hash table is empty and **false** if it contains at least one key.

keys

public synchronized Enumeration keys( )

This method returns an enumeration of the keys contained in the hash table.

put

public synchronized Object put(Object *key*, Object *value*)

This method inserts a key and a value into the hash table. It returns null if *key* is not already in the hash table, or the previous value associated with *key* if *key* is already in the hash table. It can throw a **NullPointerException**.

rehash

protected void rehash( )

This method increases the size of the hash table and rehashes all of its keys.

remove

public synchronized Object remove(Object *key*)

This method removes *key* and its value. It returns the value associated with *key*. If *key* is not in the hash table, a null object is returned.

size

public int size( )

This method returns the number of entries in the hash table.

toString

public synchronized String toString( )

This method returns the **String** equivalent of the invoking object.

7

THE LOCALE CLASS

The **Locale** class is instantiated to produce objects that describe a geographical or cultural region. It is one of several classes that provide you with the ability to write programs that can execute in several different international environments.

The **Locale** class defines a number of constants that are useful for dealing with the most common locales. These are **CANADA, CANADA_FRENCH, CHINA, CHINESE, ENGLISH, FRANCE, FRENCH, GERMAN, GERMANY, ITALIAN, ITALY, JAPAN, JAPANESE, KOREA, KOREAN, PRC, SIMPLIFIED_CHINESE, TAIWAN, TRADITIONAL_CHINESE, UK,** and **US.**

This class was introduced in Java specification 1.1.

The following sections outline only one of the constructors and one of the methods associated with this class.

Locale

public Locale(String *language*, String *country*, String *data*)

This constructor builds a locale object to represent a specific *language* and *country*. Some auxiliary browser and vendor-specific information can be provided in *data*.

setDefault

public static synchronized void setDefault(Locale *localeObj*)

This method is used to set the default locale to *localeObj*.

THE OBSERVABLE CLASS

The **Observable** class is used to create subclasses that other parts of your program can observe. When an object of such a subclass undergoes a change, observing classes are notified. Observing classes must implement the **Observer** interface, which defines the **update( )** method. The **update( )** method is called when an observer is notified of a change in an observed object.

An object that is being observed must follow two simple rules. First, if it has changed, it must call **setChanged( )**. Second, when it is ready to notify observers of this change, it must call **notifyObservers( )**. This causes the **update( )** method in the observing object(s) to be called. Be careful—if the object calls **notifyObservers( )** without having previously called **setChanged( )**, no action will take place. The observed object must call both **setChanged( )** and **notifyObservers( )** before **update( )** will be called.

Notice that **notifyObservers( )** has two forms: one that takes an argument and one that does not. If you call **notifyObservers( )** with an argument, this object is passed to the observer's **update( )** method as its second parameter. Otherwise, null is passed to **update( )**. You can use the second parameter for passing any type of object that is appropriate for your application.

Related interface: **Observer**

Observable

public Observable( )

This is the default constructor.

addObserver

public synchronized void addObserver(Observer *obj*)

This method adds *obj* to the list of objects observing the invoking object.

clearChanged

protected synchronized void clearChanged( )

This method changes the status of the invoking object to "unchanged."

countObservers

public synchronized int countObservers( )

This method returns the number of objects observing the invoking object.

7

deleteObserver

public synchronized void deleteObserver(Observer *obj*)

This method removes *obj* from the list of objects observing the invoking object.

deleteObservers

public synchronized void deleteObservers( )

This method removes all observers for the invoking object.

hasChanged

public synchronized boolean hasChanged( )

This method tests whether the invoking object has been modified.

notifyObservers

public void notifyObservers( )

This method notifies all observers of the invoking object that it has changed by calling **update( )**. A null is passed as the second argument to **update( )**.

public void notifyObservers(Object *obj*)

This method notifies all observers of this invoking object that it has changed by calling **update( )**. *obj* is passed as an argument to **update( )**.

setChanged

protected synchronized void setChanged( )

This method is called when the invoking object has changed.

THE OBSERVER INTERFACE

To observe an observable object, you must implement the **Observer** interface.

Related class: **Observable**

7

update

public abstract void update(Observable *observOb*, Object *arg*)

Here, *observOb* is the object being observed and *arg* is the value passed by **notifyObservers( )**. The **update( )** method is called when a change in the observed object takes place.

Programming Tip

Here is an example that demonstrates an observable object. It creates an observer class, called **Watcher**, that implements the **Observer** interface. The class being monitored is called **BeingWatched**. It extends **Observable**. Inside **BeingWatched** is the method **counter( )**, which simply counts down from a specified value. It uses **sleep( )** to wait a tenth of second between counts. Each time the count changes, **notifyObservers( )** is called with the current count passed as its argument. This causes the

update( ) method inside **Watcher** to be called, which displays the current count. Inside **main( )**, a **Watcher** and a **BeingWatched** object, called **observing** and **observed**, respectively, are created. Then, **observing** is added to the list of observers for **observed**. This means that **observing.update( )** will be called each time **counter( )** calls **notifyObservers( )**.

```java
/* Demonstrate the Observable class and the
   Observer interface.
*/

import java.util.*;

// This is the observing class.
class Watcher implements Observer {
  public void update(Observable obj, Object arg) {
    System.out.println("update() called, count is " +
                       ((Integer)arg).intValue());
  }
}

// This is the class being observed.
class BeingWatched extends Observable {
  void counter(int period) {
    for( ; period >=0; period--) {
      setChanged();
      notifyObservers(new Integer(period));
      try {
        Thread.sleep(100);
      } catch(InterruptedException e) {
        System.out.println("Sleep interrupted");
      }
    }
  }
}

class ObserverDemo {
  public static void main(String args[]) {
    BeingWatched observed = new BeingWatched();
    Watcher observing = new Watcher();

    /* Add the observing to the list of observers for
       observed object.  */
```

```
    observed.addObserver(observing);

    observed.counter(10);
  }
}
```

The output from this program is shown here:

```
update() called, count is 10
update() called, count is 9
update() called, count is 8
update() called, count is 7
update() called, count is 6
update() called, count is 5
update() called, count is 4
update() called, count is 3
update() called, count is 2
update() called, count is 1
update() called, count is 0
```

The **Observable** class and the **Observer** interface allow you to implement sophisticated program architectures based on the document/view methodology. They are also useful in multithreaded situations.

THE PROPERTIES CLASS

Properties is a subclass of **Hashtable**. It is used to maintain lists of values in which the key is a **String** and the value is also a **String**. The **Properties** class is used by several other Java classes. For example, it is the type of object returned by **System.getProperties( )** when obtaining environmental values.

One useful capability of the **Properties** class is that you can specify a default property that will be returned if there is no value associated with a certain key. For example, a default value may be specified along with the key in the **getProperty( )**

method, as in **getProperty("name", "default value")**. If the "name" value is not found, then "default value" is returned. In addition, when you construct a **Properties** object, you can pass another instance of **Properties** to be used as the default properties for the new instance. In this case, if you call **getProperty("foo")** on a given **Property** object and "foo" does not exist, Java will look for "foo" in the default **Properties** object. This allows for arbitrary nesting of levels of default properties.

Properties

public Properties( )

The default constructor creates an object that has no default values.

public Properties(Properties *propDefault*)

This constructor creates an object that uses *propDefault* for its default values.

getProperty

public String getProperty(String *key*)

This method returns the value associated with *key*. A null object is returned if *key* is not in the list or in the default property list.

public String getProperty(String *key*, String *defaultProperty*)

This method returns the value associated with *key*. *defaultProperty* is returned if *key* is not in the list or in the default property list.

list

public void list(PrintStream *streamOut*)

This method sends the property list to the output stream linked to *streamOut.*

public void list(PrintWriter *streamOut*)

This method sends the property list to the output stream linked to *streamOut.*

This method was introduced in Java specification 1.1.

load

public synchronized void load(InputStream *streamIn*)

This method inputs a property list from the input stream linked to *streamIn.* It can throw an **IOException**.

propertyNames

public Enumeration propertyNames( )

This method returns an enumeration of the keys. This includes those keys found in the default property list, too.

save

public synchronized void save(OutputStream *streamOut*, String *description*)

After writing the string specified by *description,* this method writes the property list to the output stream linked to *streamOut.*

THE RANDOM CLASS

The **Random** class is a generator of pseudorandom numbers. These numbers are called pseudorandom because they are simply uniformly distributed sequences.

Random

public Random( )

This is the default constructor. It creates a number generator that uses the current time as the start or seed value.

public Random(long *seed*)

This constructor allows you to specify the seed value manually. If you initialize a **Random** object with a seed, you define the starting point for the random sequence. If you use the same seed to initialize another **Random** object, you will extract the same random sequence. If you want to generate different sequences, specify different seed values. The easiest way to do this is to use the current time to seed a **Random** object. This approach reduces the possibility of getting repeated sequences.

next

protected synchronized int next(int *randomBits*)

This method returns the next random number. *randomBits* is a set of random bits.

This method was introduced in Java specification 1.1.

nextBytes

public void nextBytes(byte *byteArray*[ ])

This method places a set of random bytes in *byteArray*.

This method was introduced in Java specification 1.1.

nextDouble

public double nextDouble( )

This method returns the next **double** random number.

nextFloat

public float nextFloat( )

This method returns the next **float** random number.

nextGaussian

public synchronized double nextGaussian( )

This method returns the next Gaussian random number. **nextGaussian( )** returns a **double** value centered at 0.0 with a standard deviation of 1.0. This is what is known as a *bell curve*.

nextInt

public int nextInt( )

This method returns the next **int** random number.

nextLong

public long nextLong( )

This method returns the next **long** random number.

setSeed

public synchronized void setSeed(long *newSeed*)

This method sets the seed value (i.e., the starting point for the random number generator) to that specified by *newSeed*.

THE SIMPLETIMEZONE CLASS

The **SimpleTimeZone** class is a subclass of **TimeZone**. It allows you to work with time zones for a Gregorian Calendar. It also computes daylight saving time.

Related classes: **Calendar**, **Date**, **GregorianCalendar**, **TimeZone**

This class was introduced in Java specification 1.1.

The most commonly used constructors and methods in this class are described here.

SimpleTimeZone

public SimpleTimeZone(int *timeDelta*, String *tzName*)

This constructor creates a **SimpleTimeZone** object. *timeDelta* specifies the offset relative to Greenwich Mean Time (GMT). *tzName* is the name of the time zone.

getOffset

public int getOffset(int *era*, int *year*, int *month*, int *day*, int *dayOfWeek*, int *milliseconds*)

This method returns the offset that should be added to Greenwich Mean Time to compute local time. This value is adjusted for daylight saving time. The parameters to the method represent date and time components.

getRawOffset

public int getRawOffset( )

This method returns the raw offset that should be added to Greenwich Mean Time to compute local time. This value is not adjusted for daylight saving time.

inDaylightTime

public boolean inDaylightTime(Date *d*)

This method tests whether the date represented by *d* is in daylight saving time in the invoking object.

useDaylightTime

public boolean useDaylightTime( )

This method tests whether the invoking object uses daylight saving time.

THE STACK CLASS

Stack is a subclass of **Vector** that implements a standard last-in, first-out stack. **Stack** defines only the default constructor, which creates an empty stack. **Stack** includes all of the methods defined by **Vector** and adds several of its own.

To put an object on the top of the stack, call **push( )**. To remove and return the top element, call **pop( )**. An **EmptyStackException** is thrown if you call **pop( )** when the invoking stack is empty. You can use **peek( )** to return, but not remove, the top object. The **empty( )** method will return **true** if there is nothing on the stack. The **search( )** method determines whether an object exists on the stack and returns the number of pops that would be required to bring it to the top of the stack.

Stack

public Stack( )

This is the default constructor.

empty

public boolean empty( )

This method returns **true** if the stack is empty and **false** if it contains elements.

peek

public synchronized Object peek( )

This method returns the element on the top of the stack, but does not remove it. It can throw an **EmptyStackException**.

pop

public synchronized Object pop( )

This method returns the element on the top of the stack, removing it in the process. It can throw an **EmptyStackException**.

push

public Object push(Object *element*)

This method pushes *element* onto the stack. *element* is also returned.

search

public synchronized int search(Object *element*)

This method searches for *element* in the stack. If found, its offset from the top of the stack is returned. Otherwise, −1 is returned.

THE STRINGTOKENIZER CLASS

StringTokenizer is used to break a string into its individual tokens. To use **StringTokenizer**, you specify an input string and a string that contains delimiters. The delimiters are characters that separate tokens. Each character in the delimiters string is considered a valid delimiter; for example, ",,::" sets the delimiters to a comma, semicolon, and colon.

Once you have created a **StringTokenizer** object, the **nextToken( )** method is used to extract consecutive tokens. The **hasMoreTokens( )** method returns **true** while there are more tokens to be extracted. Since **StringTokenizer** implements **Enumeration**, the **hasMoreElements( )** and **nextElement( )** methods are also implemented and act the same as **hasMoreTokens( )** and **nextToken( )**, respectively.

StringTokenizer

public StringTokenizer(String *str*)

This constructor returns a **StringTokenizer** object. *str* is the string that will be tokenized. The default delimiters (space, tab, newline, and carriage return) are used.

public StringTokenizer(String *str*, String *delimiters*)

This constructor returns a **StringTokenizer** object. *str* is the string that will be tokenized. *delimiters* is a string that specifies the delimiters.

public StringTokenizer(String *str*, String *delimiters*, boolean *delimAsToken*)

This constructor returns a **StringTokenizer** object. *str* is the string that will be tokenized. *delimiters* is a string that specifies the delimiters. If *delimAsToken* is **true**, then the delimiters are also returned as tokens when the string is parsed. Otherwise, the delimiters are not returned. (Delimiters are not returned as tokens by the first two forms of the constructor.)

countTokens

public int countTokens( )

Using the current set of delimiters, this method determines the number of tokens left to be parsed and returns the result.

hasMoreElements

public boolean hasMoreElements( )

This method returns **true** if one or more tokens remain in the string and **false** if there are none.

hasMoreTokens

public boolean hasMoreTokens( )

This method returns **true** if one or more tokens remain in the string and **false** if there are none.

nextElement

public Object nextElement( )

This method returns the next token as an **Object**. It can throw a **NoSuchElementException**.

nextToken

public String nextToken( )

This method returns the next token as a **String**. It can throw a **NoSuchElementException**.

public String nextToken(String *delimiters*)

This method returns the next token as a **String** and sets the delimiters string to that specified by *delimiters*. It can throw a **NoSuchElementException**.

THE TIMEZONE CLASS

The **TimeZone** class allows you to work with time zone offsets from Greenwich Mean Time (GMT). It also computes daylight saving time.

Related classes: **Calendar, Date, SimpleTimeZone**

This class was introduced in Java specification 1.1.

The most commonly used methods in this class are described here.

TimeZone

public TimeZone( )

This is the default constructor.

getAvailableIDs

public static synchronized String[ ] getAvailableIDs( )

This method returns an array of **String** objects representing the names of all time zones.

public static synchronized String[ ] getAvailableIDs(int *timeDelta*)

This method returns an array of **String** objects representing the names of all time zones that are *timeDelta* offset from Greenwich Mean Time.

getDefault

public static synchronized TimeZone getDefault( )

This method returns a **TimeZone** object that represents the default time zone used on the host computer.

getOffset

public abstract int getOffset(int *era*, int *year*, int *month*, int *day*, int *dayOfWeek*, int *millisec*)

This method returns the offset that should be added to Greenwich Mean Time to compute local time. This value is adjusted for daylight saving time. The parameters to the method represent date and time components.

getRawOffset

public abstract int getRawOffset( )

This method returns the raw offset that should be added to Greenwich Mean Time to compute local time. This value is not adjusted for daylight saving time.

getTimeZone

public static synchronized TimeZone getTimeZone(String *tzName*)

This method returns the **TimeZone** object for the time zone named *tzName.*

inDaylightTime

public abstract boolean inDaylightTime(Date *d*)

This method tests whether the date represented by *d* is in daylight saving time in the invoking object.

7

setDefault

public static synchronized void setDefault(TimeZone *tz*)

This method allows you to set the default time zone to be used on this host. *tz* is a reference to the **TimeZone** object to be used.

useDaylightTime

public abstract boolean useDaylightTime( )

This method tests whether the invoking object uses daylight saving time.

THE VECTOR CLASS

A vector is essentially a variable length array of object references. That is, a vector may dynamically increase or decrease in size. Vectors are created with an initial size. When this size is exceeded, the vector is automatically enlarged. When objects are removed, the vector is shrunk.

All vectors start with an initial capacity. Once this initial capacity has been reached, the next time you attempt to store an object in the vector, the vector will automatically allocate space for that object, plus extra room for additional objects. By allocating more than just the required memory, the vector reduces the number of allocations that must take place. This is important because allocations are costly in terms of time. The amount of extra space allocated during each reallocation is determined by the increment you specify when you create the vector. If you do not specify an increment, then the vector's size is doubled by each allocation cycle. Usually, you will want to specify an increment value.

Vector has three protected data members. The increment value is stored in **capacityIncrement**. The number of elements currently in the vector is stored in **elementCount**, and the array that holds the vector is stored in **elementData**.

Vector

public Vector( )

This is the default constructor. It creates an empty vector with a default initial size.

public Vector(int *size*)

This constructor creates a vector whose initial size is specified by *size.*

public Vector(int *size*, int *incr*)

This constructor creates a vector whose initial size is specified by *size* and whose increment is specified by *incr.*

addElement

public final synchronized void addElement(Object *element*)

The object specified by *element* is added to the vector.

capacity

public final int capacity( )

This method returns the capacity of the vector.

clone

public synchronized Object clone( )

This method returns a duplicate of the invoking vector.

contains

public final boolean contains(Object *element*)

This method returns **true** if *element* is contained by the vector and **false** if it is not.

copyInto

**public final synchronized void
    copyInto(Object *array*[ ])**

This method copies the elements in the vector into *array*.

elementAt

**public final synchronized Object
    elementAt(int *index*)**

This method returns the element at position *index*. It can throw an **ArrayIndexOutOfBoundsException**.

elements

public final synchronized Enumeration elements( )

This method returns an enumeration of the elements in the vector.

ensureCapacity

**public final synchronized void
    ensureCapacity(int *size*)**

This method sets the minimum capacity of the vector to *size*.

firstElement

public final synchronized Object firstElement( )

This method returns the first element in the vector. It can throw
a **NoSuchElementException**.

indexOf

public final int indexOf(Object *element*)

This method returns the index of the first occurrence of *element*.
If the object is not in the vector, −1 is returned.

**public final synchronized int
    indexOf(Object *element*, int *start*)**

This method returns the index of the first occurrence of *element*.
The search begins at position *start*. If the object is not in the
vector, −1 is returned.

insertElementAt

**public final synchronized void
    insertElementAt(Object *element*, int *index*)**

This method adds *element* to the vector at the location specified
by *index*. It can throw an **ArrayIndexOutOfBoundsException**.

isEmpty

public final boolean isEmpty( )

This method tests whether the vector is empty.

lastElement

public final synchronized Object lastElement( )

This method returns the last element in the vector. It can throw a **NoSuchElementException**.

lastIndexOf

public final int lastIndexOf(Object *element*)

This method returns the index of the last occurrence of *element*. If the object is not in the vector, −1 is returned.

public final synchronized int lastIndexOf(Object *element*, int *start*)

This method returns the index of the last occurrence of *element* before *start*. The search proceeds backwards from *start*. If the object is not in that portion of the vector, −1 is returned.

removeAllElements

public final synchronized void removeAllElements( )

This method empties the vector. After this method executes, the size of the vector will be zero.

removeElement

public final synchronized boolean removeElement(Object *element*)

This method removes *element* from the vector. If more than one instance of the specified object exists in the vector, the first one is removed. This method returns **true** if successful and **false** if the object is not found.

removeElementAt

public final synchronized void removeElementAt(int *index*)

This method removes the element at the location specified by *index*. It can throw an **ArrayIndexOutOfBoundsException**.

setElementAt

public final synchronized void setElementAt(Object *element*, int *index*)

This method assigns *element* to the location specified by *index*. It can throw an **ArrayIndexOutOfBoundsException**.

setSize

public final synchronized void setSize(int *size*)

This method sets the number of elements in the vector to *size*. If the new size is less than the old size, elements are lost. If the new size is larger than the old size, null elements are added.

size

public final int size( )

This method returns the number of elements currently in the vector.

toString

public final synchronized String toString( )

This method returns the **String** equivalent of the vector.

trimToSize

public final synchronized void trimToSize( )

This method sets the vector's capacity equal to the number of elements that it currently holds.

Programming Tip

Given their power, vectors are surprisingly easy to use. Once you have instantiated a **Vector**, you can add an element to it by calling **addElement( )**. To obtain the element at a specific location, call **elementAt( )**. To determine whether a vector contains a certain element, call **contains( )**. To obtain the first element in the vector, call **firstElement( )**. To retrieve the last element, call **lastElement( )**. You can obtain the index of an element using **indexOf( )** and **lastIndexOf( )**. To remove an element, call **removeElement( )** or **removeElementAt( )**. The following program demonstrates **Vector** and several of its methods.

```java
// Demonstrate various Vector operations.
import java.util.Vector;
import java.util.Enumeration;

class VectorDemo {
  public static void main(String args[]) {
    // Initial size is 3, increment is 2.
    Vector v = new Vector(3, 2);

    System.out.println("Initial size: " + v.size());
    System.out.println("Initial capacity: "
                       + v.capacity() + "\n");

    // Add some integers.
    v.addElement(new Integer(1));
    v.addElement(new Integer(2));
    v.addElement(new Integer(3));
    v.addElement(new Integer(4));

    System.out.println("Capacity after four additions:"
                       + v.capacity());

    // Add some doubles.
    v.addElement(new Double(5.45));
    v.addElement(new Double(6.08));
    v.addElement(new Integer(7));

    System.out.println("Capacity after adding three"+
                       " more: " + v.capacity() + "\n");

    System.out.println("First element in vector is: "
                       + (Integer)v.firstElement());
    System.out.println("Last element in vector is: "
                       + (Integer)v.lastElement());

    if(v.contains(new Integer(3)))
      System.out.println("Vector contains a 3\n");

    // Enumerate the elements in the vector.
    Enumeration vEnum = v.elements();
```

7

```
    System.out.println("Elements in vector:");
    while(vEnum.hasMoreElements())
      System.out.print(vEnum.nextElement() + " ");
    System.out.println("\n");

    System.out.println("Element at 3 is " +
                        v.elementAt(3));

    System.out.println("Next, remove that element");
    // remove element 3
    v.removeElement(v.elementAt(3));
    System.out.println("Now element at 3 is " +
                        v.elementAt(3));
  }
}
```

The output produced by this program is shown here:

```
Initial size: 0
Initial capacity: 3

Capacity after four additions: 5
Capacity after adding three more: 7

First element in vector is: 1
Last element in vector is: 7
Vector contains a 3

Elements in vector:
1 2 3 4 5.45 6.08 7

Element at 3 is 4
Next, remove that element
Now element at 3 is 5.45
```

One important aspect of vectors demonstrated by the program is the fact that the same vector can hold a variety of different types of objects. Because **Vector**'s methods operate on objects of type **Object** (which is a superclass of all objects), any type of object can be stored in a vector. The only restriction is that the elemental types (**int, char,** etc.) must be encapsulated within a class wrapper.

Chapter 8—The Input/Output Classes and Interfaces

This chapter explores **java.io**, which provides support for I/O operations.

The I/O classes defined by **java.io** are shown here:

BufferedInputStream	FileWriter	PipedOutputStream
BufferedOutputStream	FilterInputStream	PipedReader
BufferedReader	FilterOutputStream	PipedWriter
BufferedWriter	FilterReader	PrintStream
ByteArrayInputStream	FilterWriter	PrintWriter
ByteArrayOutputStream	InputStream	PushbackInputStream
CharArrayReader	InputStreamReader	PushbackReader
CharArrayWriter	LineNumberInputStream	RandomAccessFile
DataInputStream	LineNumberReader	Reader
DataOutputStream	ObjectInputStream	SequenceInputStream
File	ObjectOutputStream	StreamTokenizer
FileDescriptor	ObjectStreamClass	StringBufferInputStream
FileInputStream	OutputStream	StringReader
FileOutputStream	OutputStreamWriter	StringWriter
FileReader	PipedInputStream	Writer

The following interfaces are defined by **java.io**.

DataInput	FilenameFilter	ObjectOutput
DataOutput	ObjectInput	Serializable
Externalizable	ObjectInputValidation	

The following classes and interfaces are new to Java specification 1.1:

BufferedReader, BufferedWriter, CharArrayReader, CharArrayWriter, FileReader, FileWriter, FilterReader,

FilterWriter, InputStreamReader, LineNumberReader, ObjectInputStream, ObjectOutputStream, ObjectStreamClass, OutputStreamWriter, PipedReader, PipedWriter, PrintWriter, PushbackReader, Reader, StringReader, StringWriter, Writer, Externalizable, ObjectInput, ObjectInputValidation, ObjectOutput, and **Serializable.**

The following classes and interfaces are infrequently used and are not discussed in this book: **ObjectInputStream, ObjectOutputStream, ObjectStreamClass, PipedInputStream, PipedOutputStream, PipedReader, PipedWriter, PushbackInputStream, PushbackReader, SequenceInputStream, StringBufferInputStream, Externalizable, ObjectInput, ObjectInputValidation, ObjectOutput,** and **Serializable.**

THE BUFFEREDINPUTSTREAM CLASS

The **BufferedInputStream** class allows you to "wrap" any **InputStream** into a buffered stream and achieve a performance improvement. Buffering an input stream also provides the foundation required to support moving backward in the stream within the available buffer.

There are five instance variables. **buf** is a protected byte array that holds the data. **count** is a protected **int** that indicates the next position to write in **buf. marklimit** is a protected **int** that indicates the maximum number of bytes allowed between a mark and a reset. **markpos** is a protected **int** that indicates the current mark position. **pos** is a protected **int** that indicates the position of the next byte to read from **buf.**

Related classes: **FilterInputStream, InputStream**

BufferedInputStream

public BufferedInputStream(InputStream *istream*)

This constructor creates a buffered stream using a buffer size of 512 bytes.

public BufferedInputStream(InputStream *istream*, int *bufSize*)

This constructor creates a buffered stream using a buffer size of *bufSize*.

available

public synchronized int available( )

This method returns the number of bytes currently available in the invoking stream. It can throw an **IOException**.

mark

public synchronized void mark(int *size*)

This method marks the current position in the invoking stream. At a later time, the **reset( )** method can be used to return to this position. The *size* parameter indicates the maximum number of bytes you expect the stream to store between mark and reset operations.

markSupported

public boolean markSupported( )

This method tests whether the invoking stream supports the ability for you to do mark and reset operations.

read

public synchronized int read( )

This method reads and returns a byte from the invoking stream. A value of −1 is returned when an end-of-stream condition occurs. The method blocks until data is available. It can throw an **IOException**.

public synchronized int read(byte *buffer*[ ], int *start*, int *size*)

This method reads *size* bytes from the invoking stream. The bytes are read into *buffer* beginning at the index specified by *start*. The return value is the number of bytes that were placed into *buffer*. A value of −1 is returned when an end-of-stream condition occurs. The method waits until data is available. It can throw an **IOException**.

reset

public synchronized void reset( )

This method resets the invoking stream position to that of the previous mark. It can throw an **IOException**.

skip

public synchronized long skip(long *number*)

This method ignores (i.e., skips) *number* bytes in the invoking stream. The return value is the number of bytes that were actually ignored. This method can throw an **IOException**.

THE BUFFEREDOUTPUTSTREAM CLASS

The **BufferedOutputStream** class allows you to "wrap" any **OutputStream** into a buffered stream and achieve a performance improvement. There are two instance variables. **buf** is a protected byte array that holds the data. **count** is a protected **int** that indicates the next position to write in **buf**.

Related classes: **FilterOutputStream**, **OutputStream**

BufferedOutputStream

public BufferedOutputStream(OutputStream *outputStream*)

The constructor creates a buffered stream using a buffer size of 512 bytes.

public BufferedOutputStream(OutputStream *outputStream*, int *bufSize*)

The constructor creates a buffered stream using a buffer size of *bufSize*.

flush

public synchronized void flush( )

This method flushes the invoking stream. It can throw an **IOException**.

write

public synchronized void write(byte *buffer*[ ], int *start*, int *size*)

This method writes *size* bytes to the invoking stream. The bytes are written from *buffer* beginning at the index specified by *start*. This method can throw an **IOException**.

public synchronized void write(int *b*)

This method writes the low-order byte in *b* to the invoking stream. It can throw an **IOException**.

THE BUFFEREDREADER CLASS

The **BufferedReader** class buffers data from a character input stream. You can use the functionality of this class in conjunction with any subclass of **Reader**.

Related class: **Reader**

This class was introduced in Java specification 1.1.

BufferedReader

public BufferedReader(Reader *r*)

This constructor creates an object that buffers data from a **Reader** object *r*. A default size is used for the buffer.

public BufferedReader(Reader *r*, int *size*)

This constructor creates an object that buffers data from a **Reader** object *r*. *size* is the space allocated for the buffer. This constructor can throw an **IllegalArgumentException**.

close

public void close( )

This method closes the invoking stream. It can throw an **IOException**.

mark

public void mark(int *size*)

This method marks the current position in the invoking stream. At a later time, the **reset( )** method can be used to return to this position. The *size* parameter indicates the maximum number of characters you expect the stream to store between mark and reset operations. This method can throw an **IOException**.

markSupported

public boolean markSupported( )

This method tests whether the invoking stream supports the ability to do mark and reset operations.

read

public int read( )

This method reads and returns a character from the invoking stream. A value of -1 is returned when an end-of-stream condition occurs. It can throw an **IOException**.

public int read(char *buffer*[ ], int *start*, int *size*)

This method reads *size* characters from the invoking stream. The characters are read into *buffer* beginning at the index specified by *start*. The return value is the number of characters that were placed into *buffer*. A value of -1 is returned when an end-of-stream condition occurs. The method can throw an **IOException**.

readLine

public String readLine( )

This method reads and returns a line of text. The line-termination characters are carriage return, linefeed, or a carriage return followed immediately by a linefeed. The line-termination characters are not included in the **String** that is returned from this method. **readLine( )** returns null when an end-of-stream condition is encountered. It can throw an **IOException**.

ready

public boolean ready( )

This method tests whether there is data in either the buffers or the stream itself. It can throw an **IOException**.

reset

public void reset( )

This method resets the invoking stream position to that of the previous mark. It can throw an **IOException**.

skip

public long skip(long *number*)

This method ignores (i.e., skips) *number* characters in the invoking stream. The return value is the number of bytes that were actually ignored. This method can throw an **IOException**.

Programming Tip

One of the most common input actions that programs perform is reading a string from the keyboard. You can accomplish this manually by using **read( )** to read characters into a **byte** array and then converting the array into a **String** object. However, Java provides a more convenient, built-in method, called **readLine( )**, which automatically reads a sequence of characters from the input stream and returns them in an object of type **String**. This method is part of several classes. The one we will use is **BufferedReader**, which provides methods for reading characters and strings.

Before you can use **readLine( )**, you must obtain a **BufferedReader** object that is linked to the console. One way to do this is to use a statement like the following:

BufferedReader *inputStream* =
new BufferedReader(new InputStreamReader(System.in));

Here, *inputStream* is the new stream that is linked to **System.in** through an instance of **InputStreamReader** that is wrapped in a **BufferedReader**.

The following program applies the preceding discussion. It reads and displays lines of text until you enter the word "stop".

```
// Read strings from the console.
import java.io.*;

class ReadStr {
  public static void main(String args[])
    throws IOException
  {
    // create a buffered reader using System.in
    BufferedReader inData =
      new BufferedReader(new
                InputStreamReader(System.in));
    String str;
```

```
    System.out.println("Enter lines of text.");
    System.out.println("Enter 'stop' to quit.");
    do {
      str = inData.readLine();
      System.out.println(str);
    } while(!str.equals("stop"));
  }
}
```

At first glance you might think that having to obtain a buffered input reader is a lot of work just to read a string from the console. But this approach pays for itself many times over in larger, real-world programs. The Java I/O system provides the programmer with a unique blend of flexibility and detailed control. Once you understand its organization, the Java I/O system is very easy to use.

THE BUFFEREDWRITER CLASS

The **BufferedWriter** class buffers data to a character output stream. You can use the functionality of this class in conjunction with any subclass of **Writer**.

Related class: **Writer**

This class was introduced in Java specification 1.1.

BufferedWriter

public BufferedWriter(Writer *w*)

This constructor creates an object that buffers data to a **Writer** object *w*. A default size is used for the buffer.

public BufferedWriter(Writer *w*, int *size*)

This constructor creates an object that buffers data to a
Writer object *w*. *size* is the space allocated for the buffer.
This constructor can throw an **IllegalArgumentException**.

close

public void close( )

This method closes the invoking stream. It can throw an
IOException.

flush

8

public void flush( )

This method flushes the invoking stream. It can throw an
IOException.

newLine

public void newLine( )

This method writes a newline separator (defined by the system
property **line.separator**) to the invoking stream. It can throw an
IOException.

write

public void write(char *buffer*[ ], int *start*, int *size*)

This method writes *size* characters to the invoking stream.
The characters are written from *buffer* beginning at the index
specified by *start*. This method can throw an **IOException**.

public void write(int *c*)

This method writes a character *c* to the invoking stream. It can throw an **IOException**.

public void write(String *str*, int *start*, int *size*)

This method writes *size* characters to the invoking stream. The characters are written from *str* beginning at the index specified by *start*. This method can throw an **IOException**.

THE BYTEARRAYINPUTSTREAM CLASS

ByteArrayInputStream is an implementation of an input stream that uses a byte array as the source. There are four instance variables. **buf** is a protected byte array that holds the data. **count** is a protected **int** that indicates the next position to write in **buf**. **mark** is a protected **int** that indicates the current mark position. **pos** is a protected **int** that indicates the next byte to read from **buf**. (**mark** was introduced in Java specification 1.1.)

Related class: **InputStream**

ByteArrayInputStream

public ByteArrayInputStream(byte *array*[ ])

This constructor creates a **ByteArrayInputStream** object. *array* is the input source.

public ByteArrayInputStream(byte *array*[ ], int *start*, int *numBytes*)

This constructor creates a **ByteArrayInputStream** object from a subset of *array* that begins with the character at the index specified by *start* and is *numBytes* long.

available

public synchronized int available( )

This method returns the number of bytes currently available in the invoking stream.

mark

public void mark(int *size*)

This method marks the current position in the invoking stream. At a later time, the **reset( )** method can be used to return to this position. The *size* parameter indicates the maximum number of bytes you expect the stream to store between mark and reset operations.

This method was introduced in Java specification 1.1.

markSupported

public boolean markSupported( )

This method tests whether the invoking stream supports the ability to do mark and reset operations.

This method was introduced in Java specification 1.1.

read

public synchronized int read( )

This method reads and returns a byte from the invoking stream. A value of −1 is returned when an end-of-stream condition occurs.

public synchronized int read(byte *buffer*[ ], int *start*, int *size*)

This method reads *size* bytes from the invoking stream. The bytes are read into *buffer* beginning at the index specified by *start*. The return value is the number of bytes that were placed into *buffer*. A value of −1 is returned when an end-of-stream condition occurs.

reset

public synchronized void reset( )

This method resets the invoking stream position to that of the previous mark.

skip

public synchronized long skip(long *number*)

This method ignores (i.e., skips) *number* bytes in the invoking stream. The return value is the number of bytes that were actually ignored.

THE BYTEARRAYOUTPUTSTREAM CLASS

ByteArrayOutputStream is an implementation of an output stream that uses a byte array as the destination. There are two instance variables. **buf** is a protected byte array that holds the data. **count** is a protected **int** that indicates the next position to write in **buf**.

Related class: **OutputStream**

ByteArrayOutputStream

public ByteArrayOutputStream( )

This constructor creates an object whose buffer size is initially 32 bytes.

public ByteArrayOutputStream(int *numBytes*)

This constructor creates an object whose buffer size is specified by *numBytes*.

reset

public synchronized void reset( )

This method resets the invoking stream by discarding any data in it and setting its counters to their initial state. The stream can then be reused.

size

public int size( )

This method returns the number of data bytes that are currently in the invoking stream.

toByteArray

public synchronized byte[ ] toByteArray( )

This method returns a new byte array whose contents are equivalent to the bytes in the invoking stream.

toString

public String toString( )

This method returns the **String** equivalent of the invoking object.

public String toString(int *upperByte*)

This method returns the **String** equivalent of the invoking object. *upperByte* is used for the upper 8 bits of each character.

This method is deprecated in Java specification 1.1.

public String toString(String *encoding*)

This method returns the **String** equivalent of the invoking object. *encoding* is the name of the character encoding that will be used to perform the byte-to-character translation. This method can throw an **UnsupportedEncodingException**.

This method was introduced in Java specification 1.1.

write

public synchronized void write(int *data*)

This method writes the low-order byte in *data* to the invoking stream.

public synchronized void write(byte *buffer*[ ], int *start*, int *size*)

This method writes *size* bytes to the invoking stream. The bytes are written from *buffer* beginning at the index specified by *start*.

writeTo

public synchronized void writeTo(OutputStream *outStream*)

This method writes the **ByteArrayOutputStream** data to the stream specified by *outStream*. It can throw an **IOException**.

THE CHARARRAYREADER CLASS

The **CharArrayReader** class allows you to use a character array as an input stream. There are four instance variables. **buf** is a protected character array that holds the data. **count** is a protected **int** that indicates the number of valid characters in **buf**. **markedPos** is a protected **int** that indicates the current mark position. **pos** is a protected **int** that indicates the position of the next character to read from **buf**.

Related class: **Reader**

This class was introduced in Java specification 1.1.

CharArrayReader

public CharArrayReader(char *carray*[ ])

This constructor creates a **CharArrayReader** object that can read from the character array *carray.*

public CharArrayReader(char *carray*[ ], int *start,* int *size*)

This constructor creates a **CharArrayReader** object that can read from the character array *carray. start* is the position in *carray* at which to begin reading characters. *size* is the number of characters to read.

close

public void close( )

This method closes the invoking stream.

mark( )

public void mark(int *size*)

This method marks the current position in the invoking stream. At a later time, the **reset( )** method can be used to return to this position. The *size* parameter is not used in this class. The method can throw an **IOException.**

markSupported

public boolean markSupported( )

This method tests whether the invoking stream supports the ability to do mark and reset operations.

read

public int read( )

This method reads and returns a character from the invoking stream. A value of −1 is returned when an end-of-stream condition occurs. This method can throw an **IOException**.

public int read(char *buffer*[ ], int *start*, int *size*)

This method reads *size* characters from the invoking stream. The characters are read into *buffer* beginning at the index specified by *start*. The return value is the number of characters that were placed into *buffer*. A value of −1 is returned when an end-of-stream condition occurs. This method can throw an **IOException**.

ready

public boolean ready( )

This method returns **true** because the stream is always ready for input. It can also throw an **IOException**.

reset

public void reset( )

This method resets the invoking stream position to that of the previous mark. It can throw an **IOException**.

skip

public long skip(long *number*)

This method ignores (i.e., skips) *number* characters in the invoking stream. The return value is the number of characters that were actually ignored. This method can throw an **IOException**.

THE CHARARRAYWRITER CLASS

The **CharArrayWriter** class allows you to use a character buffer as an output stream. There are two instance variables. **buf** is a protected character array that holds the data. **count** is a protected **int** that indicates the next position to write in **buf**.

Related class: **Writer**

This class was introduced in Java specification 1.1.

CharArrayWriter

public CharArrayWriter( )

This constructor creates a **CharArrayWriter** object with a default initial size.

public CharArrayWriter(int *numChars*)

This constructor creates a **CharArrayWriter** object with a buffer whose initial size is specified by *numChars*.

close

public void close( )

This method closes the invoking stream.

flush

public void flush( )

This method flushes the invoking stream.

reset

public void reset( )

This method resets the invoking stream by discarding any data in it and setting its counters to their initial state. The stream can then be used again.

size

public int size( )

This method returns the size of the buffer.

toCharArray

public char[ ] toCharArray( )

This method returns a new **char** array whose contents are equivalent to the characters in the stream buffer.

toString

public String toString( )

This method returns the **String** equivalent of the invoking object.

write

public void write(char *buffer*[ ], int *start*, int *size*)

This method writes *size* characters to the invoking stream. The characters are written from *buffer* beginning at the index specified by *start*.

public void write(int *data*)

This method writes the character value in *data* to the invoking stream.

public void write(String *str*, int *start*, int *size*)

This method writes *size* characters to the invoking stream. The characters are written from *str* beginning at the index specified by *start*.

writeTo

public void writeTo(Writer *w*)

This method writes the current contents of the invoking object's character buffer to the **Writer** *w*. It can throw an **IOException**.

THE DATAINPUT INTERFACE

The **DataInput** interface provides a set of methods that allow you to read the elemental data types from a stream.

Related interface: **DataOutput**

readBoolean

public abstract boolean readBoolean( )

This method reads and returns a **boolean** from the invoking stream. It can throw an **EOFException** or **IOException**.

readByte

public abstract byte readByte( )

This method reads and returns a **byte** from the invoking stream. It can throw an **EOFException** or **IOException**.

readChar

public abstract char readChar( )

This method reads and returns a **char** from the invoking stream. It can throw an **EOFException** or **IOException**.

readDouble

public abstract double readDouble( )

This method reads and returns a **double** from the invoking stream. It can throw an **EOFException** or **IOException**.

readFloat

public abstract float readFloat( )

This method reads and returns a **float** from the invoking stream. It can throw an **EOFException** or **IOException**.

readFully

public abstract void readFully(byte *buffer*[ ])

This method reads bytes from a stream into the *buffer*. The method does not return until *buffer* is filled. It can throw an **EOFException** or **IOException**.

public abstract void readFully(byte *buffer*[ ], int *start*, int *size*)

This method reads *size* bytes from the invoking stream. The bytes are read into *buffer* beginning at the index specified by *start*. The method does not return until all the bytes are read. It can throw an **EOFException** or **IOException**.

readInt

public abstract int readInt( )

This method reads and returns an **int** from the invoking stream. It can throw an **EOFException** or **IOException**.

readLine

public abstract String readLine( )

This method reads and returns a line of text from the invoking stream. The line-termination characters are carriage return, linefeed, or a carriage return followed immediately by a linefeed. The line-termination characters are not included in the **String** that is returned from this method. **readLine( )** returns null when an end-of-stream condition is encountered. It can throw an **IOException**.

readLong

public abstract long readLong( )

This method reads and returns a **long** from the invoking stream. It can throw an **EOFException** or **IOException**.

readShort

public abstract short readShort( )

This method reads and returns a **short** from the invoking stream. It can throw an **EOFException** or **IOException**.

readUnsignedByte

public abstract int readUnsignedByte( )

This method reads and returns an unsigned byte from the invoking stream. The byte is contained in the low-order byte of the value returned. This method can throw an **EOFException** or **IOException**.

readUnsignedShort

public abstract int readUnsignedShort( )

This method reads and returns an unsigned short integer from the invoking stream. It can throw an **EOFException** or **IOException**.

readUTF

public abstract String readUTF( )

This method reads data from a stream and returns a **String** object. The string is encoded in a modified UTF-8 format.

8

This method can throw an **EOFException**, **IOException**, or **UTFDataFormatException**.

skipBytes

public abstract int skipBytes(int *number*)

This method causes the invoking stream to ignore (i.e., skip) *number* bytes. It returns *number*. It can throw an **EOFException** or **IOException**.

THE DATAINPUTSTREAM CLASS

The **DataInputStream** class is an input stream that contains methods for reading the elemental data types. It extends **FilterInputStream** and implements **DataInput**.

DataInputStream

public DataInputStream(InputStream *istream*)

This constructor returns a **DataInputStream** object based on *istream*.

read

public final int read(byte *buffer*[ ])

This method fills *buffer* with bytes read from the invoking stream. The return value is the number of bytes that were placed into *buffer*. A value of −1 is returned when an end-of-stream condition occurs. The method waits until data is available. It can throw an **IOException**.

public final int read(byte *buffer*[ ], int *start*, int *size*)

This method reads *size* bytes from the invoking stream. The bytes are read into *buffer* beginning at the index specified by *start*. The return value is the number of bytes that were placed into *buffer*. A value of −1 is returned when an end-of-stream condition occurs. This method can throw an **IOException**.

readBoolean

public final boolean readBoolean( )

This method reads and returns a **boolean** from the invoking stream. It waits until data is available. It can throw an **EOFException** or **IOException**.

readByte

public final byte readByte( )

This method reads and returns a **byte** from the invoking stream. It waits until data is available. It can throw an **EOFException** or **IOException**.

readChar

public final char readChar( )

This method reads and returns a **char** from the invoking stream. It waits until data is available. It can throw an **EOFException** or **IOException**.

8

readDouble

public final double readDouble( )

This method reads and returns a **double** from the invoking stream. It waits until data is available. It can throw an **EOFException** or **IOException**.

readFloat

public final float readFloat( )

This method reads and returns a **float** from a stream. It waits until data is available. It can throw an **EOFException** or **IOException**.

readFully

public final void readFully(byte *buffer*[ ])

This method reads bytes from a stream into the *buffer.* The method does not return until *buffer* is filled. It can throw an **IOException** or **EOFException**.

public final void readFully(byte *buffer*[ ], int *start*, int *size*)

This method reads *size* bytes from the invoking stream. The bytes are read into *buffer* beginning at the index specified by *start.* The method does not return until *size* bytes have been read. It can throw an **IOException** or **EOFException**.

readInt

public final int readInt( )

This method reads and returns an **int** from the invoking stream. It waits until data is available. It can throw an **EOFException** or **IOException**.

readLine

public final String readLine( )

This method reads and returns a line of text. The line-termination characters are carriage return, linefeed, or a carriage return followed immediately by a linefeed. The line-termination characters are not included in the **String** that is returned from this method. **readLine( )** waits until data is available and returns null when an end-of-stream condition is encountered. It can throw an **IOException**.

This method is deprecated in Java specification 1.1.

readLong

8

public final long readLong( )

This method reads and returns a **long** from the invoking stream. It waits until data is available. It can throw an **EOFException** or **IOException**.

readShort

public final short readShort( )

This method reads and returns a **short** from the invoking stream. It waits until data is available. It can throw an **EOFException** or **IOException**.

readUnsignedByte

public final int readUnsignedByte( )

This method reads and returns an unsigned byte from the invoking stream. The byte is contained in the low-order byte of the value returned. The method waits until data is available. It can throw an **IOException** or **EOFException**.

readUnsignedShort

public final int readUnsignedShort( )

This method reads and returns an unsigned short integer from the invoking stream. The method waits until data is available. It can throw an **IOException** or **EOFException**.

readUTF

public final String readUTF( )

This method reads bytes from the invoking object. The bytes are interpreted as characters encoded in a modified UTF-8 format and are converted to Unicode characters. A string equivalent to the encoded characters is returned by this method. The method waits until all data is available. It can throw an **EOFException** or **IOException**.

public final static String readUTF(DataInput *istream*)

This method reads bytes from *istream*. The bytes are interpreted as characters encoded in a modified UTF-8 format and are converted to Unicode characters. A string equivalent to the encoded characters is returned from this method. The method waits until all data is available. It can throw an **IOException**, **EOFException**, or **UTFDataFormatException**.

skipBytes

public final int skipBytes(int *number*)

This method ignores (i.e., skips) *number* bytes in the invoking stream. It returns *number*. The method waits until data is available. It can throw an **EOFException** or **IOException**.

THE DATAOUTPUT INTERFACE

The **DataOutput** interface specifies a set of methods that allow you to write the elemental data types to a stream.

Related method: **DataInput**

write
------

public abstract void write(byte *buffer*[ ])

This method writes the contents of *buffer* to a stream. It can throw an **IOException**.

public abstract void write(byte *buffer*[ ], int *start*, int *size*)

This method writes *size* bytes to the invoking stream. The bytes are written from *buffer* beginning at the index specified by *start*. This method can throw an **IOException**.

public abstract void write(int *value*)

This method writes the low-order byte of *value* to the invoking stream. It can throw an **IOException**.

writeBoolean
------

public abstract void writeBoolean(boolean *value*)

This method writes a **boolean** to the invoking stream. It can throw an **IOException**.

writeByte

public abstract void writeByte(int *value*)

This method writes the low-order byte of *value* to the invoking stream. It can throw an **IOException**.

writeBytes

public abstract void writeBytes(String *str*)

This method writes the contents of *str* to the invoking stream. It can throw an **IOException**.

writeChar

public abstract void writeChar(int *value*)

This method writes a **char** to the invoking stream. It can throw an **IOException**.

writeChars

public abstract void writeChars(String *str*)

This method writes the contents of *str* to the invoking stream. It can throw an **IOException**.

writeDouble

public abstract void writeDouble(double *value*)

This method writes a **double** to the invoking stream. It can throw an **IOException**.

writeFloat

public abstract void writeFloat(float *value*)

This method writes a **float** to the invoking stream. It can throw an **IOException**.

writeInt

public abstract void writeInt(int *value*)

This method writes an **int** to the invoking stream. It can throw an **IOException**.

writeLong

public abstract void writeLong(long *value*)

This method writes a **long** to the invoking stream. It can throw an **IOException**.

writeShort

public abstract void writeShort(int *value*)

This method writes a **short** to the invoking stream. It can throw an **IOException**.

writeUTF

public abstract void writeUTF(String *str*)

This method writes the contents of *str* to the invoking stream. The Unicode string *str* is converted to a modified UTF-8 format. It can throw an **IOException**.

THE DATAOUTPUTSTREAM CLASS

The **DataOutputStream** class provides a set of methods that allow you to write the elemental data types to a stream. There is one instance variable. **written** is a protected **int** that indicates the number of bytes that have been written.

Related classes and interfaces: **DataOutput**, **FilterOutputStream**

DataOutputStream

public DataOutputStream(OutputStream *ostream*)

This constructor creates a **DataOutputStream** object for the **OutputStream** *ostream.*

flush

public void flush( )

This method flushes the invoking stream. It can throw an **IOException**.

size

public final int size( )

This method returns the size of the invoking stream. This is the number of bytes that have been written.

write

public synchronized void write(byte *buffer*[ ], int *start*, int *size*)

This method writes *size* bytes to the invoking stream. The bytes are written from *buffer* beginning at the index specified by *start*. This method can throw an **IOException**.

public synchronized void write(int *value*)

This method writes the low-order byte of *value* to the invoking stream. It can throw an **IOException**.

writeBoolean

public final void writeBoolean(boolean *value*)

This method writes a **boolean** to the invoking stream. It can throw an **IOException**.

writeByte

public final void writeByte(int *value*)

This method writes the low-order byte of *value* to the invoking stream. It can throw an **IOException**.

writeBytes

public final void writeBytes(String *str*)

This method writes the contents of *str* to the invoking stream. It can throw an **IOException**.

writeChar

public final void writeChar(int *value*)

This method writes a **char** to the invoking stream. It can throw an **IOException**.

writeChars

public final void writeChars(String *str*)

This method writes the contents of *str* to a stream. It can throw an **IOException**.

writeDouble

public final void writeDouble(double *value*)

This method writes a **double** to the invoking stream. It can throw an **IOException**.

writeFloat

public final void writeFloat(float *value*)

This method writes a **float** to the invoking stream. It can throw an **IOException**.

writeInt

public final void writeInt(int *value*)

This method writes an **int** to the invoking stream. It can throw an **IOException**.

writeLong

public final void writeLong(long *value*)

This method writes a **long** to the invoking stream. It can throw an **IOException**.

writeShort

public final void writeShort(int *value*)

This method writes a **short** to the invoking stream. It can throw an **IOException**.

8

writeUTF

public final void writeUTF(String *str*)

This method writes the contents of *str* to the invoking stream. The string is encoded in a modified UTF-8 format. This method can throw an **IOException**.

THE FILE CLASS

A **File** object is used to obtain or manipulate the information associated with a disk file or directory. Since **File** does not operate on streams, it is not a subclass of **InputStream** or **OutputStream**. There are four static variables. These will not be discussed in this book.

The most commonly used methods are described here.

Related class: **FileDescriptor**

File

public File(String *directoryPath*)

This constructor creates a **File** object for the file with a path name equal to *directoryPath*. It can throw a **NullPointerException**.

public File(String *directoryPath*, String *filename*)

This constructor creates a **File** object for the file with a path name equal to *directoryPath* and a file name equal to *filename*.

public File(File *dirObj*, String *filename*)

This constructor creates a **File** object for the file in the directory equivalent to *dirObj* with name *filename*.

canRead

public boolean canRead( )

This method checks whether the file referred to by the invoking object can be read by this program. It can throw a **SecurityException**.

canWrite

public boolean canWrite( )

This method checks whether the file referred to by the invoking object can be written by this program. It can throw a **SecurityException**.

delete

public boolean delete( )

This method deletes the file referred to by the invoking object. The method returns **true** only if the operation was successful. It can throw a **SecurityException**.

equals

public boolean equals(Object *obj*)

This method tests whether the invoking object and *obj* have the same value.

exists

public boolean exists( )

This method determines whether the file referred to by the invoking object exists. It can throw a **SecurityException**.

getAbsolutePath

public String getAbsolutePath( )

This method returns a **String** object equivalent to the absolute path name of the file referred to by the invoking object.

getName

public String getName( )

This method returns a **String** object that contains the name of the file referred to by the invoking object.

getParent

public String getParent( )

This method returns a **String** object that contains the parent directory.

getPath

public String getPath( )

This method returns the relative path name of the file.

hashCode

public int hashCode( )

This method returns the hash code of the invoking object.

isAbsolute

public native boolean isAbsolute( )

This method determines whether the file referred to by the invoking object has an absolute path name.

isDirectory

public boolean isDirectory( )

This method checks whether the file referred to by the invoking object is a directory. It can throw a **SecurityException**.

isFile

public boolean isFile( )

This method checks whether the invoking object refers to a normal file (i.e., not a directory or special file). It can throw a **SecurityException**.

lastModified

public long lastModified( )

This method returns the time stamp for the file referred to by the invoking object. This is the time at which it was last changed. The return value is system-dependent. It can throw a **SecurityException**.

8

length

public long length( )

This method returns the number of bytes in the file referred to by the invoking object. If the actual file does not exist, 0L is returned. It can throw a **SecurityException**.

list

public String[ ] list( )

This method returns an array of **String** objects equivalent to the names of files in the directory represented by the invoking object. It can throw a **SecurityException**.

public String[ ] list(FilenameFilter *nameFilter*)

This method returns an array of **String** objects equivalent to the names of files in the directory represented by the invoking object. Only the files that meet the criteria defined by *nameFilter* are included. This method can throw a **SecurityException**.

mkdir

public boolean mkdir( )

This method creates a directory whose name is the path name of the invoking object. It returns **true** only if the operation was successful. It can throw a **SecurityException**.

mkdirs

public boolean mkdirs( )

This method creates a directory whose name is the path name of the invoking object. If any of the parent directories are missing, these are also created. This method returns **true** only if the operation was successful. It can throw a **SecurityException**.

renameTo

public boolean renameTo(File *newName*)

This method renames the file referred to by the invoking object. The file's new name is equivalent to that of the *newName*. This method returns **true** only if the operation was successful. It can throw a **SecurityException**.

toString

public String toString( )

This method returns the **String** equivalent of the invoking object.

THE FILEDESCRIPTOR CLASS

The **FileDescriptor** class is used to create objects that represent platform-independent handles to platform-dependent file descriptors. The latter represent open files or sockets.

FileDescriptor defines three static variables that each hold references to **FileDescriptor** objects. **err** holds a reference to the standard error stream. **in** holds a reference to the standard input stream. **out** holds a reference to the standard output stream.

The most commonly used methods are described here.

Related class: **File**

FileDescriptor

public FileDescriptor( )

This is the default constructor.

valid

public native boolean valid( )

This method determines whether the invoking object refers to an open file or socket. If it does, the method returns **true**.

THE FILEINPUTSTREAM CLASS

The **FileInputStream** class creates an **InputStream** that you can use to read the contents of a file.

FileInputStream

public FileInputStream(File *fileObj*)

This constructor creates an object given a reference to *fileObj*. It can throw a **FileNotFoundException** or **SecurityException**.

public FileInputStream(FileDescriptor *fileDescObj*)

This constructor creates an object given a reference to *fileDescObj*. It can throw a **SecurityException**.

public FileInputStream(String *filepath*)

This constructor creates an object given the full path name of a file in *filepath*. It can throw a **FileNotFoundException** or **SecurityException**.

available

public native int available( )

This method returns the number of bytes currently available in the invoking stream. It can throw an **IOException**.

close

public native void close( )

This method closes the invoking stream. It can throw an **IOException**.

finalize

protected void finalize( )

This method guarantees that the **close( )** method is called for the invoking object. It can throw an **IOException**.

getFD

public final FileDescriptor getFD( )

This method returns the invoking stream's file descriptor. It can throw an **IOException**.

read

public native int read( )

This method reads and returns a byte from the invoking stream. A value of −1 is returned when an end-of-file condition occurs. The method waits until data is available. It can throw an **IOException**.

8

public int read(byte *buffer*[ ])

This method fills *buffer* with bytes read from the invoking stream. The return value is the number of bytes that were placed into *buffer*. A value of −1 is returned when an end-of-stream condition occurs. The method waits until data is available. It can throw an **IOException**.

public int read(byte *buffer*[ ], int *start*, int *size*)

This method reads *size* bytes from the invoking stream. The bytes are read into *buffer* beginning at the index specified by *start*. The return value is the number of bytes that were placed into *buffer*. A value of −1 is returned when an end-of-stream condition occurs. The method waits until data is available. It can throw an **IOException**.

skip

public native long skip(long *number*)

This method ignores (i.e., skips) *number* bytes in the invoking stream. The return value is the number of bytes that were actually ignored. This method can throw an **IOException**.

THE FILEOUTPUTSTREAM CLASS

The **FileOutputStream** class creates an **OutputStream** that you can use to write the contents of a file.

Related class: **OutputStream**

FileOutputStream

public FileOutputStream(File *fileObj*)

This constructor creates a **FileOutputStream** object given a reference to *fileObj*. It can throw an **IOException** or a **SecurityException**.

public FileOutputStream(FileDescriptor *fileDesc*)

This constructor creates a **FileOutputStream** object given a reference to *fileDesc*. It can throw a **SecurityException**.

public FileOutputStream(String *filepath*)

This constructor creates a **FileOutputStream** object given the full path name of a file in *filepath*. It can throw an **IOException** or a **SecurityException**.

public FileOutputStream(String *filename*, boolean *appendFlag*)

This constructor creates a new object for the file whose name is contained in the **String** object *filename*. If *appendFlag* is **true**, any new information is appended to the end of the file. Otherwise, any new information is written from the beginning of the file and existing information is lost. This constructor can throw an **IOException**.

This constructor was introduced in Java specification 1.1.

close

public void close( )

This method closes the invoking stream. It can throw an **IOException**.

finalize

protected void finalize( )

This method guarantees that the **close( )** method is called for the invoking object. It can throw an **IOException**.

getFD

public final FileDescriptor getFD( )

This method returns the invoking stream's file descriptor. It can throw an **IOException**.

write

public void write(byte *buffer*[ ])

This method writes the contents of *buffer* to the invoking stream. It can throw an **IOException**.

public void write(byte *buffer*[ ], int *start*, int *size*)

This method writes *size* bytes to the invoking stream. The bytes are written from *buffer* beginning at the index specified by *start*. This method can throw an **IOException**.

public void write(int *data*)

This method writes the low-order byte of *data* to the invoking stream. It can throw an **IOException**.

Programming Tip

Two of the most often used stream classes are **FileInputStream** and **FileOutputStream**. These create streams linked to files. To open a file, you can simply create an object of one of these classes, specifying the name of the file as an argument to the constructor. When an output file is opened, any preexisting file of the same name is destroyed.

When you are done with a file, you should close it by calling **close( )**. This method is defined by both **FileInputStream** and **FileOutputStream**.

To read from a file, you can use a version of **read( )** that is defined within **FileInputStream**. The one that will be used in the following example is shown here.

```
int read( )
```

Each time it is called, it reads a single byte from the file and returns it as an integer value. It returns −1 when the end of the file is encountered. If an error occurs while reading, an **IOException** is thrown.

To write to a file, you will use a version of the **write( )** method defined by **FileOutputStream**. This is the form used in the example:

```
void write(int b)
```

This method writes the byte specified by *b* to the file. Although *b* is declared as an integer, only the low-order 8 bits are written to the file. If an error occurs while writing, an **IOException** is thrown.

The following example demonstrates how to read and write to a file. It copies a text file. Both the source and destination file names must be specified on the command line.

```
/* Copy a text file.

   To use this program, specify the name
   of the source file and the destination file.
   For example, to copy a file called FIRST.TXT,
   to a file called SECOND.TXT, use the following
   command line:

   java CopyFile FIRST.TXT SECOND.TXT
*/

import java.io.*;

class CopyFile {
  public static void main(String args[])
    throws IOException
  {
    int i;
    FileInputStream fin;
    FileOutputStream fout;

    try {
      fin = new FileInputStream(args[0]);
      fout = new FileOutputStream(args[1]);
    } catch(FileNotFoundException e) {
      System.out.println("File Not Found");
      return ;
    } catch(IOException e) {
      System.out.println("Error Opening Output File");
      return ;
    } catch(ArrayIndexOutOfBoundsException e) {
      System.out.println("Usage: CopyFile From To");
      return ;
    }
```

8

```
   // Copy File
   try {
     do {
       i = fin.read();
       if(i != -1) fout.write(i);
     } while(i != -1);
   } catch(IOException e) {
     System.out.println("File Error");
   }

   fin.close();
   fout.close();
  }
}
```

Pay close attention to the error handling in the program. Unlike most other computer languages, including C and C++, which use error codes to report file errors, Java uses its exception-handling mechanism. Not only does this make file handling cleaner, but it also allows Java to easily differentiate the end-of-file condition from file errors when input is being performed. In C/C++, many input functions return the same value when an error occurs as when the end of the file is reached. (That is, in C/C++, often an EOF condition is mapped to the same value as an input error.) This usually means that the programmer must include extra program statements to determine which event actually occurred. In Java, errors are passed to your program via exceptions and not by return values. Thus, when **read( )** returns −1, it means only one thing: that the end of the file has been encountered.

THE FILENAMEFILTER INTERFACE

The **FilenameFilter** interface allows you to limit the files returned by the **list( )** method of the **File** class to include only those files that match a certain file-name pattern of filter.

Related class: **File**

accept

public abstract boolean accept(File *directory*, String *filename*)

This method determines whether a specific file should be accepted by the invoking object. If its name meets the criteria, then **accept( )** returns **true.**

THE FILEREADER CLASS

The **FileReader** class allows you to read character files. It uses the default character encoding.

Related classes: **FileWriter, InputStreamReader, Reader**

This class was introduced in Java specification 1.1.

FileReader

public FileReader(File *f*)

This constructor creates a **FileReader** object for the **File** *f.* It can throw a **FileNotFoundException**.

public FileReader(FileDescriptor *fd*)

This constructor creates a **FileReader** object for the **FileDescriptor** *fd.*

public FileReader(String *str*)

This constructor creates a **FileReader** object for the file whose name is contained in the **String** *str.* It can throw a **FileNotFoundException**.

THE FILEWRITER CLASS

The **FileWriter** class allows you to write character files. It uses the default character encoding and buffer size.

Related classes: **FileReader**, **OutputStreamWriter**, **Writer**

This class was introduced in Java specification 1.1.

FileWriter

public FileWriter(File *f*)

This constructor creates a **FileWriter** object for the **File** *f*. It can throw an **IOException**.

public FileWriter(FileDescriptor *fd*)

This constructor creates a **FileWriter** object for the **FileDescriptor** *fd*.

public FileWriter(String *str*)

This constructor creates a **FileWriter** object for the file whose name is contained in the **String** *str*. It can throw an **IOException**.

public FileWriter(String *str*, boolean *appendFlag*)

This constructor creates a **FileWriter** object for the file whose name is contained in the **String** *str*. If *appendFlag* is **true,** any new information is appended to the end of the file. Otherwise, any new information is written from the beginning of the file, and existing information is lost. This constructor can throw an **IOException**.

THE FILTERINPUTSTREAM CLASS

The **FilterInputStream** class provides an implementation of the abstract methods in the **InputStream** class. It has one instance variable: **in** is a protected reference to the **InputStream** that is being filtered.

Related class: **InputStream**

FilterInputStream

protected FilterInputStream(InputStream *istream*)

This constructor creates a **FilterInputStream** object for *istream.*

available( )

public int available( )

This method returns the number of bytes currently available in the invoking stream. It can throw an **IOException**.

close

public void close( )

This method closes the invoking stream. It can throw an **IOException.**

mark

public synchronized void mark(int *size*)

This method marks the current position in the invoking stream. At a later time, the **reset( )** method can be used to return to this position. The *size* parameter indicates the maximum number of bytes you expect the stream to store between mark and reset operations.

markSupported

public boolean markSupported( )

This method tests whether the invoking stream supports the ability to do mark and reset operations.

read

public int read( )

This method reads and returns a byte from the invoking stream. A value of −1 is returned when an end-of-stream condition occurs. The method waits until data is available. It can throw an **IOException.**

public int read(byte *buffer*[ ])

This method fills *buffer* with bytes read from the invoking stream. The return value is the number of bytes that were placed into *buffer.* A value of −1 is returned when an end-of-stream condition occurs. The method waits until data is available. It can throw an **IOException.**

public int read(byte *buffer* [ ], int *start*, int *size*)

This method reads *size* bytes from the invoking stream. The bytes are read into *buffer* beginning at the index specified by *start.* The return value is the number of bytes that were placed into *buffer.* A value of −1 is returned when an end-of-stream condition occurs. The method waits until data is available. It can throw an **IOException.**

reset

public synchronized void reset( )

This method resets the stream position to that of the previous mark. It can throw an **IOException**.

skip

public long skip(long *number*)

This method ignores (i.e., skips) *number* bytes in the invoking stream. The return value is the number of bytes that were actually ignored. This method can throw an **IOException**.

THE FILTEROUTPUTSTREAM CLASS

The **FilterOutputStream** class provides an implementation of the abstract methods in the **OutputStream** class. It has one instance variable: **out** is a protected reference to the **OutputStream** that is being filtered.

Related class: **OutputStream**

FilterOutputStream

public FilterOutputStream(OutputStream *ostream*)

This constructor creates a **FilterOutputStream** object for *ostream.*

close

public void close( )

This method closes the invoking stream. It can throw an **IOException**.

flush

public void flush( )

This method flushes the invoking stream. It can throw an **IOException**.

write

public void write(byte *buffer*[ ])

This method writes the contents of *buffer* to the invoking stream. It can throw an **IOException**.

public void write(byte *buffer*[ ], int *start*, int *size*)

This method writes *size* bytes to the invoking stream. The bytes are written from *buffer* beginning at the index specified by *start*. This method can throw an **IOException**.

public void write(int *data*)

This method writes the low-order byte of *data* to the invoking stream. It can throw an **IOException**.

THE FILTERREADER CLASS

The abstract **FilterReader** class allows you to read filtered character streams. It has one instance variable: **in** is a protected reference to the **Reader** that is being filtered.

Related class: **Reader**

This class was introduced in Java specification 1.1.

FilterReader

protected FilterReader(Reader *r*)

This constructor creates an object for reading filtered character streams. *r* is a reference to the **Reader** object.

close

public void close( )

This method closes the invoking stream. It can throw an **IOException**.

mark

public void mark(int *size*)

This method marks the current position in the invoking stream. At a later time, the **reset( )** method can be used to return to this position. The *size* parameter indicates the maximum number of characters you expect the stream to store between mark and reset operations. This method can throw an **IOException**.

markSupported

public boolean markSupported( )

This method tests whether the invoking stream supports the ability to do mark and reset operations.

read

public int read( )

This method reads and returns a character from the invoking stream. A value of -1 is returned when an end-of-stream condition occurs. This method can throw an **IOException**.

public int read(char *buffer*[ ], int *start*, int *size*)

This method reads *size* characters from the invoking stream. The characters are read into *buffer* beginning at the index specified by *start*. The return value is the number of characters that were placed into *buffer*. A value of -1 is returned when an end-of-stream condition occurs. This method can throw an **IOException**.

ready

public boolean ready( )

This method tests whether there is data in either the buffers or the stream itself. It can throw an **IOException**.

reset

public void reset( )

This method resets the stream position to that of the previous mark. It can throw an **IOException**.

skip

public long skip(long *number*)

This method ignores (i.e., skips) *number* characters in the invoking stream. The return value is the number of characters that were actually ignored. This method can throw an **IOException**.

THE FILTERWRITER CLASS

8

The abstract **FilterWriter** class allows you to write filtered character streams. It has one instance variable: **out** is a protected reference to the **Writer** that is being filtered.

Related class: **Writer**

This class was introduced in Java specification 1.1.

FilterWriter

protected FilterWriter(Writer *w*)

This constructor creates an object for writing filtered character streams. *w* is a reference to the **Writer** object.

close

public void close( )

This method closes the invoking stream. It can throw an **IOException**.

flush

public void flush( )

This method flushes the invoking stream. It can throw an **IOException**.

write

public void write(char *buffer*[ ], int *start*, int *size*)

This method writes *size* characters to the invoking stream. The characters are written from *buffer* beginning at the index specified by *start*. This method can throw an **IOException**.

public void write(int *c*)

This method writes the character *c* to the invoking stream. It can throw an **IOException**.

public void write(String *str*, int *start*, int *size*)

This method writes *size* characters to the invoking stream. The characters are written from *str* beginning at the index specified by *start*. This method can throw an **IOException**.

THE INPUTSTREAM CLASS

InputStream is an abstract class that defines Java's model of streaming input.

Related classes: **BufferedInputStream, ByteArrayInputStream, DataInputStream, FilterInputStream, OutputStream**

InputStream

public InputStream( )

This is the default constructor.

available( )

public int available( )

This method returns the number of bytes currently available in the invoking stream. It can throw an **IOException**.

close

public void close( )

This method closes the invoking stream. It can throw an **IOException**.

mark

public synchronized void mark(int *size*)

This method marks the current position in the invoking stream. At a later time, the **reset( )** method can be used to return to this position. The *size* parameter indicates the maximum number of bytes you expect the stream to store between mark and reset operations.

markSupported

public boolean markSupported( )

This method tests whether the invoking stream supports the ability to do mark and reset operations.

read

public abstract int read( )

This method reads and returns a byte from the invoking stream. A value of −1 is returned when an end-of-stream condition occurs. The method waits until data is available. It can throw an **IOException**.

public int read(byte *buffer*[ ])

This method fills *buffer* with bytes read from the invoking stream. The return value is the number of bytes that were placed into *buffer*. A value of −1 is returned when an end-of-stream condition occurs. The method waits until data is available. It can throw an **IOException**.

public int read(byte *buffer*[ ], int *start*, int *size*)

This method reads *size* bytes from the invoking stream. The bytes are read into *buffer* beginning at the index specified by *start*. The return value is the number of bytes that were placed into *buffer*. A value of −1 is returned when an end-of-stream condition occurs. The method waits until data is available. It can throw an **IOException**.

reset

public synchronized void reset( )

This method resets the stream position to that of the previous mark. It can throw an **IOException**.

skip

public long skip(long *number*)

This method ignores (i.e., skips) *number* bytes in the invoking stream. The return value is the number of bytes that were actually ignored. It can throw an **IOException**.

THE INPUTSTREAMREADER CLASS

The **InputStreamReader** class reads bytes from an input stream and converts these to characters.

Related class: **Reader**

This class was introduced in Java specification 1.1.

InputStreamReader

public InputStreamReader(InputStream *istream*)

This constructor creates an **InputStreamReader** object for the **InputStream** *istream*. Default character encoding is used.

public InputStreamReader(InputStream *istream*, String *encoding*)

This constructor creates an **InputStreamReader** object for the **InputStream** *istream*. *encoding* is the name of the character encoding that will be used. This constructor can throw an **UnsupportedEncodingException**.

close

public void close( )

This method closes the invoking stream. It can throw an **IOException**.

getEncoding

public String getEncoding( )

This method returns the name of the character-encoding algorithm that is being used.

read

public int read( )

This method reads and returns a character from the invoking stream. A value of −1 is returned when an end-of-stream condition occurs. The method can throw an **IOException**.

public int read(char *buffer*[ ], int *start*, int *size*)

This method reads *size* characters from the invoking stream. The characters are read into *buffer* beginning at the index specified by *start*. The return value is the number of characters that were placed into *buffer*. A value of −1 is returned when an end-of-stream condition occurs. This method can throw an **IOException**.

ready

public boolean ready( )

This method tests whether there is data in either the buffers or the stream itself. It can throw an **IOException**.

THE LINENUMBERINPUTSTREAM CLASS

The **LineNumberInputStream** class provides an input stream that counts lines.

Related classes: **FilterInputStream, InputStream, LineNumberReader**

This class is deprecated in Java specification 1.1. You should use **LineNumberReader.**

8

LineNumberInputStream

public LineNumberInputStream(InputStream *istream*)

This constructor creates a **LineNumberInputStream** object for the **InputStream** *istream*.

available

public int available( )

This method returns the number of bytes currently available in the invoking stream. It can throw an **IOException**.

getLineNumber

public int getLineNumber( )

This method returns the current line number associated with the invoking stream.

mark

public void mark(int *numBytes*)

This method places a mark at the current point in the input stream that will remain valid until *numBytes* bytes are read.

read

public int read( )

This method reads and returns a byte from the invoking stream. A value of -1 is returned when an end-of-stream condition occurs. The method waits until data is available. It can throw an **IOException**.

public int read(byte *buffer*[ ], int *start*, int *size*)

This method reads *size* bytes from the invoking stream. The bytes are read into *buffer* beginning at the index specified by *start*. The return value is the number of bytes that were placed into *buffer*. A value of -1 is returned when an end-of-stream condition occurs. The method waits until data is available. It can throw an **IOException**.

reset

public void reset( )

This method resets the stream position to that of the previous mark. It can throw an **IOException**.

setLineNumber

public void setLineNumber(int *linenum*)

This method sets the line number associated with the invoking object.

skip

public long skip(long *number*)

This method ignores (i.e., skips) *number* bytes in the invoking stream. The return value is the number of bytes that were actually ignored. This method can throw an **IOException**.

THE LINENUMBERREADER CLASS

The **LineNumberReader** class provides a buffered stream that reads characters and counts lines.

Related classes: **BufferedReader**, **Reader**

This class was introduced in Java specification 1.1.

LineNumberReader

public LineNumberReader(Reader *r*)

This constructor creates a **LineNumberReader** object for the **Reader** *r*. A default is used for the size of the input buffer.

public LineNumberReader(Reader *r*, int *size*)

This constructor creates a **LineNumberReader** object for the **Reader** *r*. *size* is the size of the input buffer.

getLineNumber

public int getLineNumber( )

This method returns the current line number associated with the invoking stream.

mark

public void mark(int *numChars*)

This method places a mark at the current point in the input stream that will remain valid until *numChars* characters are read. It can throw an **IOException**.

read

public int read( )

This method reads and returns a character from the invoking stream. A value of −1 is returned when an end-of-stream condition occurs. The method waits until data is available. It can throw an **IOException**.

public int read(char *buffer*[ ], int *start*, int *size*)

This method reads *size* characters from the invoking stream. The characters are read into *buffer* beginning at the index specified by *start*. The return value is the number of characters that were placed into *buffer*. A value of −1 is returned when an end-of-stream condition occurs. The method waits until data is available. It can throw an **IOException**.

readLine

public String readLine( )

This method reads and returns a line of text. The line-termination characters are carriage return, linefeed, or a carriage return followed immediately by a linefeed. The line-termination characters are not included in the **String** that is returned from this method. **readLine( )** returns null when an end-of-stream condition is encountered. It can throw an **IOException**.

reset

public void reset( )

This method resets the stream position to that of the previous mark. It can throw an **IOException**.

setLineNumber

public void setLineNumber(int *linenum*)

This method sets the line number associated with the invoking object.

skip

public long skip(long *number*)

This method ignores (i.e., skips) *number* bytes in the invoking stream. The return value is the number of bytes that were actually ignored. This method can throw an **IOException**.

THE OUTPUTSTREAM CLASS

OutputStream is an abstract class that defines Java's model of streaming output.

Related classes: **BufferedOutputStream, ByteArrayOutputStream, DataOutputStream, FilterOutputStream, InputStream**

OuputStream

public OutputStream( )

This is the default constructor.

close

public void close( )

This method closes the invoking stream. It can throw an **IOException**.

flush

public void flush( )

This method flushes the invoking stream. It can throw an **IOException**.

write

public void write(byte *buffer*[ ])

This method writes contents of *buffer* to the invoking stream. It can throw an **IOException**.

public void write(byte *buffer*[ ], int *start*, int *size*)

This method writes *size* bytes to the invoking stream. The bytes are written from *buffer* beginning at the index specified by *start*. This method can throw an **IOException**.

public abstract void write(int *value*)

This method writes the low-order byte of *value* to the invoking stream. It can throw an **IOException**.

THE OUTPUTSTREAMWRITER CLASS

The **OutputStreamWriter** class converts characters to bytes and writes these to an output stream.

Related class: **Writer**

This class was introduced in Java specification 1.1.

OutputStreamWriter

public OutputStreamWriter(OutputStream *ostream*)

This constructor creates an **OutputStreamWriter** object for the **OutputStream** *ostream*. Default character encoding is used.

public OutputStreamWriter(OutputStream *ostream*, String *encoding*)

This constructor creates an **OutputStreamWriter** object for the **OutputStream** *ostream*. *encoding* is the name of the character encoding that will be used. This constructor can throw an **UnsupportedEncodingException**.

close

public void close( )

This method closes the invoking stream. It can throw an **IOException**.

8

flush

public void flush( )

This method flushes the invoking stream. It can throw an **IOException**.

getEncoding

public String getEncoding( )

This method returns the name of the character-encoding algorithm that is being used.

write

public void write(char *buffer*[ ], int *start*, int *size*)

This method writes *size* characters to the invoking stream. The characters are written from *buffer* beginning at the index specified by *start*. This method can throw an **IOException**.

public void write(int *c*)

This method writes the character *c* to the invoking stream. It can throw an **IOException**.

public void write(String *str*, int *start*, int *size*)

This method writes *size* characters to the invoking stream. The characters are written from *str* beginning at the index specified by *start*. This method can throw an **IOException**.

THE PRINTSTREAM CLASS

The **PrintStream** class contains methods that make it easy to generate formatted output.

Related classes: **FilterOutputStream**, **OutputStream**, **PrintWriter**

This class is deprecated in Java specification 1.1. You should use **PrintWriter**.

PrintStream

public PrintStream(OutputStream *ostream*)

This constructs a **PrintStream** object for *ostream.*

public PrintStream(OutputStream *ostream*, boolean *flushOnNewline*)

This constructs a **PrintStream** object for *ostream.* If *flushOnNewline* is **true**, the stream is flushed every time a newline character is output.

checkError

public boolean checkError( )

This method tests whether an error has occurred on the invoking stream.

close

public void close( )

This method closes the invoking stream.

flush

public void flush( )

This method flushes the invoking stream.

print

public void print(boolean *b*)

This method outputs the string equivalent of **boolean** *b.*

public void print(char *c*)

This method outputs *c.*

public void print(char *carray*[ ])

This method outputs the **char** array *carray.*

public void print(double *d*)

This method outputs the string equivalent of **double** *d.*

public void print(float *f*)

This method outputs the string equivalent of **float** *f.*

public void print(int *i*)

This method outputs the string equivalent of integer *i.*

public void print(long *l*)

This method outputs the string equivalent of **long** *l.*

public void print(Object *obj*)

This method outputs the string equivalent of **Object** *obj*.

public void print(String *str*)

This method outputs *str*.

println

public void println( )

This method writes a newline to the invoking stream.

public void println(boolean *b*)

This method outputs the string equivalent of **boolean** *b*. A newline is also output.

public void println(char *c*)

This method outputs *c*. A newline is also output.

public void print(char *carray*[ ])

This method outputs the **char** array *carray*. A newline is also output.

public void println(double *d*)

This method outputs the string equivalent of **double** *d*. A newline is also output.

public void println(float *f*)

This method outputs the string equivalent of **float** *f*. A newline is also output.

public void println(int *i*)

This method outputs the string equivalent of **int** *i*. A newline is also output.

public void println(long *l*)

This method outputs the string equivalent of **long** *l*. A newline is also output.

public void println(Object *obj*)

This method outputs a string equivalent of **Object** *obj*. A newline is also output.

public void println(String *str*)

This method outputs *str*. A newline is also output.

setError

protected void setError( )

This method is invoked if an error occurs.

write

public void write(byte *buffer*[ ], int *start*, int *size*)

This method writes *size* bytes to the invoking stream. The bytes are written from *buffer* beginning at the index specified by *start*.

public void write(int *data*)

This method writes the low-order byte of *data* to the invoking stream.

THE PRINTWRITER CLASS

The **PrintWriter** class contains methods that make it easy to generate formatted output.

Related classes: **PrintStream, Writer**

This class was introduced in Java specification 1.1. You should use it rather than **PrintStream**.

The following methods exist in both **PrintStream** and **PrintWriter**: **checkError( )**, **close( )**, **flush( )**, **print( )**, **println( )**, and **setError( )**. See the section about **PrintStream** for descriptions of those methods. The following sections cover only the additional methods in the **PrintWriter** class.

8

PrintWriter

public PrintWriter(OutputStream *ostream*)

This constructs a **PrintWriter** object for *ostream*. The stream is not flushed each time **println( )** is called.

public PrintWriter(OutputStream *ostream*, boolean *flushOnNewline*)

This constructs a **PrintWriter** object for *ostream*. If *flushOnNewline* is **true**, the stream is flushed each time **println( )** is called.

public PrintWriter(Writer *w*)

This constructs a **PrintWriter** object for *w*. The stream is not flushed each time **println( )** is called.

public PrintWriter(Writer *w*, boolean *flushOnNewline*)

This constructs a **PrintWriter** object for *w*. If *flushOnNewline* is **true**, the stream is flushed each time **println( )** is called.

write

public void write(char *buffer*[ ])

This method writes the contents of *buffer* to the invoking stream.

public void write(char *buffer*[ ], int *start*, int *size*)

This method writes *size* characters to the invoking stream. The characters are written from *buffer* beginning at the index specified by *start*.

public void write(int *c*)

This method writes the character *c* to the invoking stream.

public void write(String *str*)

This method writes the contents of *str* to the invoking stream.

public void write(String *str*, int *start*, int *size*)

This method writes *size* characters to the invoking stream. The characters are written from *str* beginning at the index specified by *start*.

THE RANDOMACCESSFILE CLASS

The **RandomAccessFile** encapsulates a random-access file. It implements the standard input and output methods, which you can use to read and write random-access files.

Related interfaces: **DataInput**, **DataOutput**

RandomAccessFile

public RandomAccessFile(File *fileObj*, String *access*)

In this form of the constructor, *fileObj* specifies the name of the file to open as a **File** object. *access* determines what type of file access is permitted. If *access* is "r", then the file may be read but not written. If it is "rw", then the file is opened in read-write mode. This constructor can throw an **IllegalArgumentException**, an **IOException**, or a **SecurityException**.

public RandomAccessFile(String *filename*, String *access*)

In this form of the constructor, the name of the file is passed in *filename,* and *access* determines what type of file access is permitted. If *access* is "r", then the file may be read but not written. If it is "rw", then the file is opened in read-write mode. This constructor can throw an **IllegalArgumentException**, an **IOException**, or a **SecurityException**.

close

public native void close( )

This method closes the file. It can throw an **IOException**.

getFD

public final FileDescriptor getFD( )

This method returns a **FileDescriptor** object that describes the file. It can throw an **IOException**.

getFilePointer

public native long getFilePointer( )

This method returns the current value of the file pointer. This is the position at which the next read or write will occur. This method can throw an **IOException**.

length

public native long length( )

This method returns the number of bytes in the file. It can throw an **IOException**.

read

public native int read( )

This method reads and returns a byte from the file. A value of -1 is returned when an end-of-file condition occurs. The method waits until data is available. It can throw an **IOException**.

public int read(byte *buffer*[ ])

This method fills *buffer* with bytes read from the invoking stream. The return value is the number of bytes that were placed into *buffer*. A value of -1 is returned when an end-of-stream condition occurs. The method waits until data is available. It can throw an **IOException**.

public int read(byte *buffer*[ ], int *start*, int *size*)

This method reads *size* bytes from the invoking stream. The bytes are read into *buffer* beginning at the index specified by *start*. The return value is the number of bytes that were placed into *buffer*. A value of −1 is returned when an end-of-stream condition occurs. The method waits until data is available. It can throw an **IOException**.

readBoolean

public final boolean readBoolean( )

This method reads and returns a **boolean** from the file. The method waits until data is available. It can throw an **EOFException** or **IOException**.

8

readByte

public final byte readByte( )

This method reads and returns a **byte** from the file. The method waits until data is available. It can throw an **EOFException** or **IOException**.

readChar

public final char readChar( )

This method reads and returns a **char** from the file. The method waits until data is available. It can throw an **EOFException** or **IOException**.

readDouble

public final double readDouble( )

This method reads and returns a **double** from the file. The method waits until data is available. It can throw an **EOFException** or **IOException**.

readFloat

public final float readFloat( )

This method reads and returns a **float** from the file. The method waits until data is available. It can throw an **EOFException** or **IOException**.

readFully

public final void readFully(byte *buffer*[ ])

This method reads bytes from the file into the *buffer.* The method does not return until *buffer* is filled. It can throw an **IOException** or **EOFException**.

public final void readFully(byte *buffer*[ ], int *start,* int *size)*

This method reads *size* bytes from the invoking stream. The bytes are read into *buffer* beginning at the index specified by *start.* The method does not return until *size* bytes are read. It can throw an **IOException** or **EOFException**.

readInt

public final int readInt( )

This method reads and returns an **int** from the file. The method waits until data is available. It can throw an **EOFException** or **IOException**.

readLine

public final String readLine( )

This method reads and returns a line of text. The line-termination characters are carriage return, linefeed, or a carriage return followed immediately by a linefeed. The line-termination characters are included in the **String** that is returned from this method. **readLine( )** waits until data is available and returns null when an end-of-file condition is encountered. It can throw an **IOException**.

readLong

public final long readLong( )

This method reads and returns a **long** from the file. The method waits until data is available. It can throw an **EOFException** or **IOException**.

readShort

public final short readShort( )

This method reads and returns a **short** from the file. The method waits until data is available. It can throw an **EOFException** or **IOException**.

readUnsignedByte

public final int readUnsignedByte( )

This method reads and returns an unsigned byte from the file. The byte is contained in the low-order byte of the value returned. The method waits until data is available. It can throw an **EOFException** or **IOException**.

readUnsignedShort

public final int readUnsignedShort( )

This method reads and returns an unsigned short integer from the file. The method waits until data is available. It can throw an **EOFException** or **IOException**.

readUTF

public final String readUTF( )

This method reads bytes from the file. The bytes are interpreted as characters encoded in the UTF-8 format and are converted to Unicode characters. A string equivalent to the encoded characters is returned. The method waits until data is available. It can throw an **EOFException**, **IOException**, or **UTFDataFormatException**.

seek

public native void seek(long *offset*)

This method changes the current file position to *offset.* It can throw an **IOException**.

skipBytes

public int skipBytes(int *number*)

This method ignores (i.e., skips) *number* bytes in the invoking stream. It returns *number.* The method waits until the operation is complete. It can throw an **EOFException** or **IOException**.

write

public void write(byte *buffer*[ ])

This method writes the contents of *buffer* to the file. It can throw an **IOException**.

public void write(byte *buffer*[ ], int *start*, int *size*)

This method writes *size* bytes to the invoking stream. The bytes are written from *buffer* beginning at the index specified by *start*. This method can throw an **IOException**.

public native void write(int *value*)

This method writes the low-order byte of *value* to the file. It can throw an **IOException**.

writeBoolean

public final void writeBoolean(boolean *value*)

This method writes a **boolean** to the file. It can throw an **IOException**.

writeByte

public final void writeByte(int *value*)

This method writes the low-order byte of *value* to the file. It can throw an **IOException**.

writeBytes

public final void writeBytes(String *str*)

This method writes the contents of *str* to the file. Only the lowest 8 bits of each character are output. This method can throw an **IOException**.

writeChar

public final void writeChar(int *value*)

This method writes a **char** to the file. It can throw an **IOException**.

writeChars

public final void writeChars(String *str*)

This method writes the contents of *str* to the file. It can throw an **IOException**.

writeDouble

public final void writeDouble(double *value*)

This method writes a **double** to the file. It can throw an **IOException**.

writeFloat

public final void writeFloat(float *value*)

This method writes a **float** to the file. It can throw an **IOException**.

writeInt

public final void writeInt(int *value*)

This method writes an **int** to the file. It can throw an **IOException**.

writeLong

public final void writeLong(long *value*)

This method writes a **long** to the file. It can throw an **IOException**.

writeShort

public final void writeShort(short *value*)

This method writes a **short** to the file. It can throw an **IOException**.

writeUTF

public final void writeUTF(String *str*)

This method writes data from **String** *str* to the file. The Unicode string *str* is converted to a modified UTF-8 format. This method can throw an **IOException**.

THE READER CLASS

The abstract **Reader** class allows you to read from a character stream.

It has one instance variable. **lock** is a protected reference to an **Object** that is used to synchronize the activities of multiple threads that are concurrently doing read operations.

Related classes: **BufferedReader, CharArrayReader, FileReader, FilterReader, InputStreamReader, LineNumberReader, StringReader, Writer**

This class was introduced in Java specification 1.1.

Reader

protected Reader( )

This constructor creates an object that can read a stream of characters.

protected Reader(Object *lock*)

This constructor creates an object that can read a stream of characters. *lock* is an **Object** that is used to synchronize the activities of multiple threads that are concurrently doing read operations.

close

public abstract void close( )

This method closes the invoking stream. It can throw an **IOException**.

mark

public void mark(int *size*)

This method marks the current position in the invoking stream. At a later time, the **reset( )** method can be used to return to this position. The *size* parameter indicates the maximum number of characters you expect the stream to store between mark and reset operations. This method can throw an **IOException**.

markSupported

public boolean markSupported( )

This method tests whether the invoking stream supports the ability to do mark and reset operations.

read

public int read( )

This method reads and returns a character from the invoking stream. A value of −1 is returned when an end-of-stream condition occurs. This method waits until data becomes available. It can throw an **IOException.**

public int read(char *buffer*[ ])

This method reads characters from the invoking stream, filling *buffer.* The return value is the number of characters that were placed into *buffer.* A value of −1 is returned when an end-of-stream condition occurs. This method waits until data becomes available. It can throw an **IOException.**

public abstract int read(char *buffer*[ ], int *start,* int *size*)

This method reads *size* characters from the invoking stream. The characters are read into *buffer* beginning at the index specified by *start.* The return value is the number of characters that were placed into *buffer.* A value of −1 is returned when an end-of-stream condition occurs. This method waits until data becomes available. It can throw an **IOException**.

ready

public boolean ready( )

This method tests whether there is data in either the buffers or the stream itself. It can throw an **IOException**.

reset

public void reset( )

This method resets the stream position to that of the previous mark. It can throw an **IOException**.

skip

public long skip(long *number*)

This method ignores (i.e., skips) *number* characters in the invoking stream. The return value is the number of characters that were actually ignored. The method waits until some data is available. It can throw an **IOException**.

THE STREAMTOKENIZER CLASS

The **StreamTokenizer** class breaks up an **InputStream** into tokens that are delimited by sets of characters. **StreamTokenizer** defines four **int** constants: **TT_EOF**, **TT_EOL**, **TT_NUMBER**, and **TT_WORD**.

There are three instance variables. **nval** is a public **double** that is used to hold the values of numbers as they are recognized. **sval** is a public **String** that is used to hold the value of any words as they are recognized. **ttype** is a public **int** that indicates the type of token that has just been read by the **nextToken( )** method. If the token is a word, **ttype** equals **TT_WORD**. If the token is a number, **ttype** equals **TT_NUMBER**. If the token is a single character, **ttype** contains its value. If an end-of-line condition has been encountered, **ttype** equals **TT_EOL**. (This assumes that **eolIsSignificant( )** was invoked with a **true** argument.) If the end of the stream has been encountered, **ttype** equals **TT_EOF**.

StreamTokenizer

public StreamTokenizer(InputStream *istream*)

This constructor returns a **StreamTokenizer** object that can be used to process the **InputStream** *istream.*

This constructor is deprecated in Java specification 1.1.

public StreamTokenizer(Reader *r*)

This constructor returns a **StreamTokenizer** object that can be used to process the **Reader** *r.*

This constructor was introduced in Java specification 1.1.

commentChar

public void commentChar(int *c*)

This method sets the comment character. When the **StreamTokenizer** object encounters this character, it treats all subsequent characters on the same line as a comment.

eolIsSignificant

public void eolIsSignificant(boolean *eolflag*)

This method determines whether the end-of-line characters (viz., '\ r' and '\ n') are significant. If *eolflag* is **true**, the end-

8

of-line characters are returned as tokens and the **nextToken( )** method returns the value **TT_EOL**. (A carriage return followed by a newline is treated as one end-of-line.) If *eolflag* is **false**, the end-of-line characters are ignored as white space.

lineno

public int lineno( )

This method returns the current line number.

lowerCaseMode

public void lowerCaseMode(boolean *caseFlag*)

If *caseFlag* is **true,** this method automatically converts tokens to lowercase before they are assigned to the variable **sval**.

nextToken

public int nextToken( )

This method retrieves the next token from the stream and returns its type. The type of the token is also stored in the variable **ttype**. This method can throw an **IOException**.

ordinaryChar

public void ordinaryChar(int *c*)

This method causes the **StreamTokenizer** to treat the character *c* as an ordinary character. If it is encountered in the stream, the **nextToken( )** method returns its value and the **ttype** variable also contains its value.

ordinaryChars

public void ordinaryChars(int *start*, int *end*)

This method causes the **StreamTokenizer** to treat all of the characters between *start* and *end* (inclusive) as ordinary characters. If any of them are encountered in the stream, the **nextToken( )** method returns that value and the **ttype** variable also contains that value.

parseNumbers

public void parseNumbers( )

This method causes the **StreamTokenizer** to treat the digits 0-9, the decimal point, and the minus sign as numeric characters. If any of them are encountered in the stream, the **nextToken( )** method treats these as a floating-point number and returns **TT_NUMBER**. The **nval** variable contains the value of that floating-point number.

pushBack

public void pushBack( )

This method causes the **StreamTokenizer** to push the value of the current token back to the stream. Therefore, the next invocation of the **nextToken( )** method will return this same value.

quoteChar

public void quoteChar(int *c*)

This method causes the **StreamTokenizer** to treat *c* as the delimiter for string constants. If such a string constant is encountered, the **nextToken( )** method sets the variable **ttype** to the delimiter character and the **sval** variable to the string constant. The string quote characters are not included in the string referenced by **sval**.

resetSyntax

public void resetSyntax( )

This method causes the **StreamTokenizer** to treat all characters as ordinary. As each character is encountered in the stream, the **nextToken( )** method returns its value and the **ttype** variable also contains its value.

slashSlashComments

public void slashSlashComments(boolean *commentFlag*)

If *commentFlag* is **true**, this method causes the **StreamTokenizer** to interpret two consecutive forward slash characters as the start of a comment. All characters from that point to the end of the same line are ignored.

slashStarComments

public void slashStarComments(boolean *commentFlag*)

If *commentFlag* is **true**, this method causes the **StreamTokenizer** to interpret a slash-star character sequence (i.e., /*) as the start of a comment. All characters from that point to a star-slash character sequence (i.e., */) are ignored.

toString

public String toString( )

This method returns a **String** object that is equivalent to the current token.

whitespaceChars

public void whitespaceChars(int *start*, int *end*)

This method causes the **StreamTokenizer** to treat all characters between *start* and *end* (inclusive) as white space.

wordChars

public void wordChars(int *start*, int *end*)

This method causes the **StreamTokenizer** to treat all characters between *start* and *end* (inclusive) as word characters.

8

THE STRINGREADER CLASS

The **StringReader** class reads characters from a string.

Related classes: **Reader**, **StringWriter**

This class was introduced in Java specification 1.1.

StringReader

public StringReader(String *str*)

This constructor creates a new object for reading character streams. *str* is the **String** object from which data will be read.

close

public void close( )

This method closes the invoking stream.

mark

public void mark(int *size*)

This method marks the current position in the invoking stream. At a later time, the **reset( )** method can be used to return to this position. The *size* parameter indicates the maximum number of characters you expect the stream to store between mark and reset operations. This method can throw an **IOException**.

markSupported

public boolean markSupported( )

This method tests whether the invoking stream supports the ability to do mark and reset operations.

read

public int read( )

This method reads and returns a character from the invoking stream. A value of −1 is returned when an end-of-stream condition occurs. This method can throw an **IOException**.

public int read(char *buffer*[ ], int *start*, int *size*)

This method reads *size* characters from the invoking stream. The characters are read into *buffer* beginning at the index specified by *start*. The return value is the number of characters that were placed into *buffer*. A value of −1 is returned when an end-of-stream condition occurs. This method can throw an **IOException**.

ready

public boolean ready( )

This method always returns **true**.

reset

public void reset( )

This method resets the stream position to that of the previous mark. It can throw an **IOException**.

skip

public long skip(long *number*)

This method ignores (i.e., skips) *number* characters in the invoking stream. The return value is the number of characters that were actually ignored. This method can throw an **IOException**.

THE STRINGWRITER CLASS

The **StringWriter** class allows you to stream output to a **StringBuffer** object. That object can later be used to instantiate a **String** object.

Related classes: **StringReader**, **Writer**

This class was introduced in Java specification 1.1.

StringWriter

public StringWriter( )

This constructor creates an object that can receive a stream of characters and store these in a **StringBuffer** object. A default is chosen for the initial capacity of the **StringBuffer** object.

protected StringWriter(int *size*)

This constructor creates an object that can receive a stream of characters and store these in a **StringBuffer** object. *size* is the initial capacity of the **StringBuffer** object.

close

public void close( )

This method closes the invoking stream.

flush

public void flush( )

This method flushes the invoking stream.

getBuffer

public StringBuffer getBuffer( )

This method returns the **StringBuffer** object into which the characters have been stored.

toString

public String toString( )

This method returns the **String** equivalent of the invoking object.

write

public void write(char *buffer*[ ], int *start*, int *size*)

This method writes *size* character to the invoking stream. The characters are written from *buffer* beginning at the index specified by *start*.

8

public void write(int *c*)

This method writes the character *c* to the invoking stream.

public void write(String *str*)

This method writes the contents of *str* to a stream.

public void write(String *str*, int *start*, int *size*)

This method writes *size* characters to the invoking stream. The characters are written from *str* beginning at the index specified by *start*.

THE WRITER CLASS

The abstract **Writer** class allows you to write to a character stream. It has one instance variable. **lock** is a protected reference to an **Object** that is used to synchronize the activities of different threads that are doing output.

Related classes: **BufferedWriter, CharArrayWriter, FileWriter, FilterWriter, OutputStreamWriter, StringWriter, Reader**

This class was introduced in Java specification 1.1.

Writer

protected Writer( )

This constructor creates an object that can write a stream of characters.

protected Writer(Object *lock*)

This constructor creates an object that can write a stream of characters. *lock* is an **Object** that is used to synchronize the activities of multiple threads that are concurrently doing write operations.

close

public abstract void close( )

This method closes the invoking stream. It can throw an **IOException**.

flush

public abstract void flush( )

This method flushes the invoking stream. It can throw an **IOException**.

write

public void write(char *buffer*[ ])

This method writes the contents of *buffer* to the invoking stream. It can throw an **IOException**.

public abstract void write(char *buffer*[ ], int *start*, int *size*)

This method writes *size* characters to the invoking stream. The characters are written from *buffer* beginning at the index specified by *start*. This method can throw an **IOException**.

8

public void write(int *c*)

This method writes the character *c* to the invoking stream. It can throw an **IOException**.

public void write(String *str*)

This method writes the contents of *str* to the invoking stream. It can throw an **IOException**.

public void write(String *str*, int *start*, int *size*)

This method writes *size* characters to the invoking stream. The characters are written from *str* beginning at the index specified by *start*. This method can throw an **IOException**.

Chapter 9—The Networking Classes and Interfaces

The Java library includes an assortment of networking classes that make Web-based programming easy. The networking classes are contained in **java.net**. They are shown here:

ContentHandler	InetAddress	URL
DatagramPacket	MulticastSocket	URLConnection
DatagramSocket	ServerSocket	URLEncoder
DatagramSocketImpl	Socket	URLStreamHandler
HttpURLConnection	SocketImpl	

java.net also defines these interfaces:

ContentHandlerFactory	SocketImplFactory
FileNameMap	URLStreamHandlerFactory

9

The following classes and interfaces are new to Java specification 1.1: **DatagramSocketImpl**, **HttpURLConnection**, **MulticastSocket**, and **FileNameMap**.

The following classes and interfaces are less frequently used and are not discussed in this book: **ContentHandler**, **DatagramSocketImpl**, **HttpURLConnection**, **MulticastSocket**, **SocketImpl**, **URLConnection**, **URLStreamHandler**, **ContentHandlerFactory**, **FileNameMap**, **SocketImplFactory**, and **URLStreamHandlerFactory**.

THE DATAGRAMPACKET CLASS

Instances of the **DatagramPacket** class represent datagram packets, which are sent from one machine to another. The underlying protocol makes no assurance that this datagram will actually be received on the remote machine. In addition, there is no assurance that a sequence of packets sent by one machine will be received in the same sequence at the remote machine.

Related classes: **DatagramSocket, InetAddress**

DatagramPacket

public DatagramPacket(byte *buffer*[ ], int *size*)

This constructor creates a **DatagramPacket** object that can be used to receive an incoming packet. The packet is stored in *buffer*. The maximum expected packet size is specified by *size*. The length of *buffer* must be at least equal to *size*.

public DatagramPacket(byte *buffer*[ ], int *size*, InetAddress *address*, int *port*)

This constructor creates a **DatagramPacket** object that can be used to transmit an outgoing packet. The packet is stored in *buffer*. The maximum expected packet size is specified by *size*. The length of *buffer* must be at least equal to *size*. Here, *address* is the Internet address of the destination machine and *port* is the software port on the destination machine.

getAddress

public synchronized InetAddress getAddress( )

This method returns an **InetAddress** object equivalent to the IP address in the packet.

getData

public synchronized byte[ ] getData( )

This method returns a byte array containing the data in the packet.

getLength

public synchronized int getLength( )

This method returns the number of bytes of data in the packet.

getPort

public synchronized int getPort( )

This method returns the port number in this packet. For a packet that is being transmitted, this value is the destination port number. For a packet that has been received, this value is the port number on the sending machine.

setAddress

public synchronized void setAddress(InetAddress *address*)

This method sets the IP address of the packet to *address*.

This method was introduced in Java specification 1.1.

setData

public synchronized void setData(byte *data*[ ])

This method sets the data of the packet to *data*.

This method was introduced in Java specification 1.1.

setLength

public synchronized void setLength(int *size*)

This method sets the length of the packet to *size.*

This method was introduced in Java specification 1.1.

setPort

public synchronized void setPort(int *portNum*)

This method sets the port number of the packet to *portNum.*

This method was introduced in Java specification 1.1.

THE DATAGRAMSOCKET CLASS

The **DatagramSocket** class provides mechanisms to send and receive **DatagramPackets**.

Related class: **DatagramPacket**

DatagramSocket

public DatagramSocket( )

This constructor creates a **DatagramSocket** object and selects an available port. It can throw a **SocketException**.

public DatagramSocket(int *port*)

This constructor creates a **DatagramSocket** object and links it to *port*. It can throw a **SocketException**.

public DatagramSocket(int *port*, InetAddress *address*)

This constructor creates a **DatagramSocket** object and links it to *port* and *address*. Here, *address* is a local Internet address. This constructor can throw a **SocketException**.

This constructor was introduced in Java specification 1.1.

close

public void close( )

This method closes the socket.

getLocalAddress

public InetAddress getLocalAddress( )

This method returns the local address of the invoking socket.

This method was introduced in Java specification 1.1.

getLocalPort

public int getLocalPort( )

This method returns the local port number of the invoking socket.

getSoTimeout

public synchronized int getSoTimeout( )

This method returns the timeout (in milliseconds) of the invoking socket. A value of zero means there is no timeout. This method can throw a **SocketException**.

This method was introduced in Java specification 1.1.

receive

public synchronized void receive(DatagramPacket *packet*)

This method receives a **DatagramPacket**. It waits until a packet arrives. The received packet contains the data, the Internet address of the originating machine, and the software port of the originating machine. This method can throw an **IOException**.

send

public void send(DatagramPacket *packet*)

This method sends a **DatagramPacket**. The transmitted packet contains the data, the Internet address, and software port of the destination machine. This method can throw an **IOException**.

setSoTimeout

public synchronized void setSoTimeout(int *milliseconds*)

This method sets the timeout period (in *milliseconds*) of the invoking socket. The timeout period determines how long **receive( )** waits. A value of zero means there is no timeout and **receive( )** waits indefinitely. This method can throw a **SocketException**. An **InterruptedIOException** is thrown if the timeout expires.

This method was introduced in Java specification 1.1.

THE INETADDRESS CLASS

The **InetAddress** class provides methods for working with
Internet addresses.

equals

public boolean equals(Object *obj*)

This method tests whether the invoking object and *obj* have the
same IP address.

getAddress

public byte[ ] getAddress( )

This method returns the raw IP address of the invoking object
in a **byte** array. In this array, the highest-order byte of the IP
address is placed at index zero.

getAllByName

public static InetAddress[ ] getAllByName(String *hostname*)

This method returns an array of **InetAddress** objects that
represent all of the IP addresses associated with the machine
named *hostname*. It throws an **UnknownHostException** if the
host is unknown.

getByName

public static InetAddress getByName(String *hostname*)

This method returns one **InetAddress** object that represents one IP address associated with the machine named *hostname*. It throws an **UnknownHostException** if the host is unknown.

getHostAddress

public String getHostAddress( )

This method returns a **String** equivalent of the IP address of the invoking object.

This method was introduced in Java specification 1.1.

getHostName

public String getHostName( )

This method returns a **String** equivalent of the host name of the invoking object. (If a **null** is returned, the IP address is for the local machine.)

getLocalHost

public static InetAddress getLocalHost( )

This method returns an **InetAddress** object for the local host. It can throw an **UnknownHostException**.

hashCode

public int hashCode( )

This method returns the hash code of the invoking object.

isMulticastAddress

public boolean isMulticastAddress( )

This method tests whether the IP address is a multicast address.

This method was introduced in Java specification 1.1.

toString

public String toString( )

This method returns a **String** equivalent of the IP address.

THE SERVERSOCKET CLASS

The **ServerSocket** class is designed to be a "listener." It waits for clients to send connection requests. There are additional methods that are not documented here.

Related class: **Socket**

ServerSocket

public ServerSocket(int *port*)

This constructor creates a **ServerSocket** object that can be used to receive an incoming request. Here, *port* is the local software port to which client machines direct connection requests. If *port* is zero, any available port is selected. The constructor can throw an **IOException**.

public ServerSocket(int *port*, int *queuesize*)

This constructor creates a **ServerSocket** object that can be used to receive an incoming request. Here, *port* is the local software port to which client machines direct connection requests. If *port* is zero, any available port is selected. The maximum number of incoming requests that can be queued is specified by *queuesize*. If a connection request arrives and *queuesize* requests are already queued, that request is refused. The constructor can throw an **IOException**.

public ServerSocket(int *port*, int *queuesize*, InetAddress *localaddress*)

This constructor creates a **ServerSocket** object that can be used to receive an incoming request. Here, *port* is the local software port to which client machines direct connection requests. If *port* is zero, any free port is selected. The maximum number of incoming requests that can be queued is specified by *queuesize*. If a connection request arrives and *queuesize* requests are already queued, that request is refused. The *localaddress* parameter designates the local IP address that the server socket should use. The constructor can throw an **IOException**.

This constructor was introduced in Java specification 1.1.

accept

public Socket accept( )

This method waits until an incoming connection request is received from a client. It returns a **Socket** object that can then be used for communicating with that client. This method can throw an **IOException**.

close

public void close( )

This method closes the invoking object. It can throw an **IOException**.

getInetAddress

public InetAddress getInetAddress( )

This method returns an **InetAddress** object that is the IP address of the invoking object.

getLocalPort

public int getLocalPort( )

This method returns the local port of the invoking object. (This is the port number to which sending machines direct requests.)

getSoTimeout

public synchronized int getSoTimeout( )

This method returns the timeout (in milliseconds) of the invoking object. A value of zero means there is no timeout. It can throw an **IOException**.

This method was introduced in Java specification 1.1.

setSoTimeout

public synchronized void setSoTimeout(long *milliseconds*)

This method sets the timeout period (in *milliseconds*) for the invoking **ServerSocket**. The timeout period determines how long **accept( )** waits for a connection request. If no request arrives within this time interval, an **InterruptedIOException** is thrown. A value of zero means that there is no timeout and **accept( )** waits indefinitely. This method can throw a **SocketException**.

This method was introduced in Java specification 1.1.

toString

public String toString( )

This method returns a **String** equivalent of the invoking object.

THE SOCKET CLASS

The **Socket** class is designed to connect to server sockets and initiate protocol exchanges. The creation of a **Socket** object implicitly establishes a connection between the client and server. There are no methods or constructors that explicitly expose the details of establishing that connection. Once the **Socket** object has been created, it can also be examined to gain access to its input and output streams.

The most commonly used constructors and methods are described here.

Related class: **ServerSocket**

Socket

public Socket(String *hostname*, int *port*)

This constructor creates a **Socket** object that can be used to communicate with a specific machine at a specific port number. Here, *hostname* is the name of the destination machine and *port* is the destination port. The constructor can throw an **IOException** or **UnknownHostException**.

public Socket(InetAddress *address*, int *port*)

This constructor creates a **Socket** object that can be used to communicate with a specific machine at a specific port number. Here, *address* is an **InetAddress** object containing the IP address of the remote machine and *port* is the destination port number. The constructor can throw an **IOException**.

close

public synchronized void close( )

This method closes the invoking object. It can throw an **IOException**.

getInetAddress

public InetAddress getInetAddress( )

This method returns an **InetAddress** object that contains the remote IP address to which the invoking socket is connected.

getInputStream

public InputStream getInputStream( )

This method returns the **InputStream** associated with the invoking object. It can throw an **IOException**.

getLocalAddress

public InetAddress getLocalAddress( )

This method returns an **InetAddress** object that contains the local IP address of the invoking socket.

This method was introduced in Java specification 1.1.

getLocalPort

public int getLocalPort( )

This method returns the local port to which the invoking object is connected.

getOutputStream

public OutputStream getOutputStream( )

This method returns the **OutputStream** associated with the invoking object. It can throw an **IOException**.

getPort

public int getPort( )

This method returns the remote port to which the invoking object is connected.

getSoTimeout

public synchronized int getSoTimeout( )

This method returns the timeout (in milliseconds) of the invoking socket. A value of zero means there is no timeout. This method can throw a **SocketException**.

This method was introduced in Java specification 1.1.

setSoTimeout

public synchronized void setSoTimeout(int *milliseconds*)

This method sets the timeout period (in *milliseconds*) for the invoking **ServerSocket**. The timeout period determines how long a call to **read( )** on the **ServerSocket**'s input stream waits for a message to arrive. If no message arrives within this time interval, an **InterruptedIOException** is thrown. A value of zero means that there is no timeout and **read( )** waits indefinitely. This method can throw a **SocketException**.

This method was introduced in Java specification 1.1.

toString

public String toString( )

This method returns a **String** equivalent of the invoking object.

9

Programming Tip

Here is a simple example that illustrates the basic technique required to create a connection to a URL and read data from it. It will connect to Osborne McGraw-Hill's Web site by default or to the URL that you specify on the command line.

```
// Connect to a URL and read data.
import java.net.*;
import java.io.*;
```

```
class NetTest {
  public static void main(String args[])
    throws MalformedURLException, IOException {
    URL url;
    int ch;

    // construct a URL
    try {
      url = new URL(args[0]);
    } catch (ArrayIndexOutOfBoundsException e) {
      url = new URL("http://www.osborne.com/");
      System.out.println("Opening osborne.com");
    }

    // open a stream to the URL
    InputStream urlIn = url.openStream();

    // read and display content
    if(urlIn != null) {
      System.out.println("Reading...");
      do {
        ch = urlIn.read();
        if(ch != -1) System.out.print((char)ch);
      } while (ch != -1);
      System.out.println();
      urlIn.close();
    }
  }
}
```

The program works like this. First, a URL object is constructed
from either the one specified on the command line or by using
`"http://www.osborne.com/"`. A reference to this URL is stored in
url. Next, **openStream( )** is called on **url**. This opens a connection
to the URL and obtains an input stream to it. Next, data is read,
one character at a time, from the URL and displayed on the
screen. This will be the HTML associated with the URL. Finally, the
input stream is closed.

As this program shows, working with URLs is incredibly easy in
Java. Of course, a program that implements a full-featured Web

browser is significantly more sophisticated (handling graphical images, hyperlinks, etc.), but this little program does illustrate the basic technique for reading data from a URL.

THE URL CLASS

The uniform resource locator (URL) provides a way to uniquely identify or address information on the Internet. The **URL** class provides a way to use URLs.

The most commonly used constructors and methods are described here.

URL

9

public URL(String *str*)

This constructor creates a **URL** object from the information in *str*. The constructor can throw a **MalformedURLException**.

public URL(String *protocol*, String *hostname*, int *port*, String *filename*)

This constructor creates a **URL** object. Here, *protocol, hostname, port,* and *filename* are the protocol, host name, port, and file name components of the URL, respectively. To specify the default port for a given protocol, pass −1 for the port. The constructor can throw a **MalformedURLException**.

public URL(String *protocol*, String *hostname*, String *filename*)

This constructor creates a **URL** object. Here, *protocol,* *hostname,* and *filename* are the protocol, host name, and file name components of the URL, respectively. In all protocols, the default port is used. The constructor can throw a **MalformedURLException**.

equals

public boolean equals(Object *obj*)

This method tests whether the invoking URL and *obj* have the same value.

getContent

public final Object getContent( )

This method returns the contents of the invoking URL. It can throw an **IOException**.

getFile

public String getFile( )

This method returns the file name component of the invoking URL.

getHost

public String getHost( )

This method returns the host name component of the invoking URL.

getPort

public int getPort( )

This method returns the port number component of the invoking URL.

getProtocol

public String getProtocol( )

This method returns the protocol component of the invoking URL.

getRef

public String getRef( )

This method returns the anchor component of the invoking URL.

9

hashCode

public int hashCode( )

This method returns the hash code of the invoking object.

openConnection

public URLConnection openConnection( )

This method creates a connection to the URL specified by the invoking object. It returns a reference to the abstract class **URLConnection**, which encapsulates URL communications. **openConnection( )** can throw an **IOException**.

openStream

public final InputStream openStream( )

This method returns a stream connected to the URL specified by the invoking object. If there is no open connection to the URL, one is created. Once the input stream has been obtained, it can be used to read data from the URL. **openStream( )** can throw an **IOException**.

sameFile

public boolean sameFile(URL *anotherURL*)

This method tests whether the invoking object and *anotherURL* refer to the same resource. The anchor information is not used in making this test.

toString

public String toString( )

This method returns a **String** equivalent of the invoking object.

THE URLCONNECTION CLASS

URLConnection is an abstract class that encapsulates the mechanism used to communicate with a remote URL. It is beyond the scope of this book to examine its members. Most often, the functionality provided by the **URL** class is sufficient unless you are creating your own communication class.

THE URLENCODER CLASS

The **URLEncoder** class contains one static method that takes a **String** object and converts it to the corresponding URL-encoded format.

encode

public static String encode(String *str*)

This method returns the URL-encoded format of *str*. Encoding follows these rules. Alphanumeric characters are not changed. Spaces are translated into the '+' character. All other characters are converted to a two-digit hexadecimal representation of the low-order byte of the character. This value is preceded by a '%' character.

9

Chapter 10—The Java Applet Class and Interfaces

The class and interfaces defined by **java.applet** manage applets. The class contained in **java.applet** is **Applet**. The interfaces defined by **java.applet** are the following:

AppletContext   **AppletStub**   **AudioClip**

The **AppletStub** interface is not discussed in this book.

THE APPLET CLASS

The **Applet** class contains several methods that give you detailed control over the execution of your applet. All applets are subclasses of **Applet**.

The most commonly used methods are described here.

Related classes: **Component**, **Container**, **Panel**

Applet

public Applet( )

This is the default constructor.

destroy

public void destroy( )

This method is called by the execution environment (i.e., the applet viewer or browser) just before an applet is terminated.

Your applet will override this method if it needs to perform any cleanup prior to its destruction.

getAppletContext

public AppletContext getAppletContext( )

This method returns the context associated with the applet.

getAppletInfo

public String getAppletInfo( )

This method returns a string that describes the applet. Your applet will normally override this method.

getAudioClip

public AudioClip getAudioClip(URL *url*)

This method returns an **AudioClip** object that represents the audio clip found at the location specified by *url*.

public AudioClip getAudioClip(URL *url*, String *clipName*)

This method returns an **AudioClip** object that represents the audio clip found at the location specified by *url* and that has the name specified by *clipName*.

getCodeBase

public URL getCodeBase( )

This method returns the URL of the invoking applet.

getDocumentBase

public URL getDocumentBase( )

This method returns the URL of the HTML document that invoked the applet.

getImage

public Image getImage(URL *url*)

This method returns an **Image** object that represents the image found at the location specified by *url*.

public Image getImage(URL *url*, String *imageName*)

This method returns an **Image** object that represents the image found at the location specified by *url* and that has the name specified by *imageName*.

getParameter

public String getParameter(String *paramName*)

This method returns the parameter associated with *paramName*. A **null** is returned if the specified parameter is not found.

getParameterInfo

public String[ ][ ] getParameterInfo( )

This method returns a **String** table that describes the parameters recognized by the applet. Each entry in the table must consist of three strings that contain the name of the parameter, a description of its type and/or range, and an explanation of its purpose.

init

public void init( )

This method is called when an applet begins execution. It is the first method called for any applet.

isActive

public boolean isActive( )

This method tests whether the applet has been started.

play

public void play(URL *url*)

If an audio clip is found at the location specified by *url*, the clip is played.

public void play(URL *url*, String *clipName*)

If an audio clip is found at the location specified by *url* with the name specified by *clipName*, the clip is played.

resize

public void resize(Dimension *dim*)

This method resizes the applet using the dimensions specified by *dim*.

public void resize(int *width*, int *height*)

This method resizes the applet using the dimensions specified by *width* and *height*.

showStatus

public void showStatus(String *str*)

This method displays *str* in the status window of the browser or applet viewer. If the browser does not support a status window, then no action takes place.

start

public void start( )

This method is called by the browser when an applet should start (or resume) execution. It is automatically called after **init( )** when an applet first begins.

stop

public void stop( )

This method is called by the browser to suspend execution of the applet. Once stopped, an applet is restarted when the browser calls **start( )**.

10

THE APPLETCONTEXT INTERFACE

AppletContext is an interface that lets you get information from the applet's execution environment.

getApplet

public abstract Applet getApplet(String *appletName*)

This method returns the applet specified by *appletName* if it is within the current applet context. Otherwise **null** is returned.

getApplets

public abstract Enumeration getApplets( )

This method returns an enumeration that contains all of the applets within the current applet context.

getAudioClip

public abstract AudioClip getAudioClip(URL *url*)

This method returns an **AudioClip** object that represents the audio clip found at the location specified by *url*.

getImage

public abstract Image getImage(URL *url*)

This method returns an **Image** object that represents the image found at the location specified by *url*.

showDocument

public abstract void showDocument(URL *url*)

This method brings the document at the URL specified by *url* into view. This method may not be supported by applet viewers.

public abstract void showDocument(URL *url*, String *where*)

This method brings the document at the URL specified by *url* into view. This method may not be supported by applet viewers. The placement of the document is specified by *where*, which can be "_blank" (a new browser window), "_parent" (the parent frame), "_self" (the current frame), "_top" (the topmost frame), or the name of a new top-level window.

showStatus

public abstract void showStatus(String *str*)

This method displays *str* in the status window.

THE AUDIOCLIP INTERFACE

AudioClip is an interface that lets you get and control audio files.

loop

10

public abstract void loop( )

This method causes the audio clip to play in an infinite loop.

play

public abstract void play( )

This method causes the audio clip to start playing from the beginning.

stop

public abstract void stop( )

This method causes the audio clip to stop playing.

Programming Tip

All but the most trivial applets override a set of methods that provide the basic mechanism by which the browser or applet viewer interfaces to the applet and controls its execution. Four of these methods—**init( )**, **start( )**, **stop( )**, and **destroy( )**—are defined by **Applet**. Another, **paint( )**, is defined by the AWT **Component** class. Default implementations for all of these methods are provided. Applets do not need to override those methods that they do not use. However, only very simple applets will not need to define all of them. These five methods can be assembled into the skeleton, shown here.

```java
// An Applet skeleton.
import java.awt.*;
import java.applet.*;
/*
  <applet code="AppletSkel" width=300 height=100>
  </applet>
*/

public class AppletSkel extends Applet {
  // Called first.
  public void init() {
    // initialization
  }

  /* Called second, after init().  Also called
     whenever the applet is restarted. */
  public void start() {
    // start or resume execution
  }

  // Called when the applet is stopped.
  public void stop() {
    // suspends execution
  }
```

```
  /* Called when applet is terminated.  This is the
     last method executed. */
  public void destroy() {
    // perform shutdown activities
  }

  // Called when an applet's window must be restored.
  public void paint(Graphics g) {
    // redisplay contents of window
  }
}
```

Although this skeleton does not do anything, it can be compiled and run. The HTML statements necessary to execute this applet are shown in the comment near the top of the program.

It is important to understand the order in which the various methods shown in the skeleton are called. When an applet begins, the following methods are called in this sequence:

init( )

start( )

paint( )

When an applet is terminated, the following sequence of method calls takes place:

stop( )

destroy( )

While real-world applets will be significantly more complex, they will all be based on the basic architecture of this applet skeleton.

10

Chapter 11—The Abstract Window Toolkit Classes and Interfaces

The abstract window toolkit (AWT) contains many classes, interfaces, and methods that help you create and manage windows. The AWT is very large. In fact, a full description would easily fill an entire book by itself. This chapter describes the most commonly used elements.

The core AWT classes are contained in the **java.awt** package. The classes found in **java.awt** are shown here:

AWTEvent	**EventQueue**	**MenuComponent**
AWTEventMulticaster	**FileDialog**	**MenuItem**
BorderLayout	**FlowLayout**	**MenuShortcut**
Button	**Font**	**Panel**
Canvas	**FontMetrics**	**Point**
CardLayout	**Frame**	**Polygon**
Checkbox	**Graphics**	**PopupMenu**
CheckboxGroup	**GridBagConstraints**	**PrintJob**
CheckboxMenuItem	**GridBagLayout**	**Rectangle**
Choice	**GridLayout**	**Scrollbar**
Color	**Image**	**ScrollPane**
Component	**Insets**	**SystemColor**
Container	**Label**	**TextArea**
Cursor	**List**	**TextComponent**
Dialog	**MediaTracker**	**TextField**
Dimension	**Menu**	**Toolkit**
Event	**MenuBar**	**Window**

java.awt also defines these interfaces:

Adjustable	**LayoutManager2**	**PrintGraphics**
ItemSelectable	**MenuContainer**	**Shape**
LayoutManager		

11

The following classes and interfaces are new to Java specification 1.1: **AWTEvent, AWTEventMulticaster, Cursor, EventQueue, MenuShortcut, PopupMenu, PrintJob, ScrollPane, SystemColor, Adjustable, ItemSelectable, LayoutManager2, PrintGraphics,** and **Shape.**

The following classes and interfaces are less frequently used and are not discussed in this book: **AWTEventMulticaster, CardLayout, Cursor, EventQueue, GridBagConstraints, GridBagLayout, GridLayout, Image, Insets, MediaTracker, MenuShortcut, Polygon, PopupMenu, PrintJob, ScrollPane, SystemColor, Adjustable, ItemSelectable, LayoutManager, LayoutManager2, MenuContainer, PrintGraphics,** and **Shape.**

THE AWTEVENT CLASS

The **AWTEvent** class encapsulates GUI events. It defines several **int** constants: **ACTION_EVENT_MASK, ADJUSTMENT_EVENT_MASK, COMPONENT_EVENT_MASK, CONTAINER_EVENT_MASK, FOCUS_EVENT_MASK, ITEM_EVENT_MASK, KEY_EVENT_MASK, MOUSE_EVENT_MASK, MOUSE_MOTION_EVENT_MASK, TEXT_EVENT_MASK,** and **WINDOW_EVENT_MASK**. These can be used to determine the type of the event.

id is one of the instance variables. It is an **int** that indicates the type of the event.

This class was introduced in Java specification 1.1. Some commonly used methods of this class are described here.

Related class: **EventObject**

AWTEvent

public AWTEvent(Event *e*)

This constructor creates an **AWTEvent** object from the **Event** object *e*.

public AWTEvent(Object *sourceObj*, int *type*)

This constructor creates an **AWTEvent** object. *sourceObj* is the object that generated the event and *type* categorizes the event.

getID

public int getID( )

This method returns the type of the event.

toString

public String toString( )

This method returns the **String** equivalent of the invoking object.

11

THE BORDERLAYOUT CLASS

The **BorderLayout** class implements a common layout style for top-level windows. It has four narrow, fixed-width components at the edges and one large area in the center. Each of these regions is referred to by name: "North," "South," "East," and "West" represent the four sides, and "Center" is the middle. The **BorderLayout** class defines the constants **NORTH**, **SOUTH**, **CENTER**, **EAST**, and **WEST**.

The constructors for this class are shown here.

BorderLayout

publicBorderLayout( )

This is the default constructor. It creates a default border layout.

publicBorderLayout(int *horz*, int *vert*)

This constructor allows you to specify the horizontal and vertical space left between components in *horz* and *vert*, respectively.

THE BUTTON CLASS

A push button is a **Button** object that contains a label and generates an event when pressed.

The most commonly used methods for this class are shown here.

Related class: **Component**

Button

public Button(String *str*)

This constructor creates a **Button** object that contains *str* as a label.

addActionListener

public synchronized void addActionListener(ActionListener *al*)

This method adds the **ActionListener** *al* to the set of objects that will receive action events generated by the invoking **Button** object.

This method was introduced in Java specification 1.1.

getActionCommand

public String getActionCommand( )

This method returns the name of the command associated with the action event generated by the invoking **Button** object.

This method was introduced in Java specification 1.1.

getLabel

public String getLabel( )

This method returns the label (i.e., the name) of the invoking **Button** object.

removeActionListener

public synchronized void removeActionListener(ActionListener *al*)

This method removes the **ActionListener** *al* from the set of objects that will receive action events generated by the invoking **Button** object.

This method was introduced in Java specification 1.1.

setActionCommand

public void setActionCommand(String *c*)

The method sets to *c* the name of command associated with the action event that will be generated by the invoking **Button** object. (The default command name is the button label.)

This method was introduced in Java specification 1.1.

11

setLabel

public synchronized void setLabel(String *str*)

This method sets the label of the invoking **Button** object to *str*.

THE CANVAS CLASS

The **Canvas** class encapsulates a blank window upon which you can draw. This class is usually used as a superclass for your own classes.

Related class: **Component**

Canvas

public Canvas( )

This constructor creates a new **Canvas** object.

paint

public void paint(Graphics *g*)

This method paints the canvas with the current background color. The graphics context is contained in *g*. Your subclasses of **Canvas** will typically override **paint( )**.

THE CHECKBOX CLASS

A **Checkbox** object is a small box that has a label. The box is either checked or cleared.

The most commonly used methods in this class are described here.

Related classes: **CheckboxGroup**, **Component**

Checkbox

public Checkbox( )

This constructor creates a new **Checkbox** object. Its label is initially blank. The state of the check box is unchecked.

public Checkbox(String *str*)

This constructor creates a new **Checkbox** object. Its label is initially set to *str*. The state of the check box is unchecked.

public Checkbox(String *str*, boolean *on*)

This constructor creates a new **Checkbox** object. Its label is initially set to *str*. The value of *on* determines the initial state of the check box. If it is **true**, the check box is initially checked.

This constructor was introduced in Java specification 1.1.

public Checkbox(String *str*, CheckboxGroup *cbGroup*, boolean *on*)

This constructor creates a new **Checkbox** object. Its label is initially set to *str*. The value of *on* determines the initial state of the check box. If it is **true**, the check box is initially checked. The **CheckboxGroup** to which the check box belongs is specified by *cbGroup*.

public Checkbox(String *str*, boolean *on*, CheckboxGroup *cbGroup*)

This constructor creates a new **Checkbox** object. Its label is initially set to *str*. The value of *on* determines the initial

11

state of the check box. If it is **true,** the check box is initially checked. The **CheckboxGroup** to which the check box belongs is specified by *cbGroup.*

This constructor was introduced in Java specification 1.1.

addItemListener

public synchronized void addItemListener(ItemListener *il*)

This method adds the **ItemListener** *il* to the set of objects that will receive item events generated by the invoking **Checkbox** object.

This method was introduced in Java specification 1.1.

getCheckboxGroup

public CheckboxGroup getCheckboxGroup( )

This method returns the **CheckboxGroup** object to which the invoking **Checkbox** object belongs.

getLabel

public String getLabel( )

This method returns the label of the invoking **Checkbox** object.

getSelectedObjects

public Object[ ] getSelectedObjects( )

If the check box is selected, this method returns an array with one element that contains the check box label. Otherwise, it returns **null**.

This method was introduced in Java specification 1.1.

getState

public boolean getState( )

This method returns the state of the invoking **Checkbox** object. It returns **true** if the check box is checked. It returns **false** if the check box is cleared.

removeItemListener

public synchronized void removeItemListener(ItemListener *il*)

This method removes the **ItemListener** *il* from the set of objects that will receive item events generated by the invoking **Checkbox** object.

This method was introduced in Java specification 1.1.

setCheckboxGroup

public void setCheckboxGroup(CheckboxGroup *group*)

This method puts the invoking **Checkbox** object into the group of check boxes specified by *group*.

setLabel

public synchronized void setLabel(String *str*)

This method sets the label of the invoking **Checkbox** object to *str*.

setState

public void setState(boolean *state*)

This method determines whether the invoking **Checkbox** object is checked or cleared. If *state* is **true**, the check box is displayed as checked. Otherwise, it is cleared.

THE CHECKBOXGROUP CLASS

To create a set of mutually exclusive check boxes, you must first define the group to which they will belong and then specify that group when you construct the check boxes. Check box groups are objects of type **CheckboxGroup**.

The most commonly used methods in this class are described here.

Related class: **Checkbox**

CheckboxGroup

public CheckboxGroup( )

This constructor creates an empty check box group.

getCurrent

public Checkbox getCurrent( )

This method returns a reference to the **Checkbox** object that is currently selected. Only one box in a group will be set at any one time.

This method was deprecated in Java specification 1.1.

getSelectedCheckbox

public Checkbox getSelectedCheckbox( )

This method returns a reference to the **Checkbox** object that is selected.

This method was introduced in Java specification 1.1.

setCurrent

public synchronized void setCurrent(Checkbox *cb*)

This method sets the check box specified by *cb*.

This method was deprecated in Java specification 1.1.

setSelectedCheckbox

public synchronized void setSelectedCheckbox(Checkbox *cb*)

This method sets the check box specified by *cb*.

This method was introduced in Java specification 1.1.

THE CHECKBOXMENUITEM CLASS

The **CheckboxMenuItem** class encapsulates a checkable menu item. The most commonly used constructors and methods in this class are described here.

Related classes: **Menu, MenuBar, MenuItem**

11

CheckboxMenuItem

public CheckboxMenuItem(String *str*)

This constructor creates an object with *str* as a label. The object is initially unchecked.

public CheckboxMenuItem(String *str*, boolean *checked*)

This constructor creates an object with *str* as a label. If *checked* is **true**, the item is checked.

This constructor was introduced in Java specification 1.1.

addItemListener

public synchronized void addItemListener(ItemListener *il*)

This method adds the **ItemListener** *il* to the set of objects that will receive item events generated by the invoking **CheckboxMenuItem** object.

This method was introduced in Java specification 1.1.

getState

public boolean getState( )

This method returns **true** if the invoking **CheckboxMenuItem** is checked. It returns **false** if the **CheckboxMenuItem** is cleared.

removeItemListener

public synchronized void removeItemListener(ItemListener *il*)

This method removes the **ItemListener** *il* from the set of objects that will receive item events generated by the invoking **CheckboxMenuItem** object.

This method was introduced in Java specification 1.1.

setState

public synchronized void setState(boolean *state*)

This method determines whether the invoking **CheckboxMenuItem** object is checked or cleared. If *state* is **true**, the check box menu item is displayed as checked. Otherwise, it is cleared.

THE CHOICE CLASS

The **Choice** class is used to create a pop-up list of items from which the user may choose. When inactive, a **Choice** component takes up only enough space to show the currently selected item; when the user clicks on it, the whole list of choices pops up and a new selection can be made. Each item in the list is a string that appears as a left-justified label in the order in which it is added to the **Choice** object.

The most commonly used methods in this class are described here.

Related class: **Component**

Choice

public Choice( )

This is the default constructor. It creates an empty **Choice** object.

add

public synchronized void add(String *str*)

This method adds the **String** object *str* to the choice list. It can throw a **NullPointerException**.

This method was introduced in Java specification 1.1.

addItem

public synchronized void addItem(String *str*)

This method adds the **String** object *str* to the choice list. It can throw a **NullPointerException**.

11

addItemListener

public synchronized void addItemListener(ItemListener *il*)

This method adds the **ItemListener** *il* to the set of objects that will receive item events generated by the invoking **Choice** object.

This method was introduced in Java specification 1.1.

countItems

public int countItems( )

This method returns the number of items in the invoking **Choice** object.

This method is deprecated in Java specification 1.1.

getItem

public String getItem(int *i*)

This method returns the item that is stored at index *i* in the invoking **Choice** object. Indexing begins at zero.

getItemCount

public int getItemCount( )

This method returns the number of items in the invoking **Choice** object.

This method was introduced in Java specification 1.1.

getSelectedIndex

public int getSelectedIndex( )

This method returns the index of the item that is currently selected in the invoking **Choice** object. Indexing begins at zero.

getSelectedItem

public synchronized String getSelectedItem( )

This method returns the item that is currently selected in the invoking **Choice** object.

getSelectedObjects

public synchronized Object[ ] getSelectedObjects( )

If the invoking **Choice** object is empty, this method returns **null**. Otherwise, it returns an array with one object, which is the item currently selected.

This method was introduced in Java specification 1.1.

insert

public synchronized void insert(String *str*, int *i*)

This method inserts a new item into the invoking **Choice** object. The item to be inserted is specified by *str*. The index at which the item is to be inserted is passed in *i*. Indexing begins at zero. This method can throw an **IllegalArgumentException**.

This method was introduced in Java specification 1.1.

remove

public synchronized void remove(String *str*)

This method removes the item matching *str* from the invoking **Choice** object. It can throw an **IllegalArgumentException**.

This method was introduced in Java specification 1.1.

public synchronized void remove(int *i*)

This method removes the item at index *i* from the invoking **Choice** object. Indexing begins at zero.

This method was introduced in Java specification 1.1.

removeAll

public synchronized void removeAll( )

This method removes all items from the invoking **Choice** object.

This method was introduced in Java specification 1.1.

removeItemListener

public synchronized void removeItemListener(ItemListener *il*)

This method removes the **ItemListener** *il* from the set of objects that will receive item events generated by the invoking **Choice** object.

This method was introduced in Java specification 1.1.

select

public synchronized void select(int *i*)

This method selects the item at index *i* in the invoking **Choice** object. Indexing begins at zero. This method can generate an **IllegalArgumentException**.

public synchronized void select(String *str*)

This method selects the item matching *str* in the invoking **Choice** object.

THE COLOR CLASS

The **Color** class defines several methods that help manipulate colors. There are several static variables that hold references to various **Color** objects. These variables are **black**, **blue**, **cyan**, **darkGray**, **gray**, **green**, **lightGray**, **magenta**, **orange**, **pink**, **red**, **white**, and **yellow**.

The most commonly used methods in this class are described here.

Color

public Color(float *r*, float *g*, float *b*)

This constructor creates a **Color** object in which the red, green, and blue components are specified by *r*, *g*, and *b*. Each of these values must be between 0.0f and 1.0f, inclusive.

public Color(int *r*, int *g*, int *b*)

This constructor creates a **Color** object in which the red, green, and blue components are specified by *r*, *g*, and *b*. Each of these values must be between 0 and 255, inclusive.

public Color(int *rgbValue*)

This constructor creates a **Color** object in which the red, green, and blue components are specified in *rgbValue*. This is a single argument that contains the mix of red, green, and blue packed into an integer. The integer is organized with red in bits 16 to 23, green in 8 to 15, and blue in 0 to 7.

brighter

public Color brighter( )

This method returns a **Color** object that represents a brighter version of the invoking object.

darker

public Color darker( )

This method returns a **Color** object that represents a darker version of the invoking object.

decode

public static Color decode(String *name*)

This method returns a **Color** object that represents a color corresponding to *name*. It can throw a **NumberFormatException**.

This method was introduced in Java specification 1.1.

equals

public boolean equals(Object *obj*)

This method tests whether the invoking object and *obj* have the same value.

getBlue

public int getBlue( )

This method returns an integer from 0 to 255 representing the blue component of the invoking object.

getColor

public static Color getColor(String *name*)

This method returns a **Color** object that represents the color specified in *name*.

This method was introduced in Java specification 1.1.

getGreen

public int getGreen( )

This method returns an integer from 0 to 255 representing the green component of the invoking object.

getHSBColor

public static Color getHSBColor(float *h*, float *s*, float *b*)

This method returns a **Color** object that has a hue of h, a saturation of s, and a brightness of b.

getRed

public int getRed( )

This method returns an integer from 0 to 255 representing the red component of the invoking object.

getRGB

public int getRGB( )

This method returns an integer containing the red, green, and blue components of the invoking **Color** object. Bits 23 to 16 are the red component. Bits 15 to 8 are the green component. Bits 7 to 0 are the blue component.

hashCode

public int hashCode( )

This method returns the hash code associated with the invoking object.

11

HSBtoRGB

public static int HSBtoRGB(float *h*, float *s*, float *b*)

Given a hue, saturation, and brightness, this method returns an integer containing equivalent red, green, and blue color components. Bits 23 to 16 are the red component. Bits 15 to 8 are the green component. Bits 7 to 0 are the blue component. The hue, saturation, and brightness are specified by *h*, *s*, and *b*, respectively.

RGBtoHSB

public static float[ ] RGBtoHSB(int *r*, int *g*, int *b*, float *hsb*[ ])

Given the red, green, and blue color components, this method returns an array of floats that represent the equivalent hue, saturation, and brightness. The red, green, and blue components are specified by *r*, *g*, and *b*, respectively. The array into which the HSB information will be written is specified by *hsb*.

toString

public String toString( )

This method returns the **String** equivalent of the invoking object.

THE COMPONENT CLASS

At the top of the AWT hierarchy is the abstract **Component** class. All of the user interface elements that are displayed on the screen and interact with the user are subclasses of **Component**. It defines almost a hundred public methods that are responsible for managing events, such as mouse and keyboard input, positioning and sizing the window, and repainting.

The most commonly used methods in this class are described here.

Component

public Component( )

This is the default constructor.

action

public boolean action(Event *evtObj*, Object *arg*)

This method is called when a control generates an event. Your program must override **action( )** in order to process these events. Your method must return **true** if it handles the event and **false** if it does not. Another approach to use when the event is not handled is to return the result of the superclass's **handleEvent( )** method.

Use of this method is deprecated in Java specification 1.1.

addComponentListener

public synchronized void addComponentListener(ComponentListener *cl*)

This method adds the **ComponentListener** *cl* to the set of objects that will receive component events generated by this component.

This method was introduced in Java specification 1.1.

11

addFocusListener

public synchronized void addFocusListener(FocusListener *fl*)

This method adds the **FocusListener** *fl* to the set of objects that will receive focus events generated by the invoking **Component** object.

This method was introduced in Java specification 1.1.

addKeyListener

public synchronized void addKeyListener(KeyListener *kl*)

This method adds the **KeyListener** *kl* to the set of objects that will receive key events generated by the invoking **Component** object.

This method was introduced in Java specification 1.1.

addMouseListener

public synchronized void addMouseListener(MouseListener *ml*)

This method adds the **MouseListener** *ml* to the set of objects that will receive mouse events generated by the invoking **Component** object.

This method was introduced in Java specification 1.1.

addMouseMotionListener

public synchronized void addMouseMotionListener(MouseMotionListener *mm*

This method adds the **MouseMotionListener** *mml* to the set of objects that will receive mouse motion events generated by the invoking **Component** object.

This method was introduced in Java specification 1.1.

getBackground

public Color getBackground( )

This method returns the background **Color** object associated with the invoking **Component** object.

getFont

public Font getFont( )

This method returns the **Font** object that is associated with the invoking **Component** object.

getFontMetrics

public FontMetrics getFontMetrics(Font *f*)

This method returns the **FontMetrics** object that is associated with the invoking **Component** object for the specified font.

11

getForeground

public Color getForeground( )

This method returns the foreground **Color** object associated with the invoking **Component** object.

getGraphics

public Graphics getGraphics( )

This method returns the **Graphics** object associated with the invoking **Component** object.

getMaximumSize

public Dimension getMaximumSize( )

This method returns the maximum size of the invoking **Component** object.

This method was introduced in Java specification 1.1.

getMinimumSize

public Dimension getMinimumSize( )

This method returns the minimum size of the invoking **Component** object.

This method was introduced in Java specification 1.1.

getParent

public Container getParent( )

This method returns a reference to the container in which the invoking **Component** object is stored.

getPreferredSize

public Dimension getPreferredSize( )

This method returns the preferred size of the invoking **Component** object.

This method was introduced in Java specification 1.1.

getSize

public Dimension getSize( )

This method returns the size of the invoking **Component** object.

This method was introduced in Java specification 1.1.

handleEvent

public boolean handleEvent(Event *evtObj*)

This method handles events for the invoking **Component** object. The **Event** object that has been generated by some component is passed in *evtObj*. The method must return **true** if it has handled the event. Otherwise, it must return **false**. Your code will typically override this method.

This method is deprecated in Java specification 1.1.

hide

public void hide( )

This method removes the invoking object from the screen.

This method is deprecated in Java specification 1.1.

keyDown

public boolean keyDown(Event *evtObj*, int *k*)

This method is a specialized event handler for processing key-down events. The **Event** object that has been generated by some component is passed in *evtObj*. The key that was pressed is contained in *k*. The method must return **true** if it has handled the event. Otherwise, it must return **false**. Your code will typically override this method.

This method is deprecated in Java specification 1.1.

11

keyUp

public boolean keyUp(Event *e*, int *k*)

This method is a specialized event handler for processing key-up events. The **Event** object that has been generated by some component is passed in *evtObj*. The key that was released is contained in *k*. The method must return **true** if it has handled the event. Otherwise, it must return **false**. Your code will typically override this method.

This method is deprecated in Java specification 1.1.

mouseDown

public boolean mouseDown(Event *evtObj*,int *x*, int *y*)

This method is called when a mouse button is pressed. The **Event** object that describes the event is passed in *evtObj*. The coordinates of the mouse pointer at the time the event was generated are passed in *x* and *y*. This method must return **true** if it handles the event. Your code will typically override this method.

This method is deprecated in Java specification 1.1.

mouseDrag

public boolean mouseDrag(Event *evtObj*, int *x*, int *y*)

This method is called when the mouse is moved when a button is pressed. The **Event** object that describes the event is passed in *evtObj*. The coordinates of the mouse pointer at the time the event was generated are passed in *x* and *y*. This method must return **true** if it handles the event. Mouse drag events continue to occur as long as the mouse is being moved within the window and a button is pressed. Your code will typically override this method.

This method is deprecated in Java specification 1.1.

mouseEnter

public boolean mouseEnter(Event *evtObj*, int *x*, int *y*)

This method is called when the mouse moves into the window. The **Event** object that describes the event is passed in *evtObj*. The coordinates of the mouse pointer at the time the event was generated are passed in *x* and *y*. This method must return **true** if it handles the event. Your code will typically override this method.

This method is deprecated in Java specification 1.1.

mouseExit

public boolean mouseExit(Event *evtObj*, int *x*, int *y*)

This method is called when the mouse moves out of the window. The **Event** object that describes the event is passed in *evtObj*. The coordinates of the mouse pointer at the time the event was generated are passed in *x* and *y*. This method must return **true** if it handles the event. Your code will typically override this method.

This method is deprecated in Java specification 1.1.

mouseMove

public boolean mouseMove(Event *evtObj*, int *x*, int *y*)

This method is called when the mouse is moved. The **Event** object that describes the event is passed in *evtObj*. The coordinates of the mouse pointer at the time the event was generated are passed in *x* and *y*. This method must return **true** if it handles the event. Mouse-move events continue to occur as long as the mouse is being moved within the window and no button is pressed. Your code will typically override this method.

This method is deprecated in Java specification 1.1.

mouseUp

public boolean mouseUp(Event *evtObj*, int *x*, int *y*)

This method is called when a mouse button is released. The **Event** object that describes the event is passed in *evtObj*. The coordinates of the mouse pointer at the time the event was generated are passed in *x* and *y*. This method must return **true** if it handles the event. Your code will typically override this method.

This method is deprecated in Java specification 1.1.

paint

public void paint(Graphics *g*)

This method paints the component onto the **Graphics** object described by *g*. Your program typically overrides this method to perform application-specific drawing.

removeComponentListener

public synchronized void removeComponentListener(ComponentListener *cl*)

This method removes the **ComponentListener** *cl* from the set of objects that will receive component events generated by the invoking **Component** object.

This method was introduced in Java specification 1.1.

removeFocusListener

public synchronized void removeFocusListener(FocusListener *fl*)

This method removes the **FocusListener** *fl* from the set of objects that will receive focus events generated by the invoking **Component** object.

This method was introduced in Java specification 1.1.

removeKeyListener

public synchronized void removeKeyListener(KeyListener *kl*)

This method removes the **KeyListener** *kl* from the set of objects that will receive key events generated by the invoking **Component** object.

This method was introduced in Java specification 1.1.

removeMouseListener

public synchronized void removeMouseListener(MouseListener *ml*)

This method removes the **MouseListener** *ml* from the set of objects that will receive mouse-listener events generated by the invoking **Component** object.

This method was introduced in Java specification 1.1.

11

removeMouseMotionListener

public synchronized void removeMouseMotionListener(MouseMotionListener *mml*)

This method removes the **MouseMotionListener** *mml* from the set of objects that will receive mouse-motion events generated by the invoking **Component** object.

This method was introduced in Java specification 1.1.

repaint

public void repaint( )

This method requests that the Java Virtual Machine schedule calls to the **update( )** and **paint( )** methods. That is, it causes the invoking object to be repainted.

setBackground

public void setBackground(Color *bc*)

This method sets the background color of the invoking **Component** object to *bc*.

setFont

public synchronized void setFont(Font *f*)

This method sets the font of the invoking **Component** object to *f*.

setForeground

public void setForeground(Color *fc*)

This method sets the foreground color of the invoking **Component** object to *fc*.

setVisible

public void setVisible(boolean *visible*)

If *visible* is **true**, the invoking object is made visible. If it is **false**, the invoking object is removed from the screen.

This method was introduced in Java specification 1.1.

show

public void show( )

This method displays the invoking object on the screen.

This method is deprecated in Java specification 1.1.

public void show(boolean *visible*)

If *visible* is **true**, the invoking object is made visible. If it is **false**, the invoking object is removed from the screen.

This method is deprecated in Java specification 1.1.

update

public void update(Graphics *g*)

The default implementation of this method sets the entire component display area to the background color and then calls the **paint( )** method. Your program can override this method to provide a different behavior.

11

THE CONTAINER CLASS

The **Container** class is an abstract subclass of **Component**. It has additional methods that allow other **Component** objects to be nested within it. A container is responsible for laying out (i.e., positioning) any components that it contains. It does this through the use of various *layout managers*.

The most commonly used methods in this class are described here.

Related class: **Component**

Container

protected Container( )

This is the default constructor. It creates an empty **Container** object.

add

public Component add(Component *c*)

This method adds the **Component** *c* to the invoking **Container** object.

public Component add(String *name*, Component *c*)

This method adds the **Component** *c* to the invoking **Container** object. *name* specifies where the component should be added, e.g., **add("North", new Button("Start"));**.

addContainerListener

public synchronized void addContainerListener(ContainerListener *cl*)

This method adds the **ContainerListener** *cl* to the set of objects that will receive container events generated by the invoking **Container** object.

This method was introduced in Java specification 1.1.

getLayout

public LayoutManager getLayout( )

This method returns the **LayoutManager** object that is associated with the invoking **Container** object.

paint

public void paint(Graphics *g*)

This method paints the invoking object on the **Graphics** object described by *g*. Your code will typically override **paint( )**.

remove

public void remove(Component *c*)

This method removes **Component** *c* from the invoking **Container** object.

setLayout

public void setLayout(LayoutManager *lm*)

This method selects *lm* as the layout manager used by the invoking **Container** object.

11

THE DIALOG CLASS

The **Dialog** class is used to construct and manage dialog boxes. These are used primarily to obtain user input. They are similar to frame windows except that dialog boxes are always child windows of a top-level window. Also, dialog boxes don't have menu bars. In other respects, dialog boxes function like frame windows. (For example, you can add controls to them in the same way that you add controls to a frame window.) Dialog boxes can be *modal* or *modeless*. When a modal dialog box is active, all input is directed to it until it is closed. This means that you cannot access other parts of your program until you have closed the dialog box. When a modeless dialog box is active, input focus can be directed to another window in your program.

Two of **Dialog**'s most commonly used constructors are described here.

Dialog

public Dialog(Frame *parentWindow*, boolean *mode*)

This constructor creates a **Dialog** object. The owner of the dialog box is *parentWindow*. If *mode* is true, the dialog box is modal. Otherwise, it is modeless. Generally, you will subclass **Dialog**, adding the functionality required by your application.

public Dialog(Frame *parentWindow*, String *title*, boolean *mode*)

This constructor creates a **Dialog** object. The owner of the dialog box is *parentWindow*. If *mode* is true, the dialog box is modal. Otherwise, it is modeless. The title of the dialog box can be passed in *title*. Generally, you will subclass **Dialog**, adding the functionality required by your application.

THE DIMENSION CLASS

The **Dimension** class has two instance variables, **height** and **width**, which are **int**s.

Dimension

public Dimension( )

This constructor creates an object whose width and height are zero.

public Dimension(Dimension *d*)

This constructor creates an object whose width and height are specified by *d*.

public Dimension(int *w*, int *h*)

This constructor creates an object whose width and height are equal to *w* and *h*, respectively.

equals

public boolean equals(Object *obj*)

This method tests whether the invoking object and *obj* have the same value.

This method was introduced in Java specification 1.1.

getSize

public Dimension getSize( )

This method returns a **Dimension** object whose properties are equal to those of the invoking object.

This method was introduced in Java specification 1.1.

setSize

public void setSize(Dimension *d*)

This method sets the width and height of the invoking object equal to those of *d*.

This method was introduced in Java specification 1.1.

11

public void setSize(int *w*, int *h*)

This method sets the width and height of the invoking object equal to *w* and *h*, respectively.

This method was introduced in Java specification 1.1.

toString

public String toString( )

This method returns the **String** equivalent of the invoking object.

THE EVENT CLASS

The **Event** class provides support for events generated by the various AWT components. There are ten instance variables. **arg** is a reference to an **Object** that provides auxiliary information about an event. **clickCount** is an **int** that records the number of consecutive mouse clicks. **evt** is a reference to an **Event** object. It is used when constructing a linked list of events. **id** is an **int** that identifies the event. **key** is an **int** that records a keypress. **modifiers** is an **int** that has the state of the modifier keys (Ctrl, Alt, Shift, and Meta keys). **target** is a reference to the **Object** that generated the event. **when** is a **long** that records the time an event occurred. **x** and **y** are **ints** that record where an event occurred.

Several **int** constants also have been defined: **ACTION_EVENT, ALT_MASK, BACK_SPACE, CAPS_LOCK, CTRL_MASK, DELETE, DOWN, END, ENTER, ESCAPE, F1, F2, F3, F4, F5, F6, F7, F8, F9, F10, F11, F12, GOT_FOCUS, HOME, INSERT, KEY_ACTION, KEY_ACTION_RELEASE, KEY_PRESS, KEY_RELEASE, LEFT, LIST_DESELECT, LIST_SELECT, LOAD_FILE, LOST_FOCUS, META_MASK, MOUSE_DOWN, MOUSE_DRAG, MOUSE_ENTER, MOUSE_EXIT, MOUSE_MOVE,**

MOUSE_UP, NUM_LOCK, PAUSE, PGDN, PGUP, PRINT_SCREEN,
RIGHT, SAVE_FILE, SCROLL_ABSOLUTE, SCROLL_BEGIN,
SCROLL_END, SCROLL_LINE_DOWN, SCROLL_LINE_UP,
SCROLL_LOCK, SCROLL_PAGE_DOWN, SCROLL_PAGE_UP,
SHIFT_MASK, TAB, UP, WINDOW_DEICONIFY,
WINDOW_DESTROY, WINDOW_EXPOSE, WINDOW_ICONIFY,
and **WINDOW_MOVED**. (Of these constants, the following
were introduced in Java specification 1.1: **BACK_SPACE,
CAPS_LOCK, DELETE, ENTER, ESCAPE, INSERT, NUM_LOCK,
PAUSE, PRINT_SCREEN, SCROLL_BEGIN, SCROLL_END,
SCROLL_LOCK**, and **TAB**.)

Some commonly used methods in this class are described here.

controlDown

public boolean controlDown( )

This method returns **true** if the control key was pressed when
the event occurred and **false** otherwise.

metaDown

public boolean metaDown( )

This method returns **true** if the meta key was pressed when the
event occurred and **false** otherwise.

shiftDown

public boolean shiftDown( )

This method returns **true** if the shift key was pressed when the
event occurred and **false** otherwise.

11

toString

public String toString( )

This method returns the **String** equivalent of the invoking object.

THE FILEDIALOG CLASS

The **FileDialog** class is used to present a modal dialog box that allows the user to select a file. There are two **int** constants, called **LOAD** and **SAVE**, that indicate whether the user is attempting to load or save a file.

The most commonly used methods in this class are described here.

Related classes: **Component**, **Container**, **Dialog**, **Window**

FileDialog

public FileDialog(Frame *parentFrame*)

This constructor creates a **FileDialog** object that is owned by *parentFrame*. The title of this dialog box is empty.

This method was introduced in Java specification 1.1.

public FileDialog(Frame *parentFrame*, String *dialogTitle*)

This constructor creates a **FileDialog** object that is owned by *parentFrame*. The title of this dialog box is *dialogTitle*.

**public FileDialog(Frame *parentFrame*,
  String *dialogTitle*, int *mode*)**

This constructor creates a **FileDialog** object that is owned by
parentFrame. The title of this dialog box is *dialogTitle*, and *mode*
is either **LOAD** or **SAVE**.

getDirectory

public String getDirectory( )

This method gets the name of the directory entered by the user.

getFile

public String getFile( )

This method gets the name of the file entered by the user.

getFilenameFilter

public FilenameFilter getFilenameFilter( )

This method returns the **FilenameFilter** associated with the
invoking **FileDialog** object.

11

getMode

public int getMode( )

This method returns the mode (either **LOAD** or **SAVE**) for the
invoking **FileDialog** object.

setDirectory

public synchronized void setDirectory(String *dirName*)

This method sets the default directory for the invoking **FileDialog** object to that specified by *dirName*.

setFile

public synchronized void setFile(String *fileName*)

This method sets the default filename for the invoking **FileDialog** object to that specified by *fileName*.

setFilenameFilter

public synchronized void setFilenameFilter(FilenameFilter *fileFilter*)

This method sets the **FilenameFilter** object associated with the invoking **FileDialog** object to that specified by *fileFilter*.

setMode

public void setMode(int *mode*)

This method sets the mode of the invoking **FileDialog** object to either **LOAD** or **SAVE**. The mode determines whether a file is being opened for input (**LOAD**) or output (**SAVE**).

This method was introduced in Java specification 1.1.

THE FLOWLAYOUT CLASS

FlowLayout implements a simple layout style, which is similar to how words flow in a text editor. Components are laid out from the upper-left corner, left to right and top to bottom. When no more components fit on a line, the next one appears on the next line. A small space is left between each component, above and below, as well as left and right.

FlowLayout defines three **int** constants: **CENTER**, **LEFT**, and **RIGHT**. These can be used to control the alignment of the components.

Related interface: **LayoutManager**

FlowLayout

public FlowLayout( )

This is the default constructor. It uses a centered alignment.

public FlowLayout(int *alignment*)

This constructor creates an object that uses the specified *alignment*.

public FlowLayout(int *alignment*, int *horizontalGap*, int *verticalGap*)

This constructor creates an object that uses the specified *alignment*. The values of *horizontalGap* and *verticalGap* specify the horizontal and vertical gap between components.

11

THE FONT CLASS

Fonts are encapsulated by the **Font** class. The AWT supports multiple type fonts.

There are three **int** constants: **BOLD**, **ITALIC**, and **PLAIN**. There are three protected instance variables. **name** is a **String** object that contains the name of a font. **style** is an **int** that indicates the style of a font. It can be **PLAIN** or **ITALIC**. **BOLD** can also be combined with **PLAIN** or **ITALIC**. **size** is an **int** that indicates the font size.

The most commonly used methods in this class are described here.

Related class: **FontMetrics**

Font

public Font(String *fontName*, int *styleId*, int *pointSize*)

This constructor creates a **Font** object. *fontName* specifies the name of the font (e.g., Courier, Helvetica), *styleId* indicates the styles, and *pointSize* is the size of the font.

decode

public static Font decode(String *fontName*)

This method returns a **Font** object for the specified *fontName*.

This method was introduced in Java specification 1.1.

getFont

public static Font getFont(String *property*, Font *defaultFont*)

This method returns the font associated with the system property specified by *property*. The font specified by *defaultFont* is returned if *property* does not exist.

public static Font getFont(String *property*)

This method returns the font associated with the system property specified by *property*. A **null** is returned if *property* does not exist.

getName

public String getName( )

This method returns the name of the invoking **Font** object.

getSize

public int getSize( )

This method returns the size, in points, of the invoking **Font** object.

getStyle

public int getStyle( )

This method returns the style values of the invoking **Font** object.

isBold

public boolean isBold( )

This method tests whether the font includes the **BOLD** style value.

isItalic

public boolean isItalic( )

This method tests whether the font includes the **ITALIC** style value.

isPlain

public boolean isPlain( )

This method tests whether the font includes the **PLAIN** style value.

toString

public String toString( )

This method returns the **String** equivalent of the invoking object.

THE FONTMETRICS CLASS

The **FontMetrics** class encapsulates various pieces of information about a font. It allows you to determine the dimensions and various other attributes of the currently selected font, including the following:

- *Height:* the top-to-bottom size of the tallest character in the font

- *Baseline:* the line to which the bottoms of characters are aligned (not counting descent)

- *Ascent:* the distance from the baseline to the top of a character

- *Descent:* the distance from the baseline to the bottom of a character

- *Leading:* the distance between the bottom of one line of text and the top of the next

There is one instance variable. **font** is a protected reference to a **Font** object.

The most commonly used methods in this class are described here.

Related class: **Font**

FontMetrics

public FontMetrics(Font *f*)

This constructor creates a **FontMetrics** object for the **Font** *f*.

getHeight

public int getHeight( )

This method returns the height of a line of text in the font currently contained in the invoking **Font** object.

stringWidth

public int stringWidth(String *str*)

This method returns the width of *str* in pixels in the font currently contained in the invoking **Font** object.

Programming Tip

Perhaps the most common use of **FontMetrics** is to determine the spacing between lines of text when outputting text in a window. The second most common use is to determine the length of a string that is being displayed. Here is how to accomplish these tasks.

In general, to display multiple lines of text in a window, your program must manually keep track of the current output position. Each time a new line is desired, the Y coordinate must be advanced to the beginning of the next line. Each time a string is displayed, the X coordinate must be set to the point at which the string ends. This allows the next string to be written so that it begins at the end of the preceding one.

To determine the spacing between lines, you need to know the total height of a line of text. The easiest way to obtain this value is to call **getHeight( )**. When outputting text, each time you want to advance to the next line, simply increment the Y coordinate by this value.

To start output at the end of previous output on the same line, you must know the length, in pixels, of each string that you display. To obtain this value, call **stringWidth( )**. You can use this value to advance the X coordinate each time you display a line.

The following applet shows how to output multiple lines of text in a window. It also displays multiple sentences on the same line. Notice the variables **curX** and **curY**. They keep track of the current text output position.

```java
// Demonstrate multiline output.
import java.applet.*;
import java.awt.*;
/*
 <applet code="MultiLine" width=300 height=100>
 </applet>
*/

public class MultiLine extends Applet {
  int curX=0, curY=0; // current position

  public void init() {
    Font f = new Font("Helvetica", Font.PLAIN, 12);
    setFont(f);
  }

  public void paint(Graphics g) {
    FontMetrics fm = g.getFontMetrics();

    nextLine("This is on line one.", g);
    nextLine("This is on line two.", g);
    sameLine(" This is on same line.", g);
    sameLine(" This, too.", g);
    nextLine("This is on line three.", g);
  }
```

```
  // Advance to next line.
  void nextLine(String s, Graphics g) {
    FontMetrics fm = g.getFontMetrics();

    curY += fm.getHeight(); // advance to next line
    curX = 0;

    g.drawString(s, curX, curY);
    // advance to end of line
    curX = fm.stringWidth(s);
  }

  // Display on same line.
  void sameLine(String s, Graphics g) {
    FontMetrics fm = g.getFontMetrics();

    g.drawString(s, curX, curY);
    // advance to end of line
    curX += fm.stringWidth(s);
  }
}
```

The window produced by this applet using the Applet Viewer is shown here.

THE FRAME CLASS

The **Frame** class encapsulates what is commonly thought of as a "window." It is a subclass of **Window** and has a title bar, menu bar, borders, and resizing handles.

The most commonly used methods in this class are described here.

Related classes: **Component**, **Container**, **Window**

Frame

public Frame( )

This constructor creates a **Frame** object (i.e., a window) with no title.

public Frame(String *title*)

This constructor creates a **Frame** object with *title* displayed in the title bar. The window will be invisible when it is first created.

setMenuBar

public synchronized void setMenuBar(MenuBar *mbar*)

This method sets the menu bar for the invoking **Frame** object to *mbar*. That is, *mbar* becomes the frame's menu bar.

setTitle

public synchronized void setTitle(String *title*)

This method sets the title for this frame to *title*.

THE GRAPHICS CLASS

The abstract **Graphics** class is the superclass for all graphics contexts.

The most commonly used methods in this class are described here.

drawLine

public abstract void drawLine(int *startX*, int *startY*, int *endX*, int *endY*)

This method displays a line in the current drawing color that begins at *startX, startY* and ends at *endX, endY*.

drawOval

public abstract void drawOval(int *top*, int *left*, int *width*, int *height*)

This method draws an ellipse within a bounding rectangle whose upper-left corner is specified by *top, left* and whose width and height are specified by *width* and *height*. To draw a circle, specify a square as the bounding rectangle.

drawRect

public void drawRect(int *top*, int *left*, int *width*, int *height*)

This method displays a rectangle whose upper-left corner is at *top, left*. The dimensions of the rectangle are specified by *width* and *height*.

drawString

public abstract void drawString(String *message*, int *x*, int *y*)

This method outputs a string at the specified *x, y* location.

11

fillOval

public abstract void fillOval(int *top*, int *left*, int *width*, int *height*)

This method draws an ellipse within a bounding rectangle whose upper-left corner is specified by *top*, *left* and whose width and height are specified by *width* and *height*. To draw a circle, specify a square as the bounding rectangle. The ellipse is filled with the current color.

fillRect

public abstract void fillRect(int *top*, int *left*, int *width*, int *height*)

This method displays a rectangle whose upper-left corner is at *top*, *left*. The dimensions of the rectangle are specified by *width* and *height*. The rectangle is filled with the current color.

setColor

public abstract void setColor(Color *c*)

This method sets the color of the invoking **Graphics** context to *c*.

setFont

public abstract void setFont(Font *f*)

This method sets the font of the invoking **Graphics** context to *f*.

THE LABEL CLASS

A **Label** object is a component that displays a string. It defines three **int** constants: **CENTER**, **LEFT**, and **RIGHT**. These can be used to control the alignment of the string.

The most commonly used methods in this class are described here.

Related class: **Component**

Label

public Label( )

This is the default constructor. It uses a blank label.

public Label(String *str*)

This constructor creates an object that displays *str*.

public Label(String *str*, int *how*)

This constructor creates an object that displays *str*. *how* specifies the alignment. The value of *how* must be **Label.LEFT**, **Label.RIGHT**, or **Label.CENTER**.

getText

public String getText( )

This method returns a **String** object that contains the text of the invoking **Label** object.

11

setText

public synchronized void setText(String *str*)

This method changes the label of the invoking **Label** object to *str*.

THE LIST CLASS

The **List** class provides a compact, multiple-choice, scrolling selection list.

The most commonly used methods in this class are described here.

Related class: **Component**

List( )

public List( )

This constructor creates an empty list component. Only one item can be selected at any one time.

public List(int *numRows*)

This constructor creates an empty list component. *numRows* specifies the number of entries in the list that will always be visible (others can be scrolled into view, as needed).

This constructor was introduced in Java specification 1.1.

public List(int *numRows*, boolean *multipleSelect*)

This constructor creates an empty list component. *numRows* specifies the number of entries in the list that will always be visible (others can be scrolled into view, as needed). If *multipleSelect* is **true**, then the user can select two or more items at a time. If it is **false**, then only one item can be selected.

addActionListener

public synchronized void
addActionListener(ActionListener *al*)

This method adds the **ActionListener** *al* to the set of objects that will receive action commands generated by the invoking **List** object.

This method was introduced in Java specification 1.1.

addItem

public void addItem(String *str*)

This method adds *str* to the end of the list contained in the invoking **List** object.

public synchronized void addItem(String *str*,
int *index*)

This method adds *str* to the list contained in the invoking **List** object. The item is added at the index specified by *index*. Indexing begins at zero.

addItemListener

public synchronized void
addItemListener(ItemListener *il*)

This method adds the **ItemListener** *il* to the set of objects that will receive item events generated by the invoking **List** object.

This method was introduced in Java specification 1.1.

11

delItem

public synchronized void delItem(int *index*)

This method deletes the item at the specified *index* from the list contained by the invoking **List** object.

getItem

public String getItem(int *index*)

This method returns the item at the specified *index* within the list contained by the invoking **List** object.

getItems

public synchronized String[ ] getItems( )

This method returns a **String** array that contains all of the items in the invoking **List** object.

This method was introduced in Java specification 1.1.

getSelectedIndex

public synchronized int getSelectedIndex( )

This method returns the index of the item that has been selected. Indexing begins at zero. If no item is selected, -1 is returned.

getSelectedIndexes

public synchronized int[ ] getSelectedIndexes( )

This method returns an array of **int**s that contains the indexes of those items that have been selected. Indexing begins at zero.

removeActionListener

public synchronized void
removeActionListener(ActionListener *al*)

This method removes the **ActionListener** *al* from the set of objects that will receive action events generated by the invoking **List** object.

This method was introduced in Java specification 1.1.

removeItemListener

public synchronized void
removeItemListener(ItemListener *il*)

This method removes the **ItemListener** *il* from the set of objects that will receive item events generated by the invoking **List** object.

This method was introduced in Java specification 1.1.

select

public synchronized void
select(int *index*)

The method selects the item at *index* within the list contained by the invoking **List** object. Indexing begins at zero.

THE MENU CLASS

A menu is contained in a menu bar. See **MenuBar** for an overview.

The most commonly used methods in this class are described here.

Related classes: **CheckboxMenuItem**, **MenuBar**,
MenuComponent, **MenuItem**

Menu

public Menu(String *menuName*)

This constructor creates a **Menu** object. *menuName* specifies
the name of the menu.

public Menu(String *menuName*, boolean *removable*)

This constructor creates a **Menu** object. *menuName* specifies
the name of the menu. If *removable* is **true**, the pop-up menu
can be removed and allowed to float free. Otherwise, it will
remain attached to the menu bar. (Removable menus are
implementation dependent.)

add

public synchronized MenuItem add(MenuItem *item*)

This method adds *item* to the menu. The return value is *item*.

public void add(String *str*)

This method adds an item whose name is passed in *str* to this
menu.

THE MENUBAR CLASS

A **MenuBar** object contains one or more **Menu** objects.
Each **Menu** object contains a list of **MenuItem** objects. Each
MenuItem object represents something that can be selected by

the user. Since **Menu** is a subclass of **MenuItem**, a hierarchy of nested submenus can be created. It is also possible to include checkable menu items. These are menu options of type **CheckboxMenuItem** and will have a check mark next to them when they are selected.

The most commonly used methods in this class are described here.

Related classes: **CheckboxMenuItem**, **Menu**, **MenuComponent**, **MenuItem**

MenuBar

public MenuBar( )

This constructor creates an empty menu bar.

add

public synchronized Menu add(Menu *m*)

This method adds the **Menu** *m* to the invoking **MenuBar** object. The return value is *m*.

getMenu

public Menu getMenu(int *pos*)

This method returns the **Menu** object at the index specified by *pos* in the invoking **MenuBar** object. Indexing begins at zero.

remove

public synchronized void remove(int *pos*)

This method removes the **Menu** object at the index specified by *pos* from the invoking **MenuBar** object. Indexing begins at zero.

public synchronized void remove(MenuComponent *mc*)

This method removes the **MenuComponent** *mc* from the invoking **MenuBar** object.

setHelpMenu

public synchronized void setHelpMenu(Menu *newHelp*)

This method sets the help menu of the invoking **MenuBar** to *newHelp*.

THE MENUCOMPONENT CLASS

The **MenuComponent** class is the superclass of **MenuBar**, **Menu**, and **MenuItem**.

The most commonly used methods in this class are described here.

MenuComponent

public MenuComponent( )

This is the default constructor.

getFont

public Font getFont( )

This method returns the font used by the invoking object.

getName

public String getName( )

This method returns the name of the invoking object.

This method was introduced in Java specification 1.1.

postEvent

public boolean postEvent(Event *evtObj*)

This method posts **Event** *evtObj* to the invoking object.

This method is deprecated in Java specification 1.1.

setFont

public void setFont(Font *f*)

This method sets the font of the invoking object to *f*.

setName

public void setName(String *str*)

This method sets the name of the invoking object to *str*.

This method was introduced in Java specification 1.1.

11

THE MENUITEM CLASS

MenuItem encapsulates an individual menu item. See **MenuBar** for an overview.

The most commonly used methods in this class are described here.

Related classes: **CheckboxMenuItem, MenuBar, MenuComponent, MenuItem**

MenuItem

public MenuItem(String *itemName*)

This constructor creates an object with *itemName* as the name of the item shown in the menu. There is no keyboard shortcut associated with the item.

addActionListener

public synchronized void addActionListener(ActionListener *al*)

This method adds the **ActionListener** *al* to the set of objects that will receive action events generated by the invoking **MenuItem** object.

This method was introduced in Java specification 1.1.

getActionCommand

public String getActionCommand( )

This method returns the name of the command associated with the action event generated by the invoking **MenuItem** object.

This method was introduced in Java specification 1.1.

removeActionListener

public synchronized void removeActionListener(ActionListener *al*)

This method removes the **ActionListener** *al* from the set of objects that will receive action commands generated by the invoking **MenuItem** object.

This method was introduced in Java specification 1.1.

setActionCommand

public void setActionCommand(String *c*)

This method sets *c* to the name of the command associated with the action event that will be generated by the invoking **MenuItem** object. (The default command name is the item's name.)

This method was introduced in Java specification 1.1.

setLabel

public synchronized void setLabel(String *str*)

This method sets the name of the menu item to *str*.

THE PANEL CLASS

The **Panel** class is a concrete subclass of **Container**. It doesn't add any new methods; it simply implements **Container**. **Panel** is the superclass for **Applet**. When screen output is directed to an applet, it is drawn on the surface of a **Panel** object. In essence, a **Panel** is a window that does not contain a title bar, menu bar, or border. This is why you don't see these items when an applet is run inside a browser. When you run an applet using an applet viewer, it is the applet viewer that provides the title and border.

Other components can be added to a **Panel** object by using its **add( )** method. Once these components have been added, you can position and resize them manually using the **move( )**, **resize( )**, or **reshape( )** methods.

The most commonly used constructors for this class are described here.

Related classes: **Component**, **Container**, **Applet**

Panel

public Panel( )

This constructor creates a **Panel** object that has a **FlowLayout** object as its default layout manager.

public Panel(LayoutManager *lm*)

This constructor creates a **Panel** object that has *lm* as its layout manager.

This method was introduced in Java specification 1.1.

THE POINT CLASS

A **Point** object encapsulates an x, y position. It contains two public **ints**, called **x** and **y**, that hold the coordinates.

The most commonly used methods in this class are described here.

Point

public Point(int *x*, int *y*)

This constructor creates an object representing location *x, y*.

public Point(Point *p*)

This constructor creates an object representing the same location as **Point** *p*.

This method was introduced in Java specification 1.1.

equals

public boolean equals(Object *obj*)

This method tests whether the invoking object and *obj* have the same value.

getLocation

public Point getLocation( )

This method returns a **Point** object that represents the same location as the invoking object.

This method was introduced in Java specification 1.1.

hashCode

public int hashCode( )

This method returns the hash code of the invoking object.

move

public void move(int *newx*, int *newy*)

This method sets the **x** and **y** fields for the invoking object to *newx* and *newy*.

setLocation

public void setLocation(int *newx*, int *newy*)

This method sets the **x** and **y** fields for the invoking object to *newx* and *newy*.

This method was introduced in Java specification 1.1.

public void setLocation(Point *newPoint*)

This method changes the **x** and **y** fields for the invoking object to those of **Point** *newPoint*.

toString

public String toString( )

This method returns the **String** equivalent of the invoking object, which is the object's x, y coordinates.

translate

public void translate(int *deltax*, int *deltay*)

This method adds *deltax* and *deltay* to the **x** and **y** fields for the invoking object.

THE RECTANGLE CLASS

A **Rectangle** object represents a rectangular shape with an upper-left corner, a width, and a height. There are four instance variables. **x** and **y** are the x and y coordinates of the upper-left corner of the rectangle. **height** and **width** represent its dimensions.

The following sections outline some of the methods of this class.

Rectangle

public Rectangle( )

This constructor creates a **Rectangle** object whose **x**, **y**, **height** and **width** properties are all zero.

public Rectangle(Dimension *d*)

This constructor creates a **Rectangle** object positioned at 0, 0 with the dimensions of *d*.

public Rectangle(int *w*, int *h*)

This constructor creates a **Rectangle** object positioned at 0, 0 with a width and height of *w* and *h*, respectively.

public Rectangle(int *xUpperLeft*, int *yUpperLeft*, int *w*, int *h*)

This constructor creates a **Rectangle** object positioned at *xUpperLeft*, *yUpperLeft* with a width and height of *w* and *h*, respectively.

public Rectangle(Point *p*)

This constructor creates a **Rectangle** object positioned at *p* with a width and height of zero.

public Rectangle(Point *p*, Dimension *d*)

This constructor creates a **Rectangle** object positioned at *p* with a width and height of *d*.

public Rectangle(Rectangle *rec*)

This constructor creates a **Rectangle** object whose position and dimensions are equivalent to *rec*.

This method was introduced in Java specification 1.1.

contains

These methods were introduced in Java specification 1.1.

public boolean contains(int *x*, int *y*)

This method returns **true** if the point specified by *x* and *y* is within the invoking **Rectangle** object and **false** otherwise.

public boolean contains(Point *p*)

This method returns **true** if the point specified by *p* is within the invoking **Rectangle** object and **false** otherwise.

equals

public boolean equals(Object *obj*)

This method tests whether the invoking object and *obj* have the same value.

inside

public boolean inside(int *x*, int *y*)

This method returns **true** if the point specified by *x* and *y* is within the invoking **Rectangle** object and **false** otherwise.

This method is deprecated in Java specification 1.1.

move

public void move(int *newx*, int *newy*)

This method sets the **x** and **y** fields for the invoking object to *newx* and *newy*.

This method is deprecated in Java specification 1.1.

setLocation

public void setLocation(int *newx*, int *newy*)

This method sets the **x** and **y** fields for the invoking object to *newx* and *newy*.

This method was introduced in Java specification 1.1.

public void setLocation(Point *newPoint*)

This method sets the **x** and **y** fields for the invoking object to those of **Point** *newPoint*.

This method was introduced in Java specification 1.1.

translate

public void translate(int *deltax*, int *deltay*)

This method adds *deltax* and *deltay* to the **x** and **y** fields for the invoking object.

11

This method is deprecated in Java specification 1.1.

THE SCROLLBAR CLASS

Scroll bars are used to select continuous values between a specified minimum and maximum. The **Scrollbar** class allows you to manage this type of component. **Scrollbar** defines two **int** constants: **HORIZONTAL** and **VERTICAL**. These can be used to select an orientation for the scroll bar.

The following sections outline some of the methods of this class.

Related class: **Component**

Scrollbar

public Scrollbar( )

This default constructor creates a vertical scroll bar.

public Scrollbar(int *style*)

This constructor allows you to choose between a horizontal or vertical orientation. *style* can be **Scrollbar.VERTICAL** or **Scrollbar.HORIZONTAL**.

public Scrollbar(int *style*, int *initialValue*, int *thumbSize*, int *min*, int *max*)

This constructor gives you greater control over the scroll bar's parameters. *style* can be **Scrollbar.VERTICAL** or **Scrollbar.HORIZONTAL**. The initial value of the scroll bar is passed in *initialValue*. The number of units represented by the height of the thumb is passed in *thumbSize*. The minimum and maximum values for the scroll bar are specified by *min* and *max*.

addAdjustmentListener

public synchronized void addAdjustmentListener(AdjustmentListener *al*)

This method adds the **AdjustmentListener** *al* to the set of objects that will receive adjustment events from the invoking **Scrollbar** object.

This method was introduced in Java specification 1.1.

getValue

public int getValue( )

This method gets the current position of the invoking **Scrollbar** object.

removeAdjustmentListener

public synchronized void removeAdjustmentListener(AdjustmentListener *al*)

This method removes the **AdjustmentListener** *al* from the set of objects that will receive adjustment events generated by the invoking **Scrollbar** object.

This method was introduced in Java specification 1.1.

THE TEXTAREA CLASS

The **TextArea** class provides a simple multiple-line editor. It defines four **int** constants: **SCROLLBARS_BOTH**, **SCROLLBARS_HORIZONTAL_ONLY**, **SCROLLBARS_NONE**, and **SCROLLBARS_VERTICAL_ONLY**. These can be used in one of the constructors to affect the visibility of the scroll bars for the text area.

The following sections outline some of the methods of this class.

Related classes: **Component**, **TextComponent**, **TextField**

11

TextArea

public TextArea(int *numLines*, int *numChars*)

This constructor creates a **TextArea** object that has *numLines* lines. Each line is *numChars* characters wide.

public TextArea(String *str*)

This constructor creates a **TextArea** object. The control is initialized using *str*.

public TextArea(String *str*, int *numLines*, int *numChars*)

This constructor creates a **TextArea** object that has *numLines* lines. Each line is *numChars* characters wide. The control is initialized using *str*.

public TextArea(String *str*, int *numLines*, int *numChars*, int *scrollbarOption*)

This constructor creates a **TextArea** object that has *numLines* lines. Each line is *numChars* characters wide. The control is initialized using *str*. The *scrollbarOption* parameter can be one of the four constants previously mentioned.

append

public synchronized void append(String *str*)

This method appends *str* to the end of any existing string in the invoking object.

This method was introduced in Java specification 1.1.

appendText

public void appendText(String *str*)

This method appends *str* to the end of any existing string in the invoking object.

This method is deprecated in Java specification 1.1.

insert

public synchronized void insert(String *str*, int *index*)

This method inserts *str* into the string currently in the invoking object at the specified *index*. Indexing begins at zero.

This method was introduced in Java specification 1.1.

insertText

public void insert(String *str*, int *index*)

This method inserts *str* into the string currently in the invoking object at the specified *index*. Indexing begins at zero.

This method is deprecated in Java specification 1.1.

replaceRange

public synchronized void replaceRange(String *str*, int *startIndex*, int *endIndex*)

This method replaces the characters between *startIndex* and *endIndex* in the invoking object with *str*.

This method was introduced in Java specification 1.1.

replaceText

public void replaceText(String *str*, int *startIndex*, int *endIndex*)

This method replaces the characters between *startIndex* and *endIndex* in the invoking object with *str*.

This method is deprecated in Java specification 1.1.

11

THE TEXTCOMPONENT CLASS

The **TextComponent** class is the superclass of the **TextArea** and **TextField** classes. There is one instance variable. **textListener** can hold a reference to a **TextListener** object.

The following sections describe some of the methods of this class.

Related classes: **Component**, **TextArea**, **TextField**

addTextListener

public synchronized void addTextListener(TextListener *tl*)

This method adds the **TextListener** *tl* to the set of objects that will receive text events from the invoking object.

This method was introduced in Java specification 1.1.

getSelectedText

public synchronized String getSelectedText( )

This method returns a **String** object containing any text that has been selected in the invoking object.

getText

public synchronized String getText( )

This method returns a **String** object containing all text in the invoking object.

isEditable

public boolean isEditable( )

This method tests whether the invoking object can be edited

removeTextListener

public void removeTextListener(TextListener *tl*)

This method removes the **TextListener** *tl* from the set of objects that will receive text events from the invoking object.

This method was introduced in Java specification 1.1.

select

public synchronized void select(int *startIndex*, int *endIndex*)

This method selects the text between positions *startIndex* and *endIndex* in the invoking object.

selectAll

public synchronized void selectAll( )

This method selects all of the text in the invoking object.

setEditable

public synchronized void setEditable(boolean *enableEdits*)

This method is used to enable or disable editing of the component. If *enableEdits* is **true**, the text in the component can be changed.

setText

public synchronized void setText(String *str*)

This method sets the text of the invoking object to *str*.

11

THE TEXTFIELD CLASS

The **TextField** class provides a single-line editor.

The following sections describe some of the methods of this class.

Related classes: **Component**, **TextArea**, **TextComponent**

TextField

public TextField(int *numChars*)

This constructor creates a new object that initially contains no text. The number of columns is specified by *numChars*.

public TextField(String *str*)

This constructor creates a new object that initially contains *str*.

public TextField(String *str*, int *numChars*)

This constructor creates a new object that initially contains text equivalent to *str*. The number of columns is specified by *numChars*.

addActionListener

public synchronized void addActionListener(ActionListener *al*)

This method adds the **ActionListener** *al* to the set of objects that will receive action events generated by the invoking **TextField** object.

This method was introduced in Java specification 1.1.

removeActionListener

public synchronized void removeActionListener(ActionListener *al*)

This method removes the **ActionListener** *al* from the set of objects that will receive action events generated by the invoking **TextField** object.

This method was introduced in Java specification 1.1.

THE TOOLKIT CLASS

Toolkit is an abstract class. It defines methods that are used in the process of creating platform-dependent peers for various GUI components. A separate subclass of **Toolkit** is created for each platform.

Two commonly used methods of this class are shown here.

getFontMetrics

public abstract FontMetrics getFontMetrics(Font *f*)

This method returns the **FontMetrics** object for the **Font** *f*.

getScreenSize

public abstract Dimension getScreenSize( )

This method returns a **Dimension** object that contains the size of the screen in pixels.

11

THE WINDOW CLASS

The **Window** class creates a *top-level window*. A top-level window is not contained within any another object; it sits directly on the desktop. Generally, you won't create **Window** objects directly. Instead, you will use a subclass of **Window** called **Frame**. The default layout manager for a **Window** is **BorderLayout**.

Some commonly used methods in this class are described here.

Related classes: **Component**, **Container**, **Window**

Window

public Window(Frame *f*)

This constructor creates a new **Window** object. *f* is the parent of this new window. The window is not initially visible.

addWindowListener

public synchronized void addWindowListener(WindowListener *wl*)

This method adds the **WindowListener** *wl* to the set of objects that will receive window events generated by the invoking **Window** object. This method was introduced in Java specification 1.1.

pack

public void pack( )

This method calculates the dimensions of the window by examining the preferred sizes of the components that are in it.

removeWindowListener

public synchronized void removeWindowListener(WindowListener *wl*)

This method removes the **WindowListener** *wl* from the set of objects that will receive window events generated by the invoking **Window** object.

This method was introduced in Java specification 1.1.

show

public void show( )

This method makes the window visible. By default, new windows are invisible.

Chapter 12—The Event Classes and Interfaces

Java specification 1.1 introduced a new event model. **java.awt.event** is a new package that contains classes and interfaces related to the new way events are handled.

The classes in **java.awt.event** are shown here:

ActionEvent	KeyAdapter
AdjustmentEvent	KeyEvent
ComponentAdapter	MouseAdapter
ComponentEvent	MouseEvent
ContainerAdapter	MouseMotionAdapter
ContainerEvent	PaintEvent
FocusAdapter	TextEvent
FocusEvent	WindowAdapter
InputEvent	WindowEvent
ItemEvent	

java.awt.event also defines these interfaces:

ActionListener	KeyListener
AdjustmentListener	MouseListener
ComponentListener	MouseMotionListener
ContainerListener	TextListener
FocusListener	WindowListener
ItemListener	

12

The following classes and interfaces are less frequently used and are not discussed in this book: **ComponentAdapter**, **ComponentEvent**, **ComponentListener**, **ContainerAdapter**, **ContainerEvent**, **ContainerListener**, **FocusAdapter**, **FocusEvent**, **InputEvent**, **KeyAdapter**, **MouseAdapter**,

MouseMotionAdapter, **PaintEvent**, **TextEvent**, **TextListener**, and **WindowAdapter**.

THE ACTIONEVENT CLASS

Instances of this class describe action events.

ActionEvent defines seven **int** constants: **ACTION_FIRST**, **ACTION_LAST**, **ACTION_PERFORMED**, **ALT_MASK**, **CTRL_MASK**, **META_MASK**, and **SHIFT_MASK**.

The most commonly used methods in this class are described here.

getActionCommand

public String getActionCommand( )

This method returns the name of the command for the invoking **ActionEvent** object.

getModifiers

public int getModifiers( )

This method returns an **int** that indicates which modifier keys (Ctrl, Alt, Shift, and Meta) were pressed when the event was generated.

THE ACTIONLISTENER INTERFACE

This interface defines a method to receive action events.

actionPerformed

public abstract void actionPerformed(ActionEvent *ae*)

This method is called when an action event takes place. The event itself is contained in *ae*.

THE ADJUSTMENTEVENT CLASS

Instances of this class describe adjustment events. A scroll bar is an example of an object that generates adjustment events.

AdjustmentEvent defines eight **int** constants: **ADJUSTMENT_FIRST**, **ADJUSTMENT_LAST**, **ADJUSTMENT_VALUE_CHANGED**, **BLOCK_DECREMENT**, **BLOCK_INCREMENT**, **TRACK**, **UNIT_DECREMENT**, and **UNIT_INCREMENT**.

The most commonly used methods in this class are described here.

getAdjustable

public Adjustable getAdjustable( )

This method returns the object that generated the event.

getAdjustmentType

public int getAdjustmentType( )

This method returns the type of this event. It will be one of the constants defined by **AdjustmentEvent**.

getValue

public int getValue( )

This method returns the amount of the adjustment.

THE ADJUSTMENTLISTENER INTERFACE

This interface defines a method to receive adjustment events.

adjustmentValueChanged

public abstract void adjustmentValueChanged(AdjustmentEvent *ae*)

This method is called when an adjustment event takes place. The event itself is contained in *ae*.

THE FOCUSLISTENER INTERFACE

This interface defines methods to receive keyboard focus events.

focusGained

public abstract void focusGained(FocusEvent *fe*)

This method is called when keyboard focus is acquired by an object. The event itself is contained in *fe*.

focusLost

public abstract void focusLost(FocusEvent *fe*)

This method is called when keyboard focus is removed from an object. The event itself is contained in *fe*.

THE ITEMEVENT CLASS

Instances of this class describe item events.

ItemEvent defines five **int** constants: **DESELECTED**, **ITEM_FIRST**, **ITEM_LAST**, **ITEM_STATE_CHANGED**, and **SELECTED**.

The most commonly used methods in this class are described here.

getItem

public Object getItem( )

This method returns the item associated with this event.

12

getItemSelectable

public ItemSelectable getItemSelectable( )

This method returns the object that generated the event.

getStateChange

public int getStateChange( )

This method returns the state change (i.e., **SELECTED** or **DESELECTED**) for the event.

THE ITEMLISTENER INTERFACE

This interface defines a method to receive item events.

itemStateChanged

public abstract void itemStateChanged(ItemEvent *ie*)

This method is called when an item event takes place. The event itself is contained in *ie*.

THE KEYEVENT CLASS

Instances of this class describe keystroke events.

KeyEvent defines many constants. Among these are **KEY_PRESSED**, **KEY_RELEASED**, and **KEY_TYPED**.

The most commonly used method in this class is described here.

getKeyChar

public char getKeyChar( )

This method returns the key that was pressed.

THE KEYLISTENER INTERFACE

This interface defines methods to receive keyboard events.

keyPressed

public abstract void keyPressed(KeyEvent *ke*)

This method is called when a key is pressed. The event itself is contained in *ke*.

keyReleased

public abstract void keyReleased(KeyEvent *ke*)

This method is called when a key is released. The event itself is contained in *ke*.

keyTyped

public abstract void keyTyped(KeyEvent *ke*)

This method is called when a key is pressed and then released. The event itself is contained in *ke*.

THE MOUSEEVENT CLASS

12

Instances of this class describe mouse events.

MouseEvent defines these **int** constants: **MOUSE_CLICKED, MOUSE_DRAGGED, MOUSE_ENTERED, MOUSE_EXITED, MOUSE_FIRST, MOUSE_LAST, MOUSE_MOVED, MOUSE_PRESSED**, and **MOUSE_RELEASED**.

The most commonly used methods in this class are described here.

getX

public int getX( )

This method returns the X coordinate of the mouse when the event occurred.

getY

public int getY( )

This method returns the Y coordinate of the mouse when the event occurred.

THE MOUSELISTENER INTERFACE

This interface defines methods to receive mouse events.

mouseClicked

public abstract void mouseClicked(MouseEvent *me*)

This method is called when the mouse is clicked. The event itself is contained in *me*.

mouseEntered

public abstract void mouseEntered(MouseEvent *me*)

This method is called when an object acquires mouse focus. The event itself is contained in *me*.

mouseExited

public abstract void mouseExited(MouseEvent *me*)

This method is called when an object loses mouse focus. The event itself is contained in *me*.

mousePressed

public abstract void mousePressed(MouseEvent *me*)

This method is called when a mouse button is pressed. The event itself is contained in *me*.

mouseReleased

public abstract void mouseReleased(MouseEvent *me*)

This method is called when a mouse button is released. The event itself is contained in *me*.

THE MOUSEMOTIONLISTENER INTERFACE

12

This interface defines methods to receive mouse-motion events.

mouseDragged

public abstract void mouseDragged(MouseEvent *me*)

This method is called when a mouse-drag operation occurs. The event itself is contained in *me*.

mouseMoved

public abstract void mouseMoved(MouseEvent *me*)

This method is called when a mouse-move operation occurs. The event itself is contained in *me*.

THE WINDOWEVENT CLASS

Instances of this class describe window events.

WindowEvent defines these **int** constants: **WINDOW_ACTIVATED, WINDOW_CLOSED, WINDOW_CLOSING, WINDOW_DEACTIVATED, WINDOW_DEICONIFIED, WINDOW_FIRST, WINDOW_ICONIFIED, WINDOW_LAST**, and **WINDOW_OPENED**.

The most commonly used methods in this class are described here.

WindowEvent

public WindowEvent(Window *src*, int *type*)

This constructor creates a **WindowEvent** object. *src* is the object that generated the event and *type* is its type.

getWindow

public Window getWindow( )

This method returns the **Window** object that generated the event.

THE WINDOWLISTENER INTERFACE

This interface defines methods to receive window events.

windowActivated

public abstract void
windowActivated(WindowEvent *we*)

This method is called when a window is activated. The event itself is contained in *we*.

windowClosed

public abstract void
windowClosed(WindowEvent *we*)

This method is called when a window is closed. The event itself is contained in *we*.

windowClosing

public abstract void
windowClosing(WindowEvent *we*)

This method is called when a window is closing. The event itself is contained in *we*.

windowDeactivated

public abstract void
windowDeactivated(WindowEvent *we*)

This method is called when a window is deactivated. The event itself is contained in *we*.

12

windowDeiconified

public abstract void
windowDeiconified(WindowEvent *we*)

This method is called when a window is restored. The event itself is contained in *we*.

windowIconified

public abstract void
windowIconified(WindowEvent *we*)

This method is called when a window is reduced to its icon. The event itself is contained in *we*.

windowOpened

public abstract void
windowOpened(WindowEvent *we*)

This method is called when a window is opened. The event itself is contained in *we*.

Programming Tip

In Java specification 1.0, an event can be processed by the component that generates it or by one of its parent containers. For example, an event-handling method such as **mouseDrag( )** returns **true** if it has completely processed that event or **false** if the event should be propagated to its parent container. In this manner, events are propagated up the GUI containment hierarchy. Also, if a programmer needs to define how a component reacts to a particular event, this is done by creating a subclass of that component and overriding the particular event-handling method.

This strategy has some disadvantages. Performance can suffer if large numbers of events are propagated up the GUI containment hierarchy. Also, it becomes inconvenient to subclass components simply to handle events they generate.

Java specification 1.1 provides a new mechanism to handle user interface events that is based on *event sources* and *event listeners*. Listeners register with sources. When an event occurs, it is sent to all of the listeners who registered an interest in that event.

The following program provides a simple example of this concept:

```java
// Demonstrate the new event model.
import java.applet.*;
import java.awt.*;
import java.awt.event.*;

public class ButtonTest {
  public static void main(String args[]) {
    Frame frame = new Frame("Button Test");
    ButtonApplet buttonApplet = new ButtonApplet();
    buttonApplet.init();
    frame.add("Center", buttonApplet);
    frame.pack();
    frame.setVisible(true);
  }
}

class ButtonApplet extends Applet
                   implements ActionListener {
  Button b1, b2, b3;
  public void init() {
    b1 = new Button("One");
    b1.addActionListener(this);
    add(b1);
    b2 = new Button("Two");
    b2.addActionListener(this);
    add(b2);
    b3 = new Button("Three");
    b3.addActionListener(this);
    add(b3);
  }
```

12

```
   public void actionPerformed(ActionEvent ae) {
     System.out.println(ae);
   }
 }
```

This program creates three buttons and registers the **ButtonApplet** object as the listener for events from these buttons. The **ActionListener** interface contains one method, **actionPerformed( )**, which is invoked when an action occurs at any of these buttons.

Note that this new event-handling mechanism allows you to more efficiently invoke an event-handler method. It also separates code that deals with user-interface elements from application logic.

INDEX

451